MAX RIDE
FIRST FLIGHT

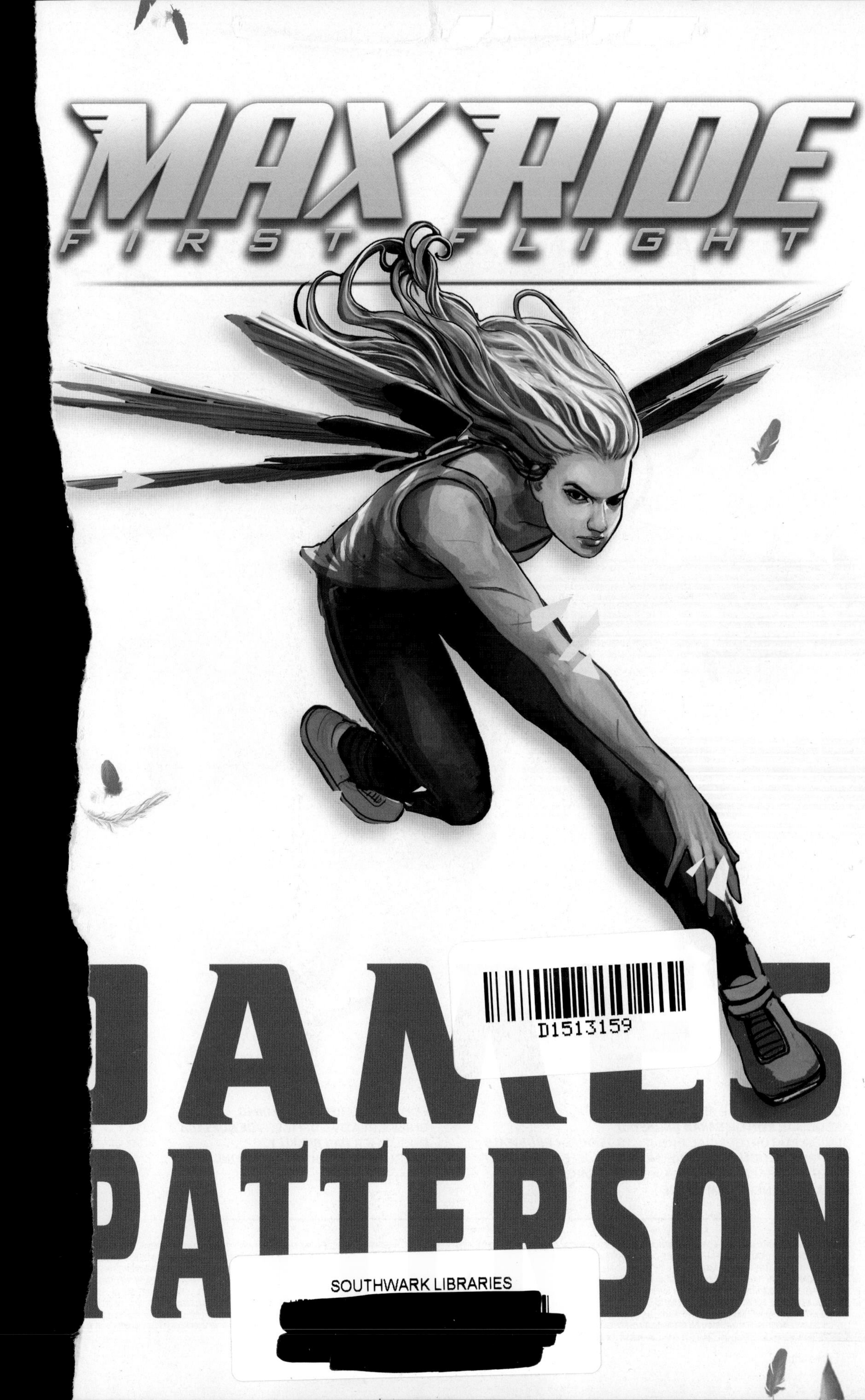

JAMES PATTERSON

COLLECTION EDITOR *MARK D. BEAZLEY*
ASSOCIATE EDITOR *SARAH BRUNSTAD*
SENIOR EDITOR, SPECIAL PROJECTS *JENNIFER GRÜNWALD*
VP, PRODUCTION & SPECIAL PROJECTS *JEFF YOUNGQUIST*
SVP PRINT, SALES & MARKETING *DAVID GABRIEL*
BOOK DESIGNER *ADAM DEL RE*

EDITOR IN CHIEF *AXEL ALONSO*
CHIEF CREATIVE OFFICER *JOE QUESADA*
PUBLISHER *DAN BUCKLEY*
EXECUTIVE PRODUCER *ALAN FINE*

MAX RIDE: FIRST FLIGHT. CONTAINS MATERIAL ORIGINALLY PUBLISHED IN MAGAZINE FORM AS MAX RIDE: FIRST FLIGHT #1-5. FIRST PRINTING 2016. ISBN# 978-0-7851-9931-1. PUBLISHED BY MARVEL WORLDWID, SUBSIDIARY OF MARVEL ENTERTAINMENT, LLC. OFFICE OF PUBLICATION: 135 WEST 50TH STREET, NEW YORK, NY 10020. COPYRIGHT © 2016 BY JAMES PATTERSON. ALL RIGHTS RESERVED. ALL CHARACTERS FEATURE ISSUE AND THE DISTINCTIVE NAMES AND LIKENESSES THEREOF, AND ALL RELATED INDICIA ARE TRADEMARKS OF JAMES PATTERSON. NO SIMILARITY BETWEEN ANY OF THE NAMES, CHARACTERS, PERSONS, AND/OR INSTI IN THIS MAGAZINE WITH THOSE OF ANY LIVING OR DEAD PERSON OR INSTITUTION IS INTENDED, AND ANY SUCH SIMILARITY WHICH MAY EXIST IS PURELY COINCIDENTAL. MARVEL AND ITS LOGOS ARE TM MARVEL CHAR INC. **PRINTED IN THE U.S.A.** ALAN FINE, PRESIDENT, MARVEL ENTERTAINMENT; DAN BUCKLEY, PRESIDENT, TV, PUBLISHING & BRAND MANAGEMENT; JOE QUESADA, CHIEF CREATIVE OFFICER; TOM BREVOORT, SVP OF PUBL DAVID BOGART, SVP OF BUSINESS AFFAIRS & OPERATIONS, PUBLISHING & PARTNERSHIP; C.B. CEBULSKI, VP OF BRAND MANAGEMENT & DEVELOPMENT, ASIA; DAVID GABRIEL, SVP OF SALES & MARKETING, PUBLISHIN YOUNGQUIST, VP OF PRODUCTION & SPECIAL PROJECTS; DAN CARR, EXECUTIVE DIRECTOR OF PUBLISHING TECHNOLOGY; ALEX MORALES, DIRECTOR OF PUBLISHING OPERATIONS; SUSAN CRESPI, PRODUCTION MANAGER, LEE, CHAIRMAN EMERITUS. FOR INFORMATION REGARDING ADVERTISING IN MARVEL COMICS OR ON MARVEL.COM, PLEASE CONTACT VIT DEBELLIS, INTEGRATED SALES MANAGER, AT VDEBELLIS@MARVEL.COM. FOR M/ SUBSCRIPTION INQUIRIES, PLEASE CALL 888-511-5480. MANUFACTURED BETWEEN 7/22/2016 AND 8/29/2016 BY R.R. DONNELLEY, INC., SALEM, VA, USA.

10 9 8 7 6 5 4 3 2 1

ADAPTED FROM THE NOVEL,

MAXIMUM RIDE
BY **JAMES PATTERSON**

WRITER
MARGUERITE BENNETT

PENCILER
ALEX SANCHEZ

INKERS
ALEX SANCHEZ (#1-3) & **MARK PENNINGTON** (#3-5)

COLORIST
ESTHER SANZ

LETTERER
VC'S TRAVIS LANHAM

COVER ARTISTS
STEPHANIE HANS & **YASMINE PUTRI** (#2)

ASSISTANT EDITOR
CHARLES BEACHAM

EDITOR
SANA AMANAT

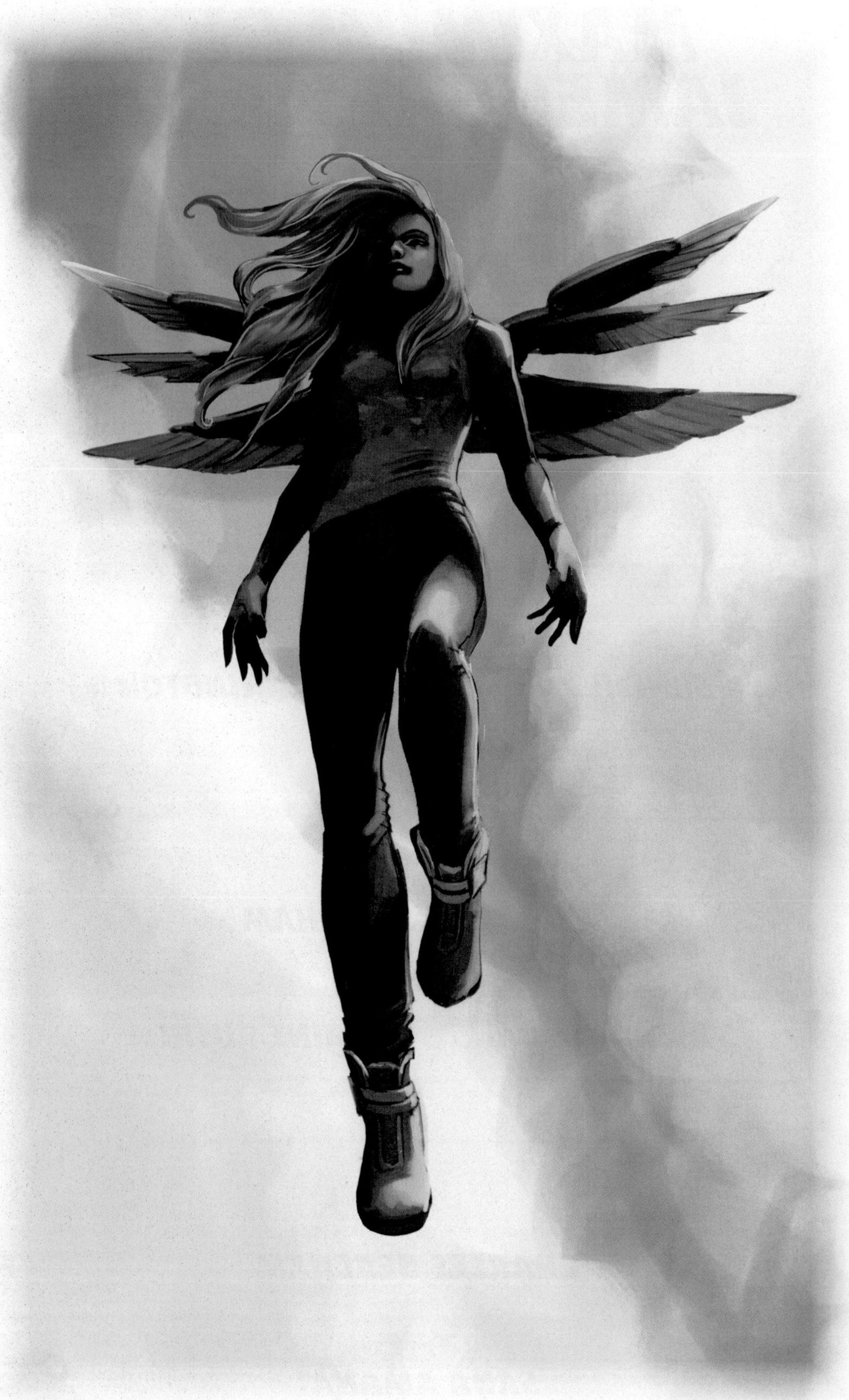

Congratulations on slipping the surly bonds of Earth! You're airborne. You're airborne with a story that has perhaps the most dedicated following of any I've written (my publisher tells me it's had more than 20 million readers, and counting). You're airborne with the wizards of Marvel, those guys who have created the most successful pantheon of heroes in the modern era. You're airborne with Maximum Ride and the greatest development in all of human evolution: your brain.

Of course, you've been up here before. Those of us who read books (illustrated and not) know a little secret, don't we? That reading a story can be a more intense and pleasurable experience than any film, game, or amusement-park ride.

It's not always the case. Some graphic novels (and many, many regular novels) don't manage to get our minds and spirits aloft. But when they work—when they're good—go ahead and grab your knees and say goodbye to terra firma.

You're a reader. You know what I'm talking about.

Anyhow, I happen to know that the Maximum Ride novels achieved this effect on many people. Tens of millions of them. No other story has generated more fan mail for me, nor generated more spontaneous online content. There are tens if not hundreds of thousands of fan videos, drawings, and fan fictions out there featuring Maximum Ride.

So when Marvel came to me and said they wanted to take a crack at doing their own rendition of Max, I was all ears. The people who brought Spider-Man, the Avengers, the X-Men, and so many more iconic cultural figures into living color have here taken their own brilliant talents to my Max, and I think she's only the better for it.

I think you'll find even if you've read the books already that this adaptation is more than an adaptation. This is a whole new flight. My only instructions to them were to make it fly, and they've done that.

I'm not going to get all gooey on you here and say Marvel's the wind beneath my wings or anything, but the writers and artists and editors did do something rare here: they took a fresh vision of an existing story and they got it (and all its characters) aloft.

Which probably is all part of some gigantic cosmic metaphor here. I mean, a big part of the reason I dreamed up Max in the first place was that I have always been fascinated by flight. That idea of being able to just take off into the air and look down on the world, to get from point A to point B (or discover undreamt-of point C) like a bird, or like a dream, or like when you're experiencing a great story—it's a pretty cool experience.

So please don't let me hold you back here. Turn the page and go take flight with a bunch of mutant kids who will change how you see the world.

Please, enjoy the elevation, and the Ride.

All my best,

JP

CHAPTER 1

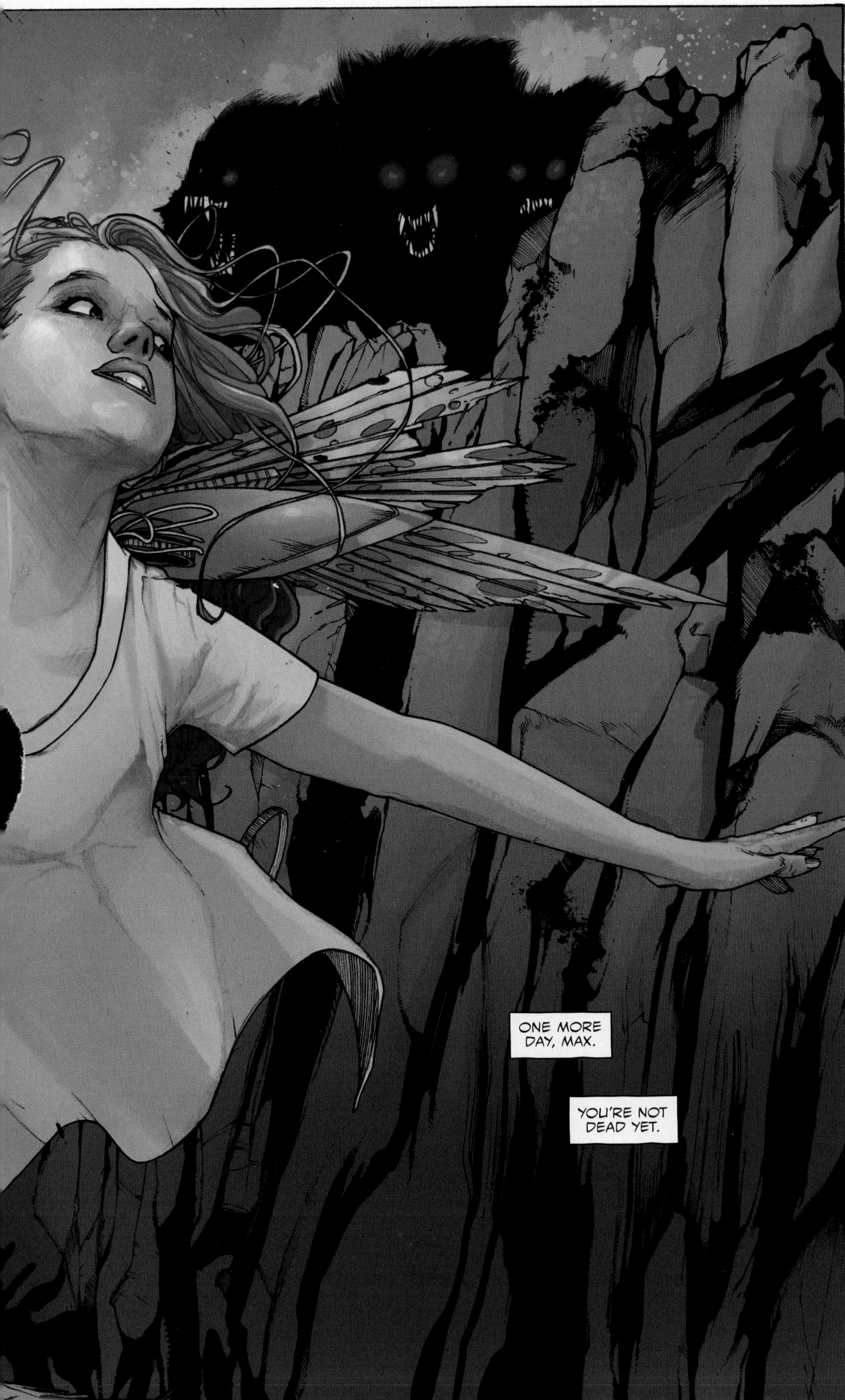
ONE MORE DAY, MAX.
YOU'RE NOT DEAD YET.

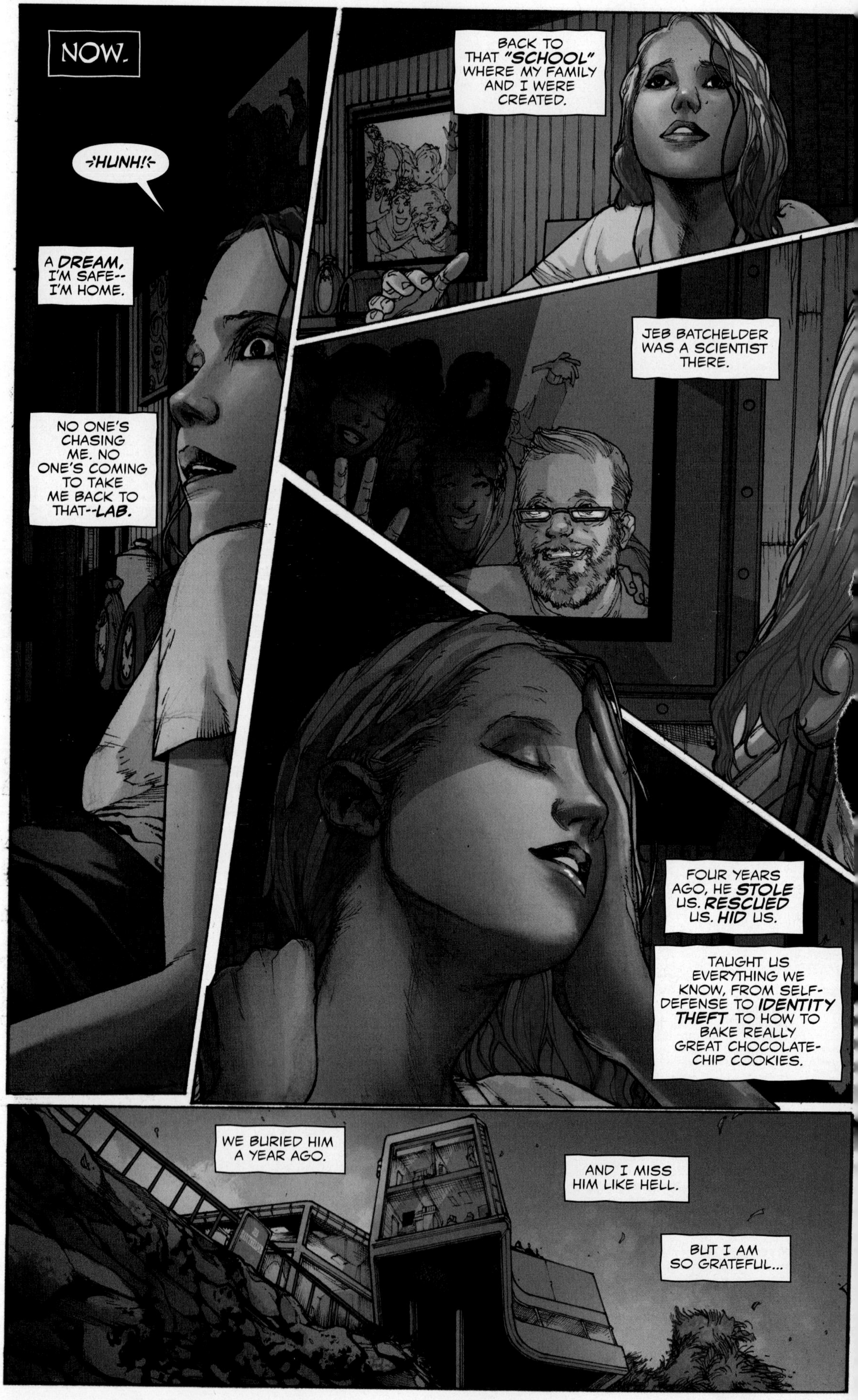
NOW.
HUNH!
A DREAM, I'M SAFE-- I'M HOME.
NO ONE'S CHASING ME. NO ONE'S COMING TO TAKE ME BACK TO THAT--LAB.
BACK TO THAT "SCHOOL" WHERE MY FAMILY AND I WERE CREATED.
JEB BATCHELDER WAS A SCIENTIST THERE.
FOUR YEARS AGO, HE STOLE US. RESCUED US. HID US.
TAUGHT US EVERYTHING WE KNOW, FROM SELF-DEFENSE TO IDENTITY THEFT TO HOW TO BAKE REALLY GREAT CHOCOLATE-CHIP COOKIES.
WE BURIED HIM A YEAR AGO.
AND I MISS HIM LIKE HELL.
BUT I AM SO GRATEFUL...

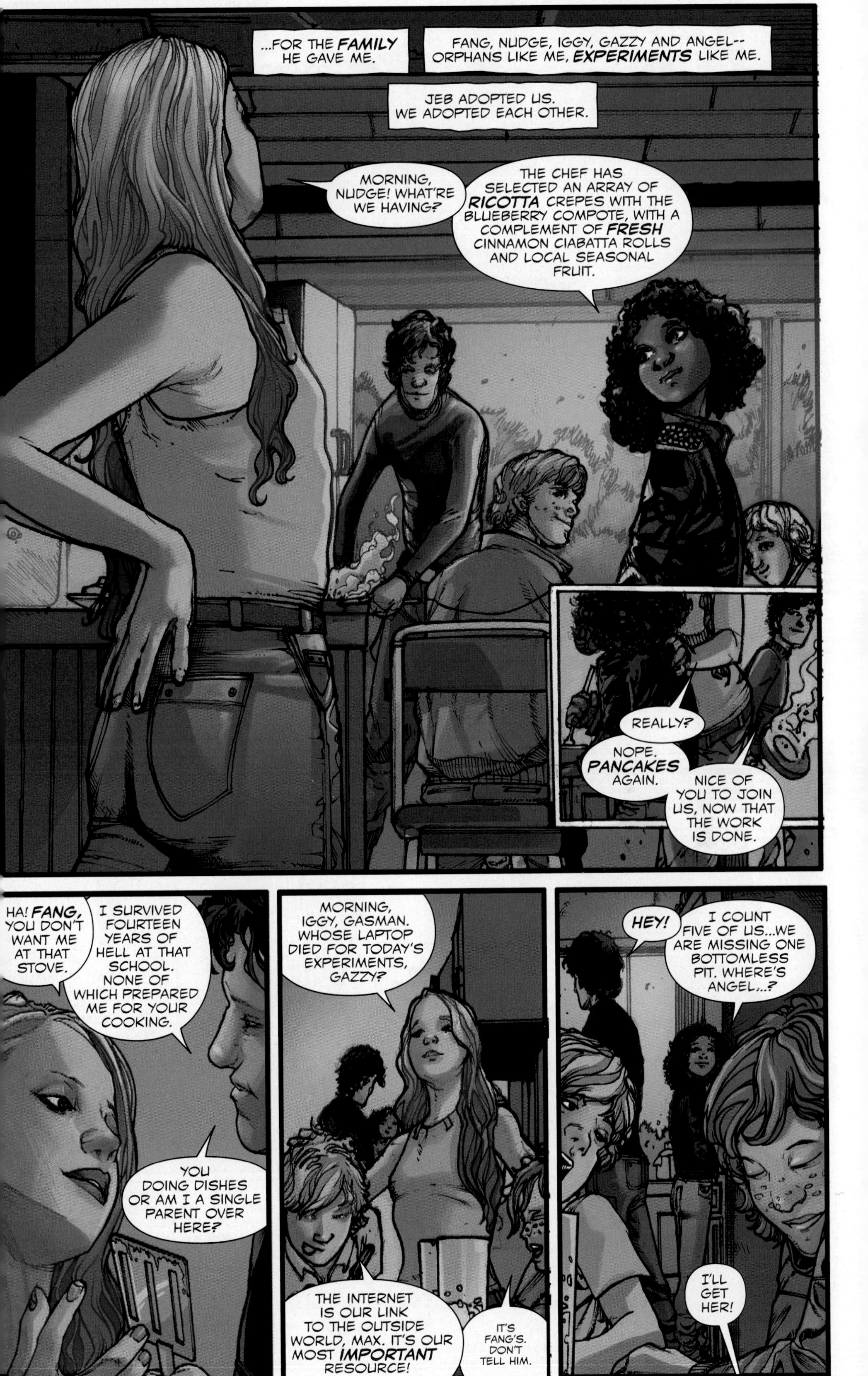

...FOR THE *FAMILY* HE GAVE ME.
FANG, NUDGE, IGGY, GAZZY AND ANGEL-- ORPHANS LIKE ME, *EXPERIMENTS* LIKE ME.
JEB ADOPTED US. WE ADOPTED EACH OTHER.
MORNING, NUDGE! WHAT'RE WE HAVING?
THE CHEF HAS SELECTED AN ARRAY OF *RICOTTA* CREPES WITH THE BLUEBERRY COMPOTE, WITH A COMPLEMENT OF *FRESH* CINNAMON CIABATTA ROLLS AND LOCAL SEASONAL FRUIT.
REALLY?
NOPE. *PANCAKES* AGAIN.
NICE OF YOU TO JOIN US, NOW THAT THE WORK IS DONE.
HA! *FANG,* YOU DON'T WANT ME AT THAT STOVE.
I SURVIVED FOURTEEN YEARS OF HELL AT THAT SCHOOL. NONE OF WHICH PREPARED ME FOR YOUR COOKING.
YOU DOING DISHES OR AM I A SINGLE PARENT OVER HERE?
MORNING, IGGY, GASMAN. WHOSE LAPTOP DIED FOR TODAY'S EXPERIMENTS, GAZZY?
THE INTERNET IS OUR LINK TO THE OUTSIDE WORLD, MAX. IT'S OUR MOST *IMPORTANT* RESOURCE!
IT'S FANG'S. DON'T TELL HIM.
HEY!
I COUNT FIVE OF US...WE ARE MISSING ONE BOTTOMLESS PIT. WHERE'S ANGEL...?
I'LL GET HER!

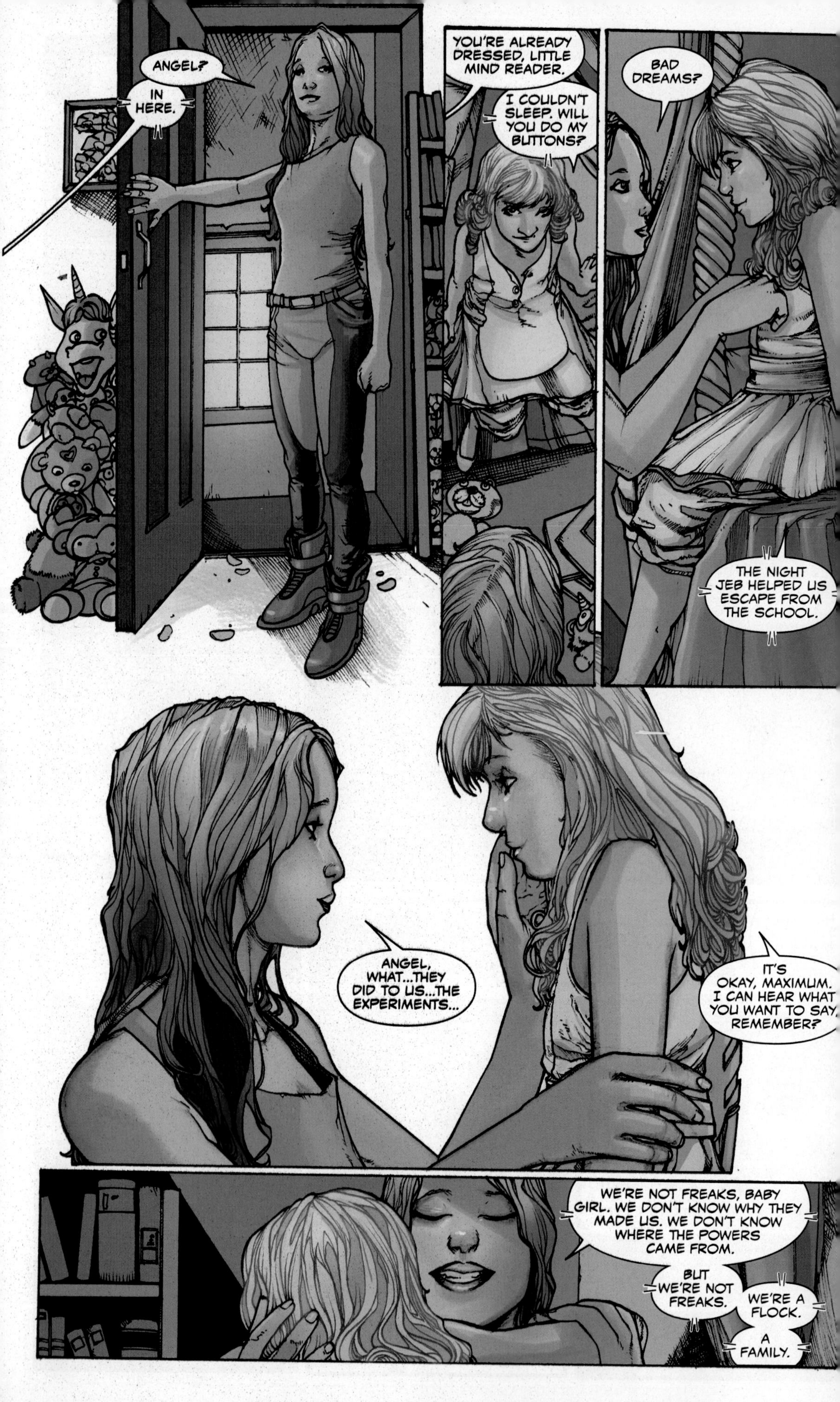
ANGEL?
IN HERE.
YOU'RE ALREADY DRESSED, LITTLE MIND READER.
I COULDN'T SLEEP. WILL YOU DO MY BUTTONS?
BAD DREAMS?
THE NIGHT JEB HELPED US ESCAPE FROM THE SCHOOL.
ANGEL, WHAT...THEY DID TO US...THE EXPERIMENTS...
IT'S OKAY, MAXIMUM. I CAN HEAR WHAT YOU WANT TO SAY, REMEMBER?
WE'RE NOT FREAKS, BABY GIRL. WE DON'T KNOW WHY THEY MADE US. WE DON'T KNOW WHERE THE POWERS CAME FROM.
BUT WE'RE NOT FREAKS.
WE'RE A FLOCK.
A FAMILY.

"NOW LET'S HAVE BREAKFAST."

I BUILT A NEW HARD DRIVE, YOU GUYS! WANNA SEE?

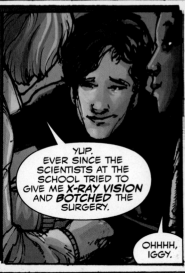

YUP. EVER SINCE THE SCIENTISTS AT THE SCHOOL TRIED TO GIVE ME *X-RAY VISION* AND *BOTCHED* THE SURGERY.

OHHHH, IGGY.

THIS IS WHY YOU'RE MY FAVORITE, IGGY.

I'M NOT YOUR FAVORITE, FANG?

I'M TOO JEALOUS OF YOUR FASHION SENSE, NUDGE. I LIE AWAKE AT NIGHT, WISHING I COULD PULL OFF BOOTY SHORTS.

THAT-- CAME OUT WRONG.

YOU CAME OUT WRONG, FANG.

HAHAHA!

YOU LEARN TO LOVE THESE STUPID MOMENTS.

BECAUSE YOU KNOW HOW QUICKLY--

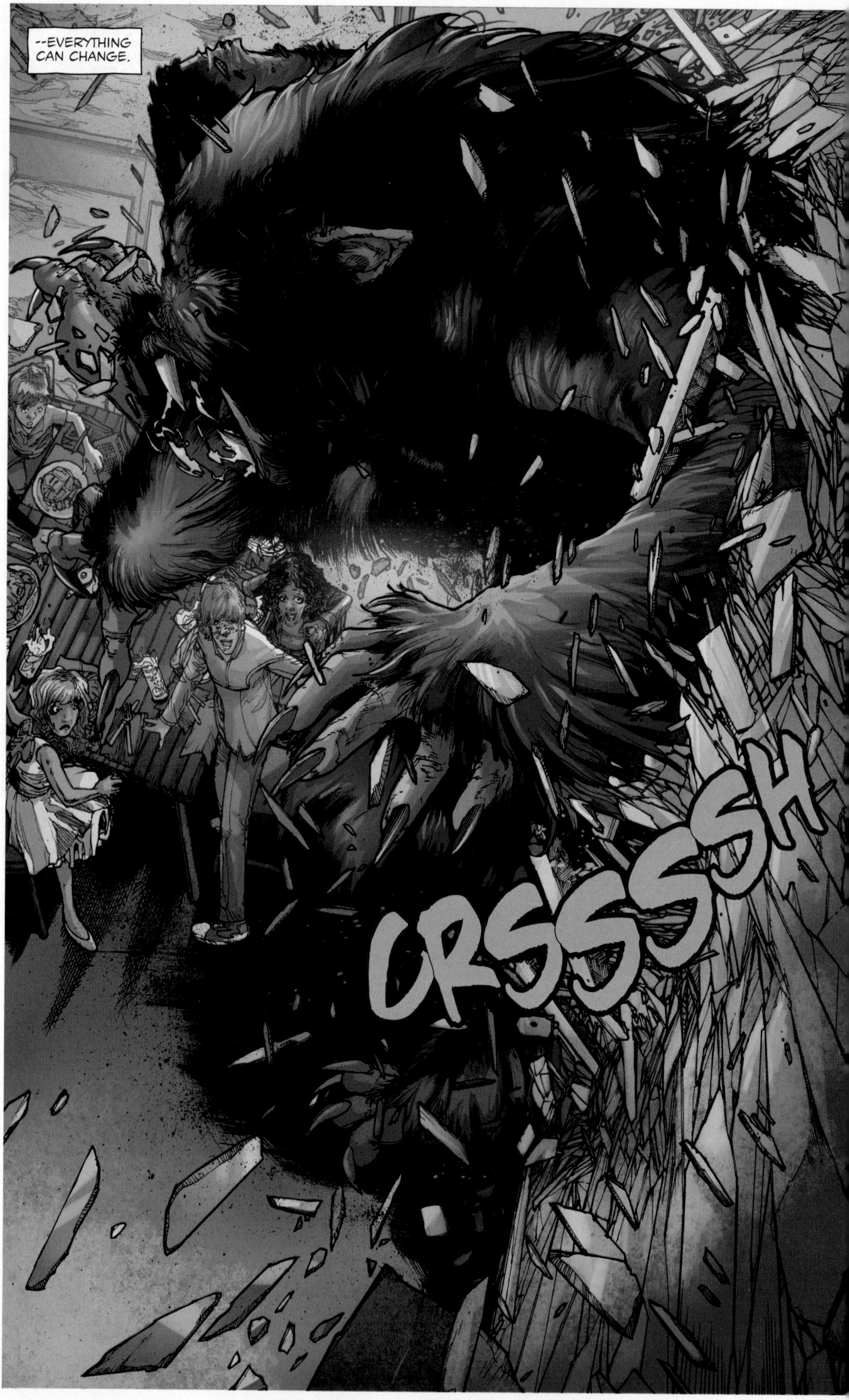
--EVERYTHING CAN CHANGE.
CRSSSSH

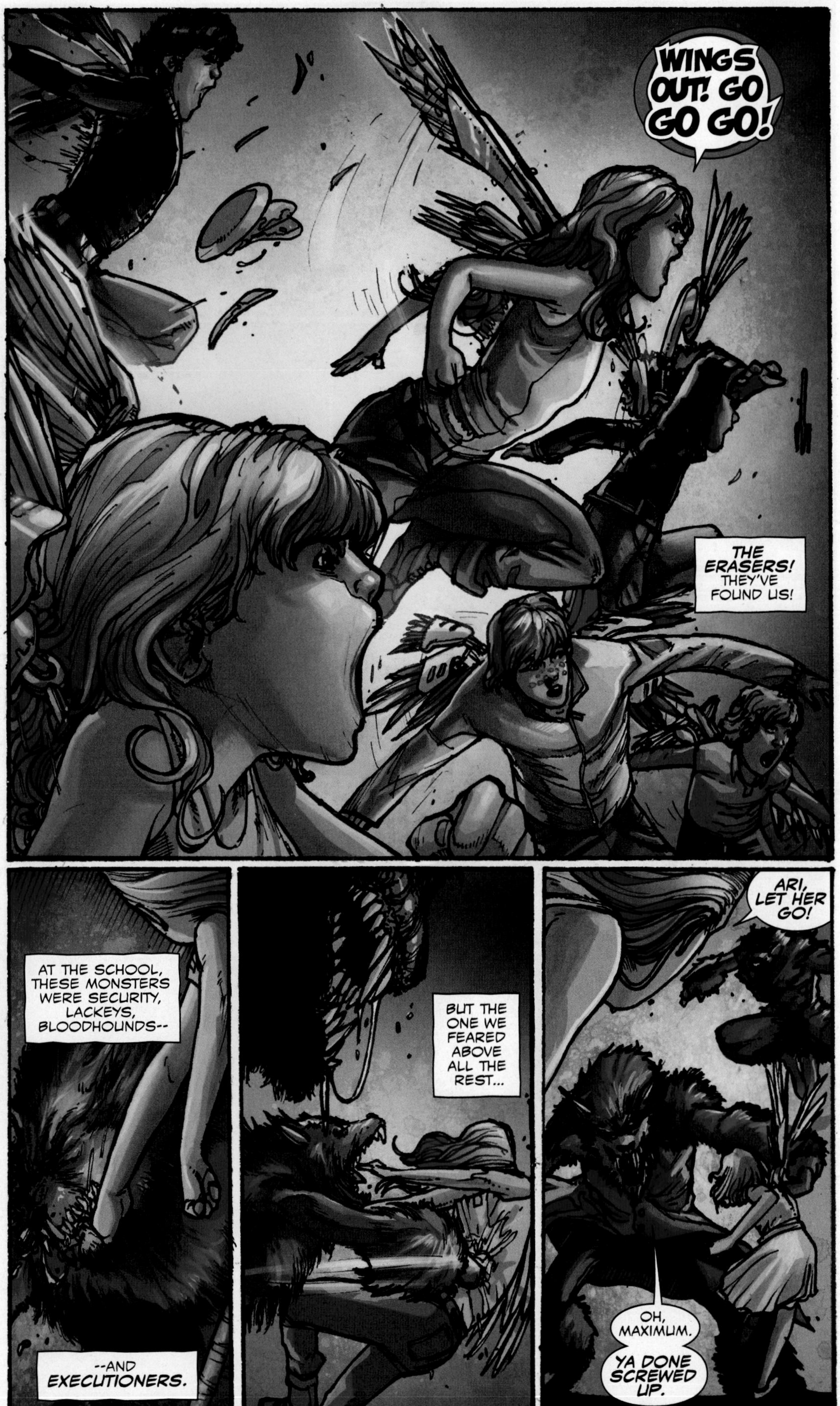
WINGS OUT! GO GO GO!
THE ERASERS! THEY'VE FOUND US!
AT THE SCHOOL, THESE MONSTERS WERE SECURITY, LACKEYS, BLOODHOUNDS--
--AND EXECUTIONERS.
BUT THE ONE WE FEARED ABOVE ALL THE REST...
ARI, LET HER GO!
OH, MAXIMUM.
YA DONE SCREWED UP.

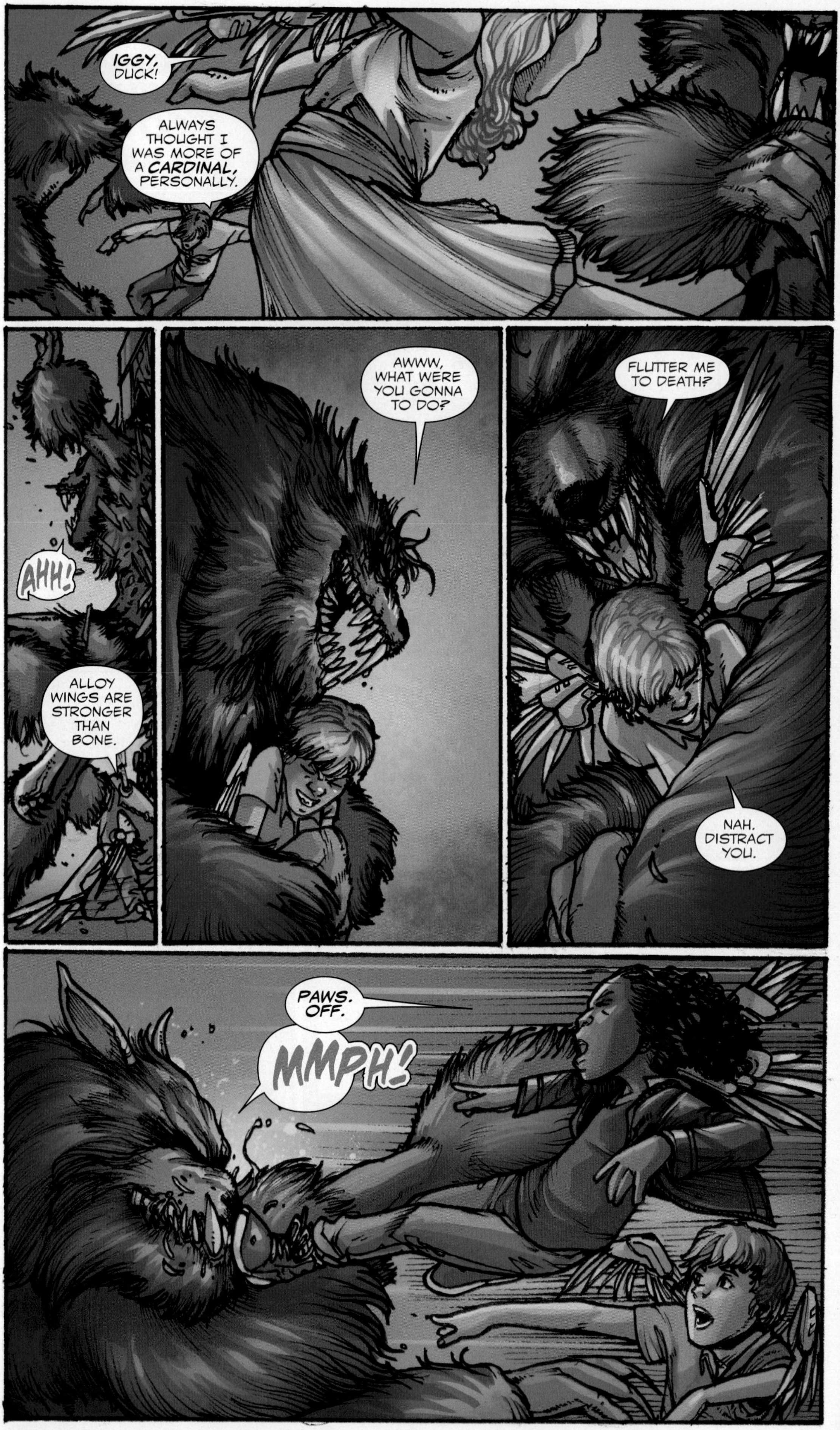
IGGY, DUCK!
ALWAYS THOUGHT I WAS MORE OF A CARDINAL, PERSONALLY.
AHH!
ALLOY WINGS ARE STRONGER THAN BONE.
AWWW, WHAT WERE YOU GONNA TO DO?
FLUTTER ME TO DEATH?
NAH. DISTRACT YOU.
PAWS. OFF.
MMPH!

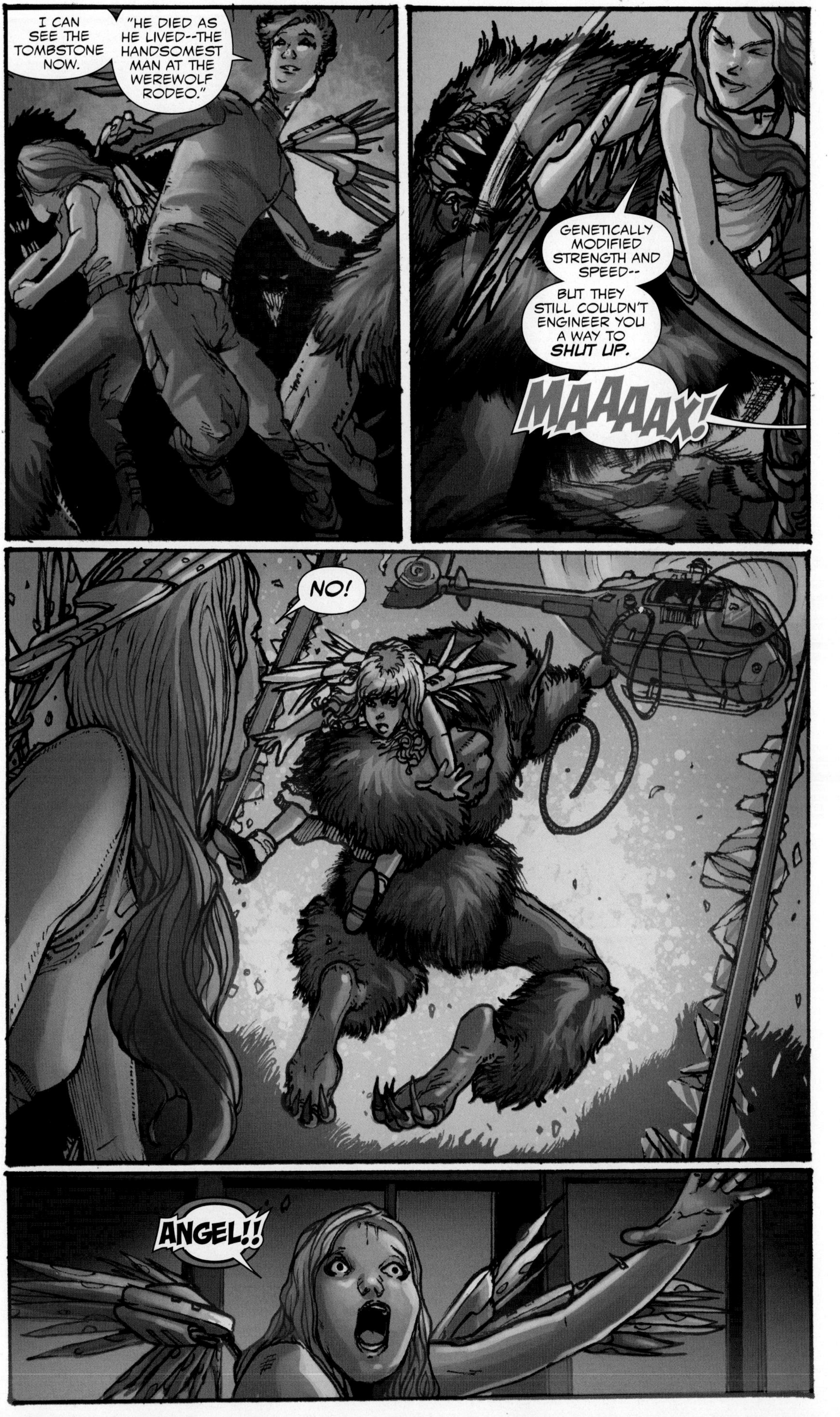
I CAN SEE THE TOMBSTONE NOW.
"HE DIED AS HE LIVED--THE HANDSOMEST MAN AT THE WEREWOLF RODEO."
GENETICALLY MODIFIED STRENGTH AND SPEED--
BUT THEY STILL COULDN'T ENGINEER YOU A WAY TO SHUT UP.
MAAAAX!
NO!
ANGEL!!

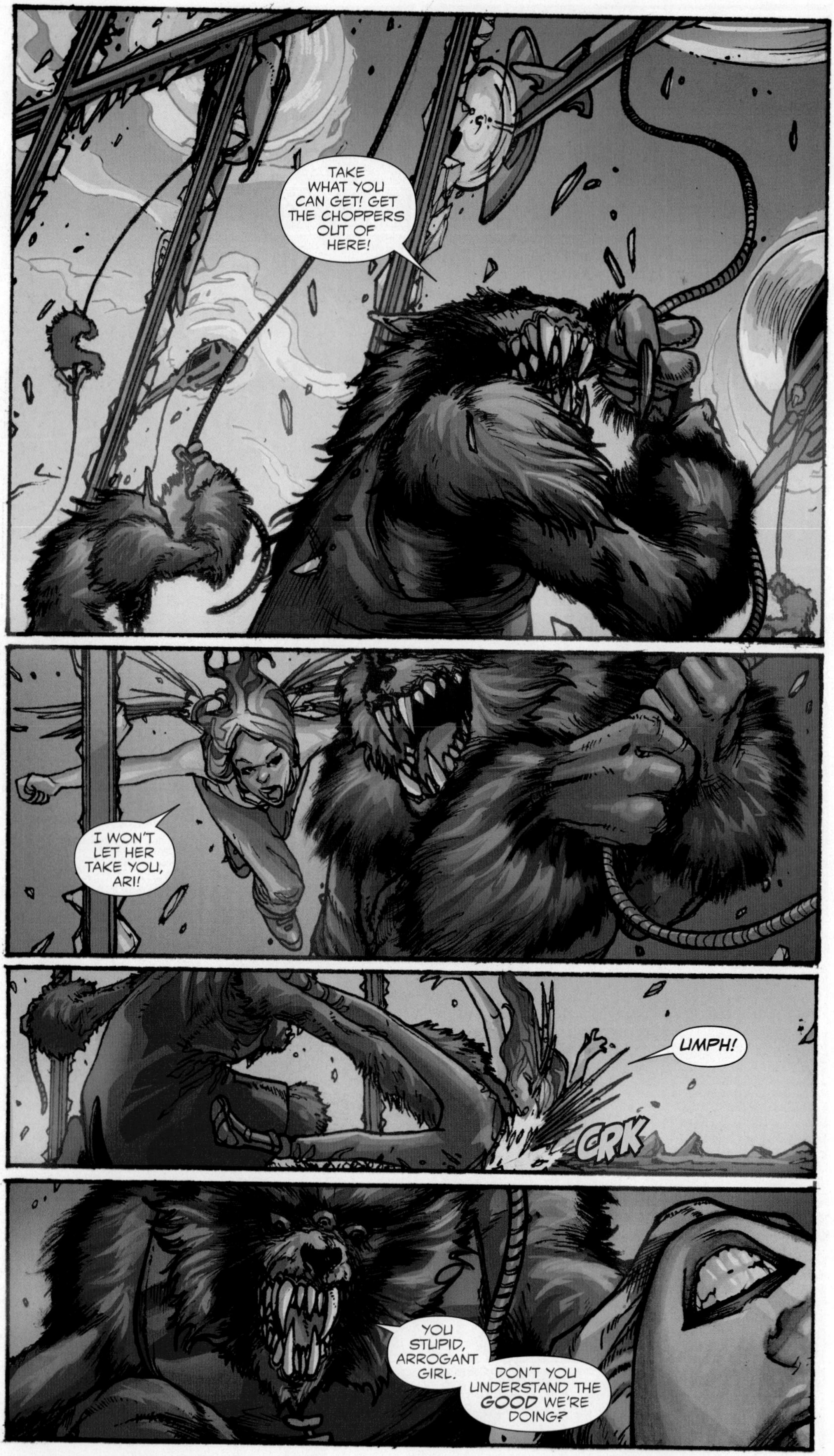
TAKE WHAT YOU CAN GET! GET THE CHOPPERS OUT OF HERE!
I WON'T LET HER TAKE YOU, ARI!
UMPH!
CRK
YOU STUPID, ARROGANT GIRL.
DON'T YOU UNDERSTAND THE GOOD WE'RE DOING?

YOU'RE A PUNK WHO ATTACKS KIDS. THAT'S A PRETTY CRAP DEFINITION OF "GOOD."
GAZZY!
WANT TO KNOW WHY THEY CALL ME THE GASMAN, ARI?
"I CAN'T READ MINDS LIKE MY SISTER.
"BUT I CAN READ MACHINES.
"AND I'M REAL GOOD WITH FIRE."

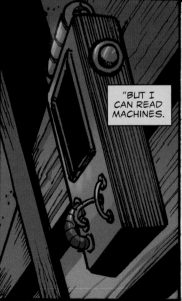

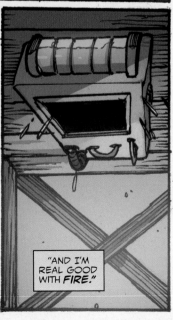

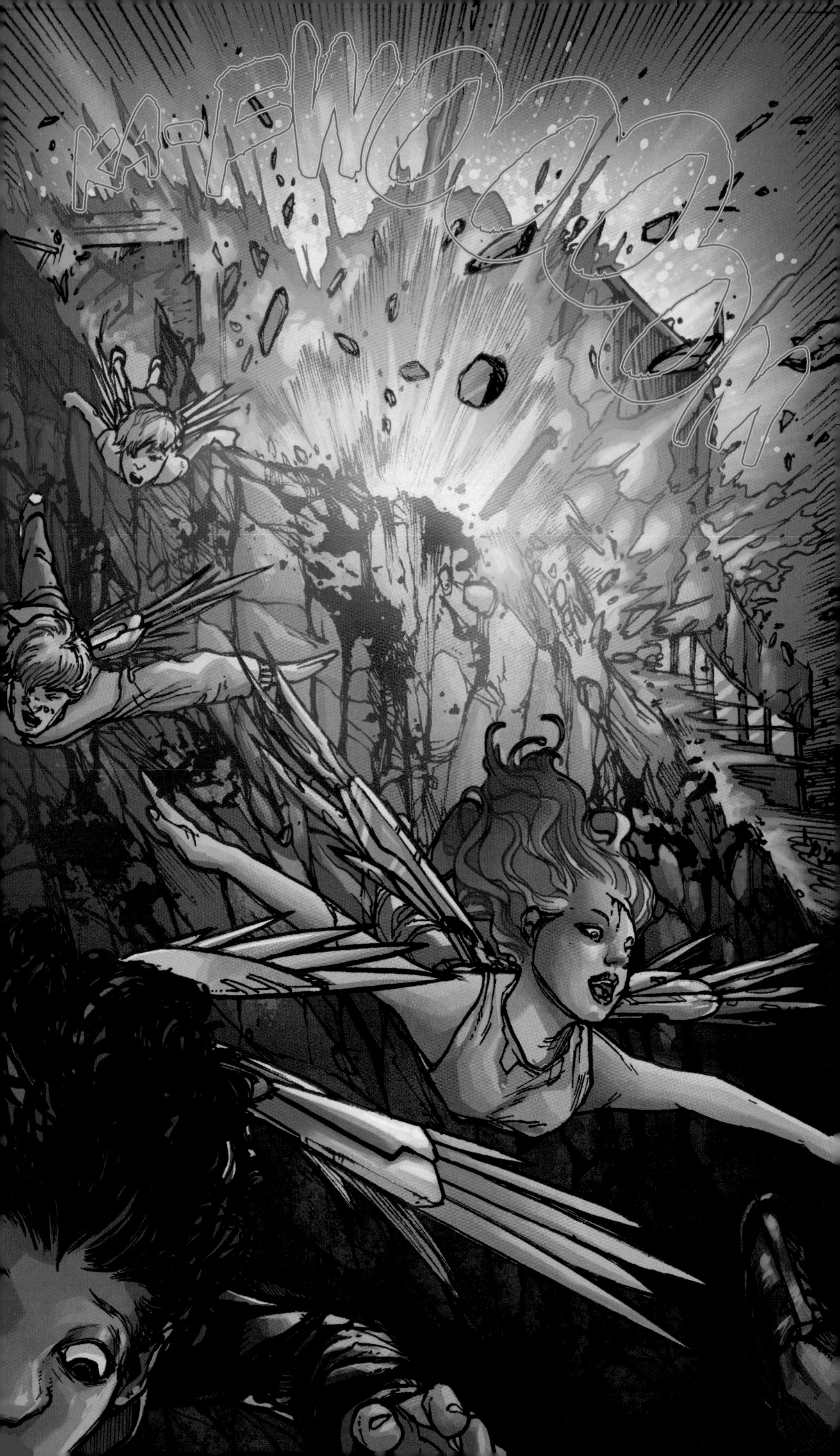
KA-FWOOOOOM!

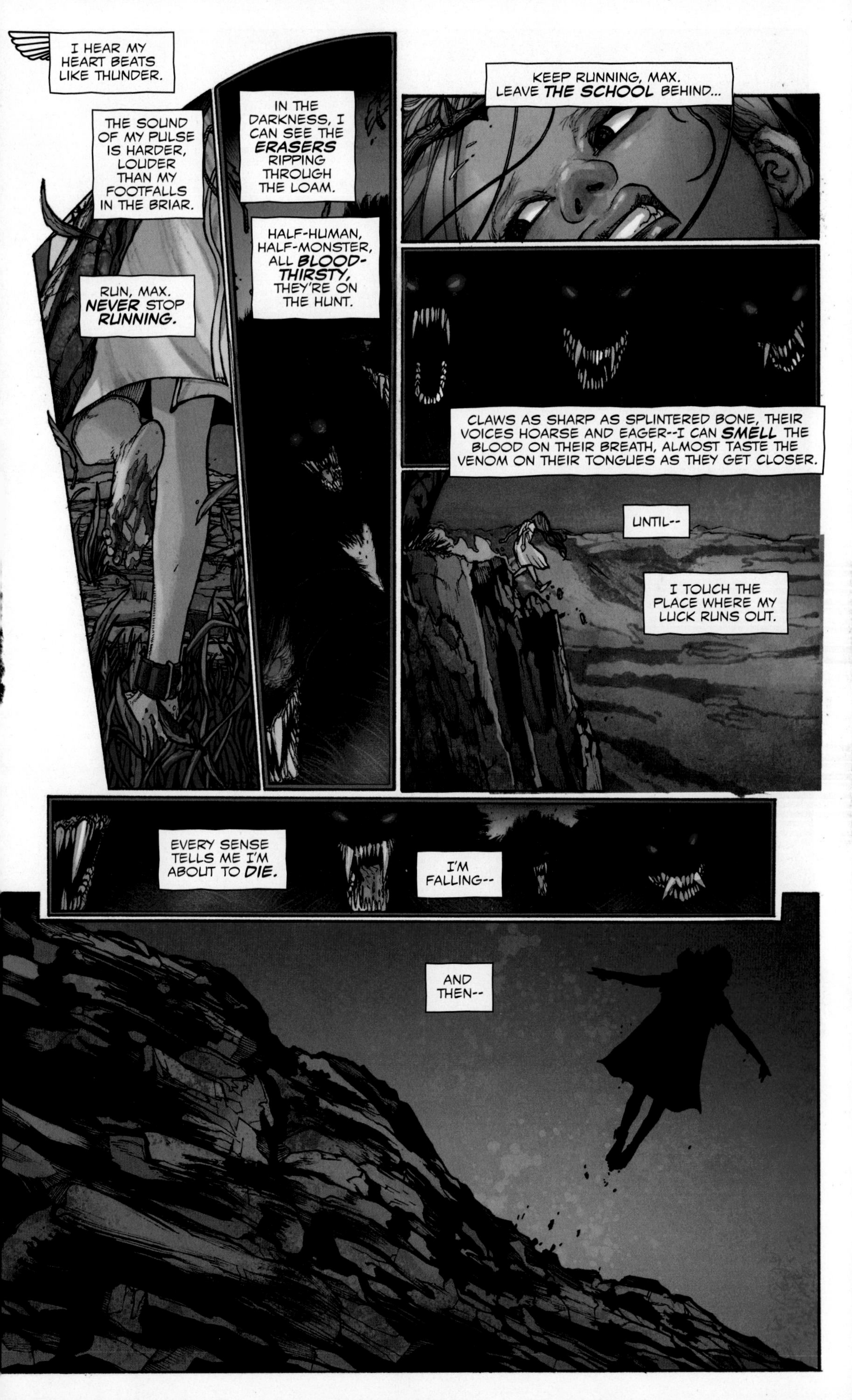

I HEAR MY HEART BEATS LIKE THUNDER.
THE SOUND OF MY PULSE IS HARDER, LOUDER THAN MY FOOTFALLS IN THE BRIAR.
RUN, MAX. NEVER STOP RUNNING.
IN THE DARKNESS, I CAN SEE THE ERASERS RIPPING THROUGH THE LOAM.
HALF-HUMAN, HALF-MONSTER, ALL BLOOD-THIRSTY, THEY'RE ON THE HUNT.
KEEP RUNNING, MAX. LEAVE THE SCHOOL BEHIND...
CLAWS AS SHARP AS SPLINTERED BONE, THEIR VOICES HOARSE AND EAGER--I CAN SMELL THE BLOOD ON THEIR BREATH, ALMOST TASTE THE VENOM ON THEIR TONGUES AS THEY GET CLOSER.
UNTIL--
I TOUCH THE PLACE WHERE MY LUCK RUNS OUT.
EVERY SENSE TELLS ME I'M ABOUT TO DIE.
I'M FALLING--
AND THEN--

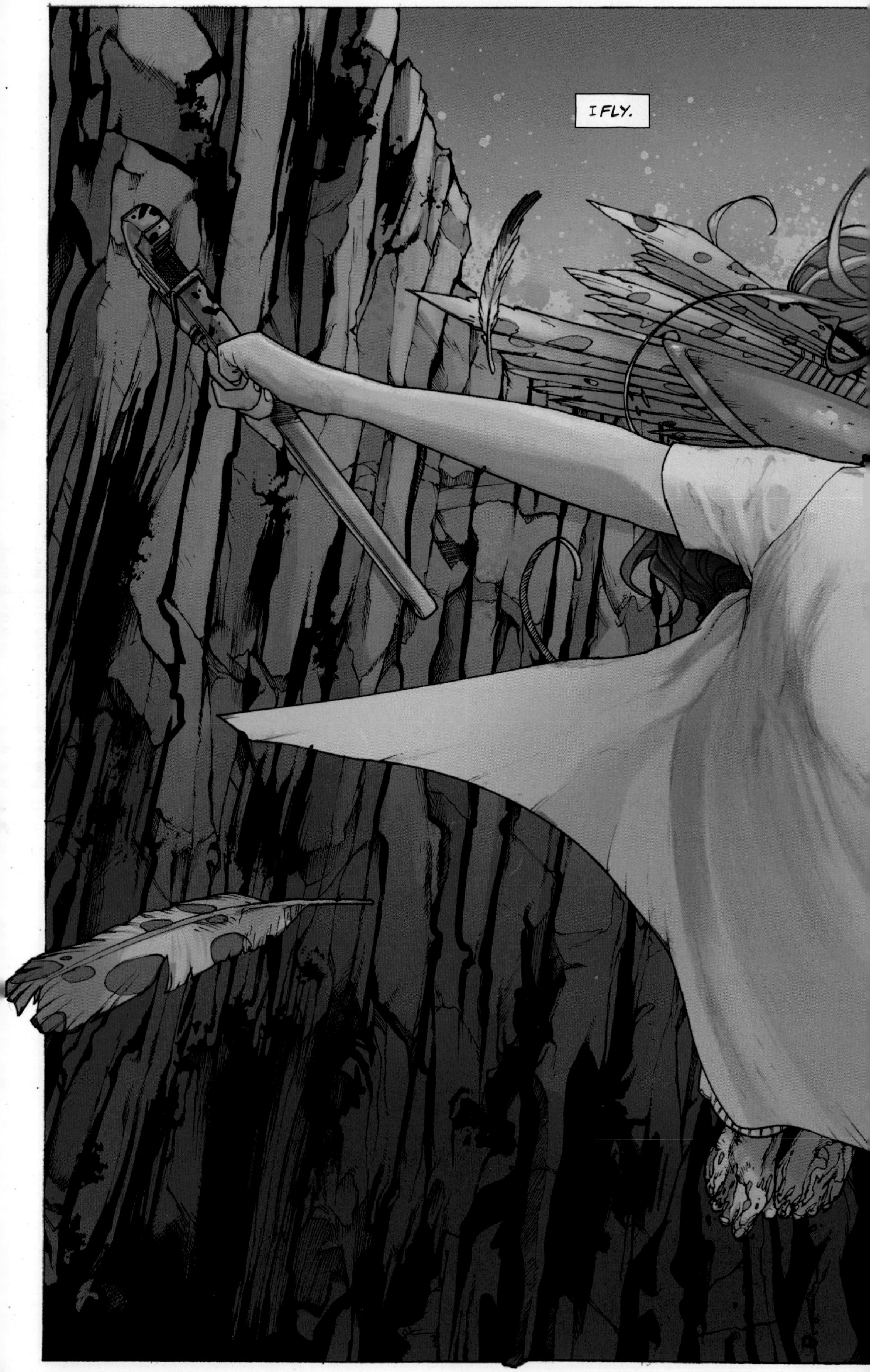
I FLY.

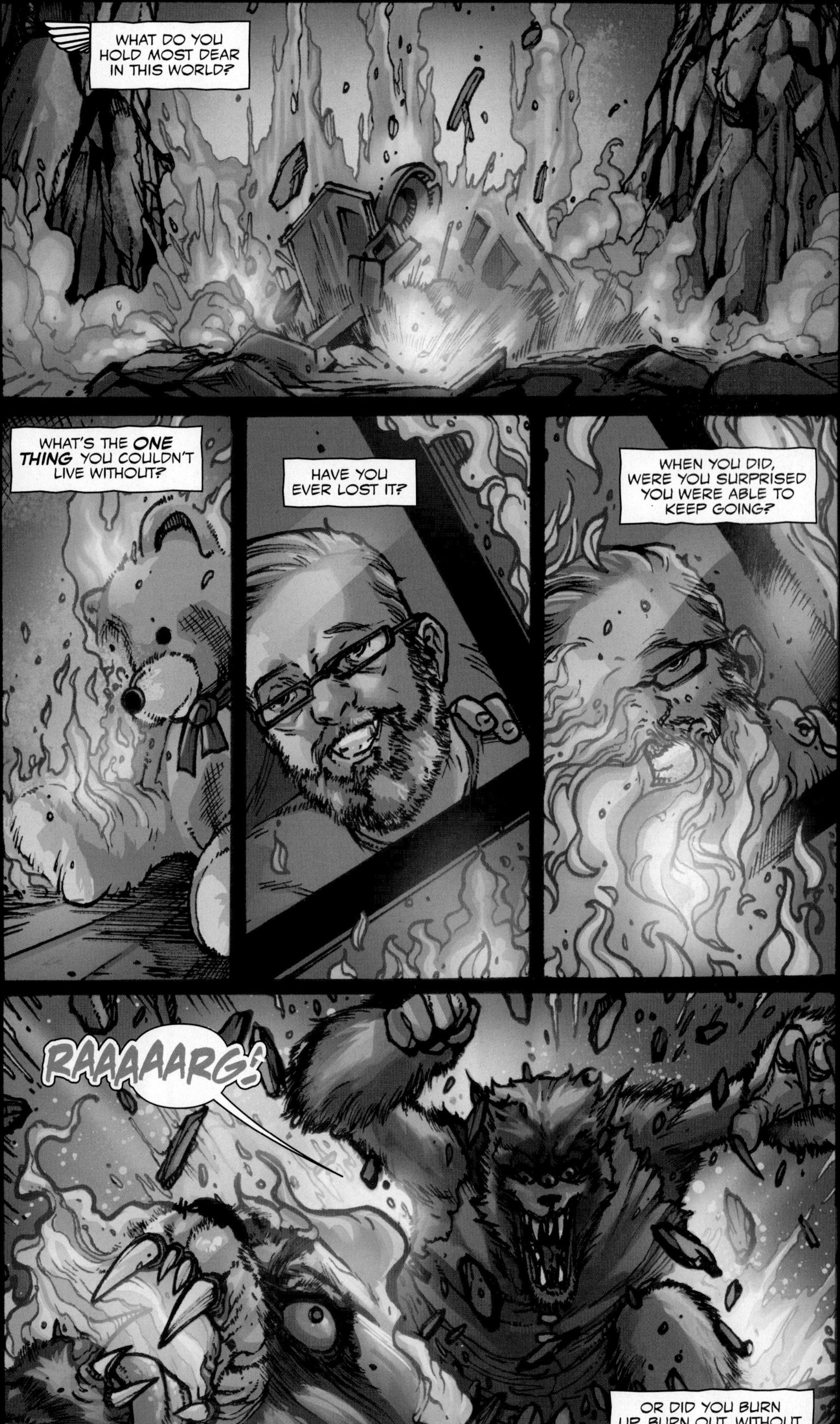
WHAT DO YOU HOLD MOST DEAR IN THIS WORLD?
WHAT'S THE ONE THING YOU COULDN'T LIVE WITHOUT?
HAVE YOU EVER LOST IT?
WHEN YOU DID, WERE YOU SURPRISED YOU WERE ABLE TO KEEP GOING?
RAAAAARG!
OR DID YOU BURN UP, BURN OUT, WITHOUT IT TO SUSTAIN YOU?

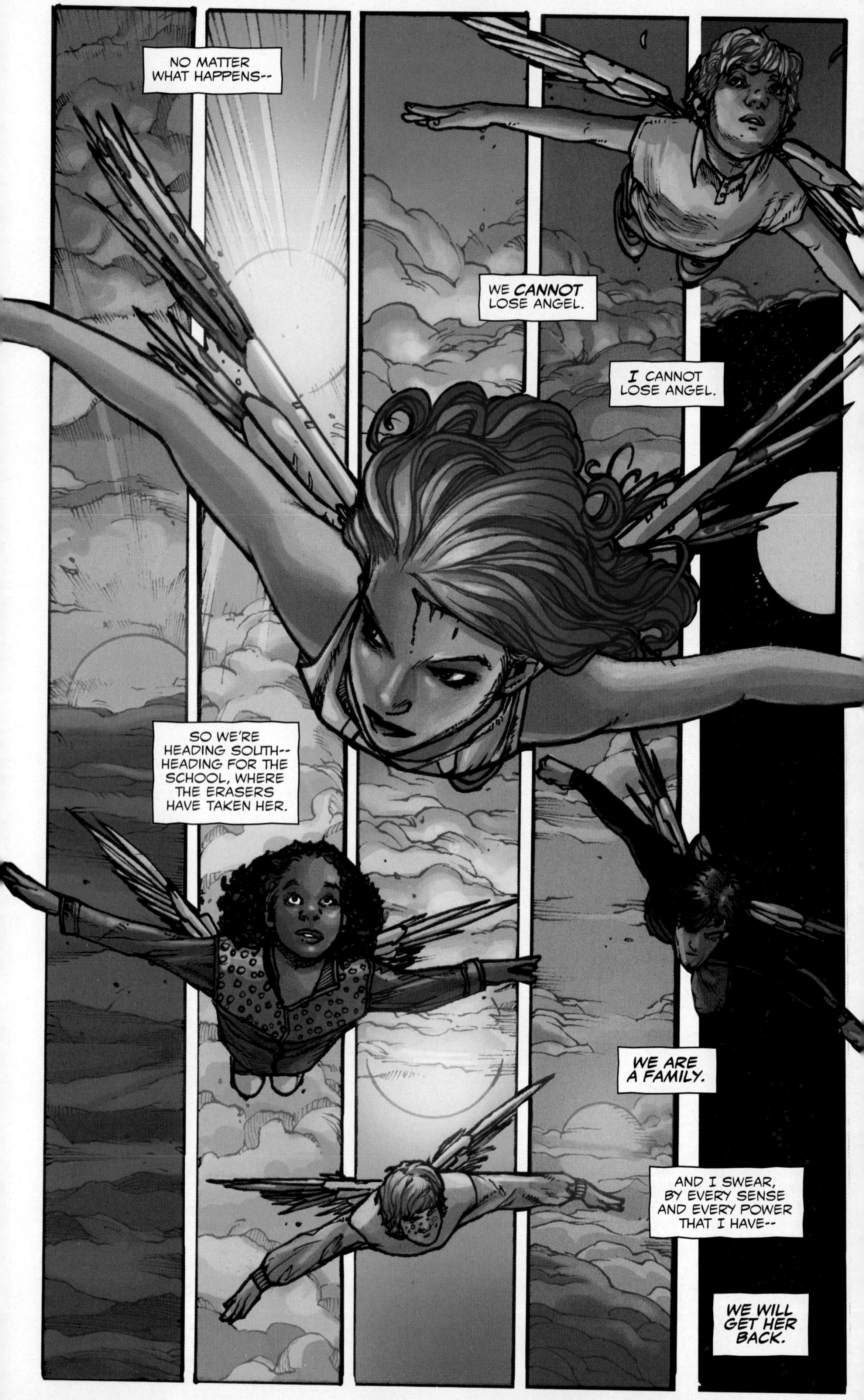
NO MATTER WHAT HAPPENS--
WE CANNOT LOSE ANGEL.
I CANNOT LOSE ANGEL.
SO WE'RE HEADING SOUTH--HEADING FOR THE SCHOOL, WHERE THE ERASERS HAVE TAKEN HER.
WE ARE A FAMILY.
AND I SWEAR, BY EVERY SENSE AND EVERY POWER THAT I HAVE--
WE WILL GET HER BACK.

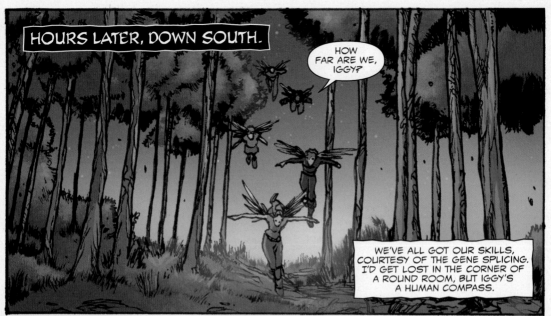

HOW FAR ARE WE, IGGY?

WE'VE ALL GOT OUR SKILLS, COURTESY OF THE GENE SPLICING. I'D GET LOST IN THE CORNER OF A ROUND ROOM, BUT IGGY'S A HUMAN COMPASS.

WE'RE DEFINITELY IN CALIFORNIA. I'M GUESSING NOT FAR FROM LAKE TAHOE.

WE'RE GOING TO NEED TO EAT SOON. OUR METABOLISMS ARE TOO HIGH TO SUSTAIN THIS MUCH ACTIVITY WITHOUT THE NUTRIENTS TO MATCH.

I'LL GO FOR SUPPLIES.

BE CAREFUL, MAX.

I'M PRETTY SURE I'M THE APEX PREDATOR AROUND HERE.

UMM, DID YOU SEE WHAT FLEW INTO OUR HOUSE?

RUDE.

HURRY BACK, MAX. WE'LL BE WAITING.

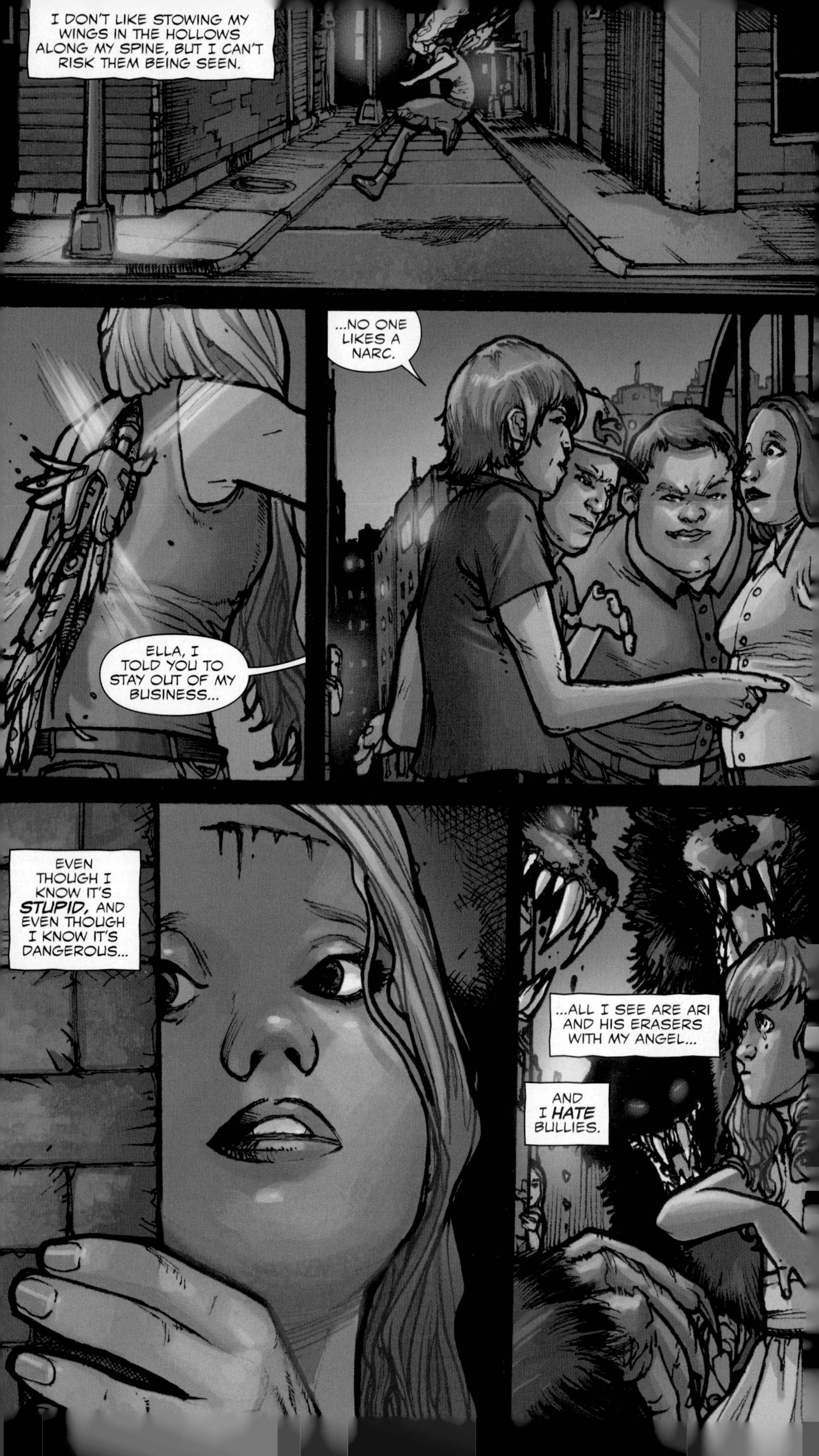
I DON'T LIKE STOWING MY WINGS IN THE HOLLOWS ALONG MY SPINE, BUT I CAN'T RISK THEM BEING SEEN.
ELLA, I TOLD YOU TO STAY OUT OF MY BUSINESS...
...NO ONE LIKES A NARC.
EVEN THOUGH I KNOW IT'S STUPID, AND EVEN THOUGH I KNOW IT'S DANGEROUS...
...ALL I SEE ARE ARI AND HIS ERASERS WITH MY ANGEL...
AND I HATE BULLIES.

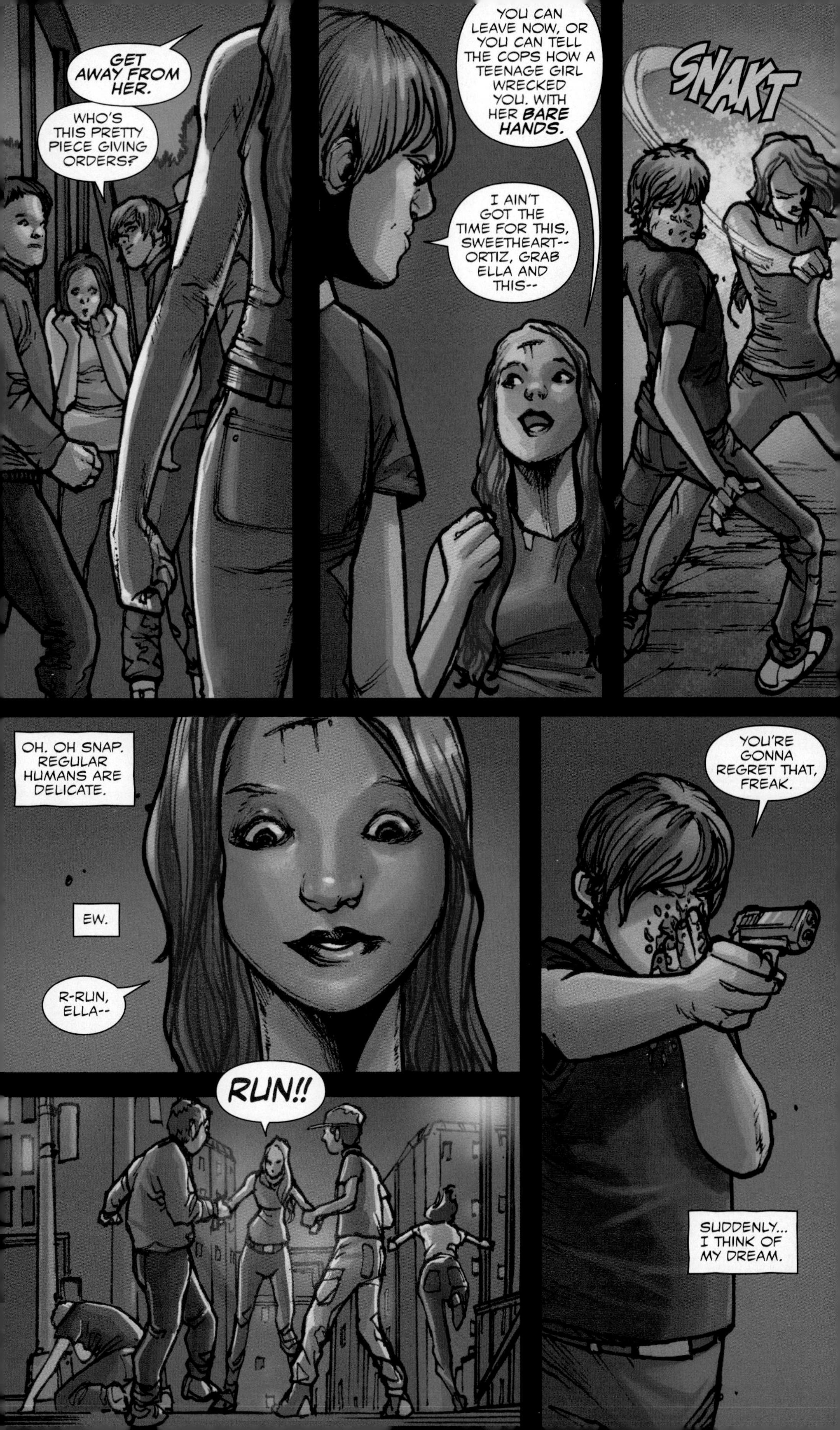
GET AWAY FROM HER.
WHO'S THIS PRETTY PIECE GIVING ORDERS?
YOU CAN LEAVE NOW, OR YOU CAN TELL THE COPS HOW A TEENAGE GIRL WRECKED YOU. WITH HER BARE HANDS.
I AIN'T GOT THE TIME FOR THIS, SWEETHEART-- ORTIZ, GRAB ELLA AND THIS--
SNAKT
OH. OH SNAP. REGULAR HUMANS ARE DELICATE.
EW.
R-RUN, ELLA--
YOU'RE GONNA REGRET THAT, FREAK.
RUN!!
SUDDENLY... I THINK OF MY DREAM.

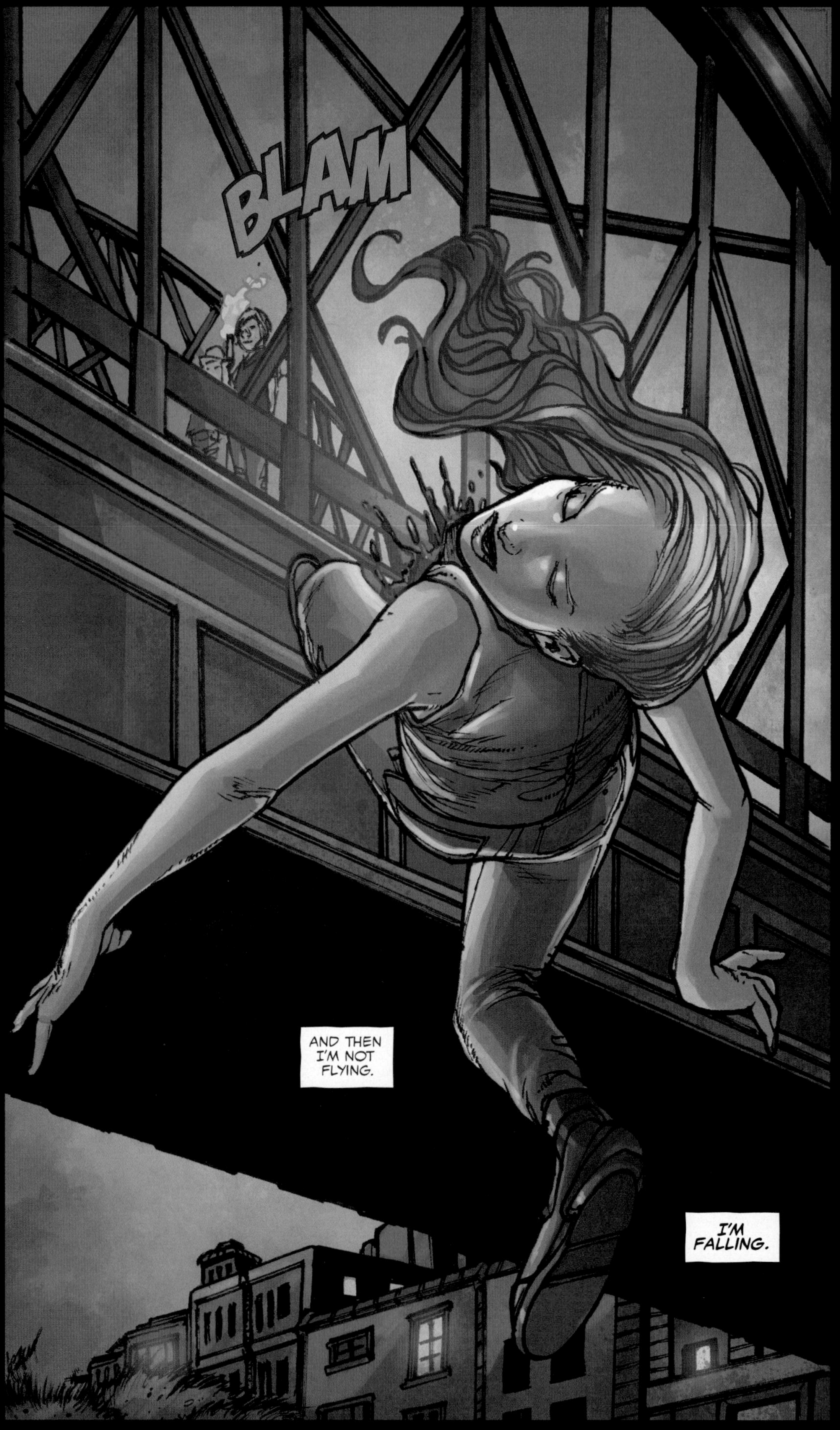
BLAM
AND THEN I'M NOT FLYING.
I'M FALLING.

CHAPTER 2

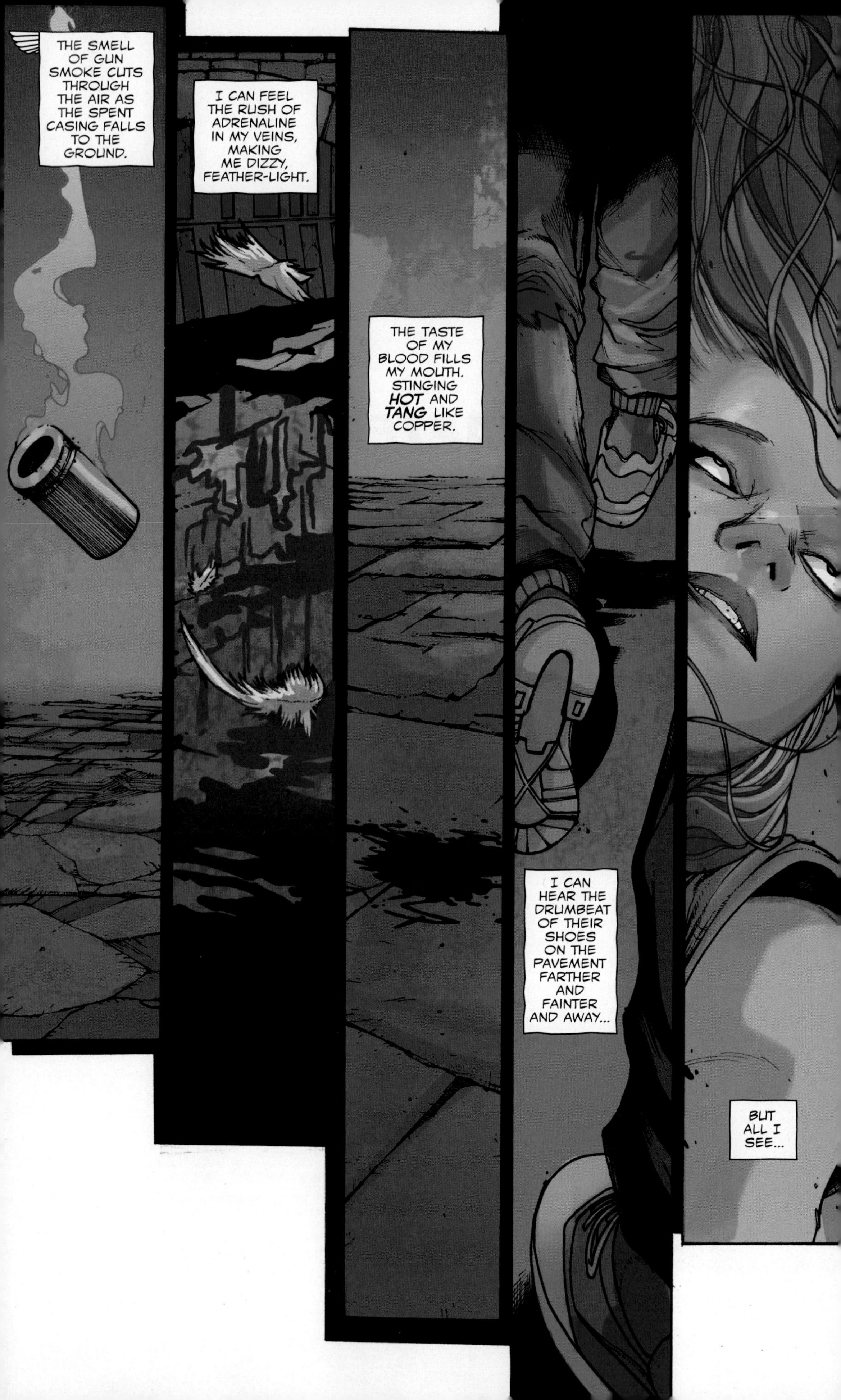
THE SMELL OF GUN SMOKE CUTS THROUGH THE AIR AS THE SPENT CASING FALLS TO THE GROUND.
I CAN FEEL THE RUSH OF ADRENALINE IN MY VEINS, MAKING ME DIZZY, FEATHER-LIGHT.
THE TASTE OF MY BLOOD FILLS MY MOUTH. STINGING HOT AND TANG LIKE COPPER.
I CAN HEAR THE DRUMBEAT OF THEIR SHOES ON THE PAVEMENT FARTHER AND FAINTER AND AWAY...
BUT ALL I SEE...

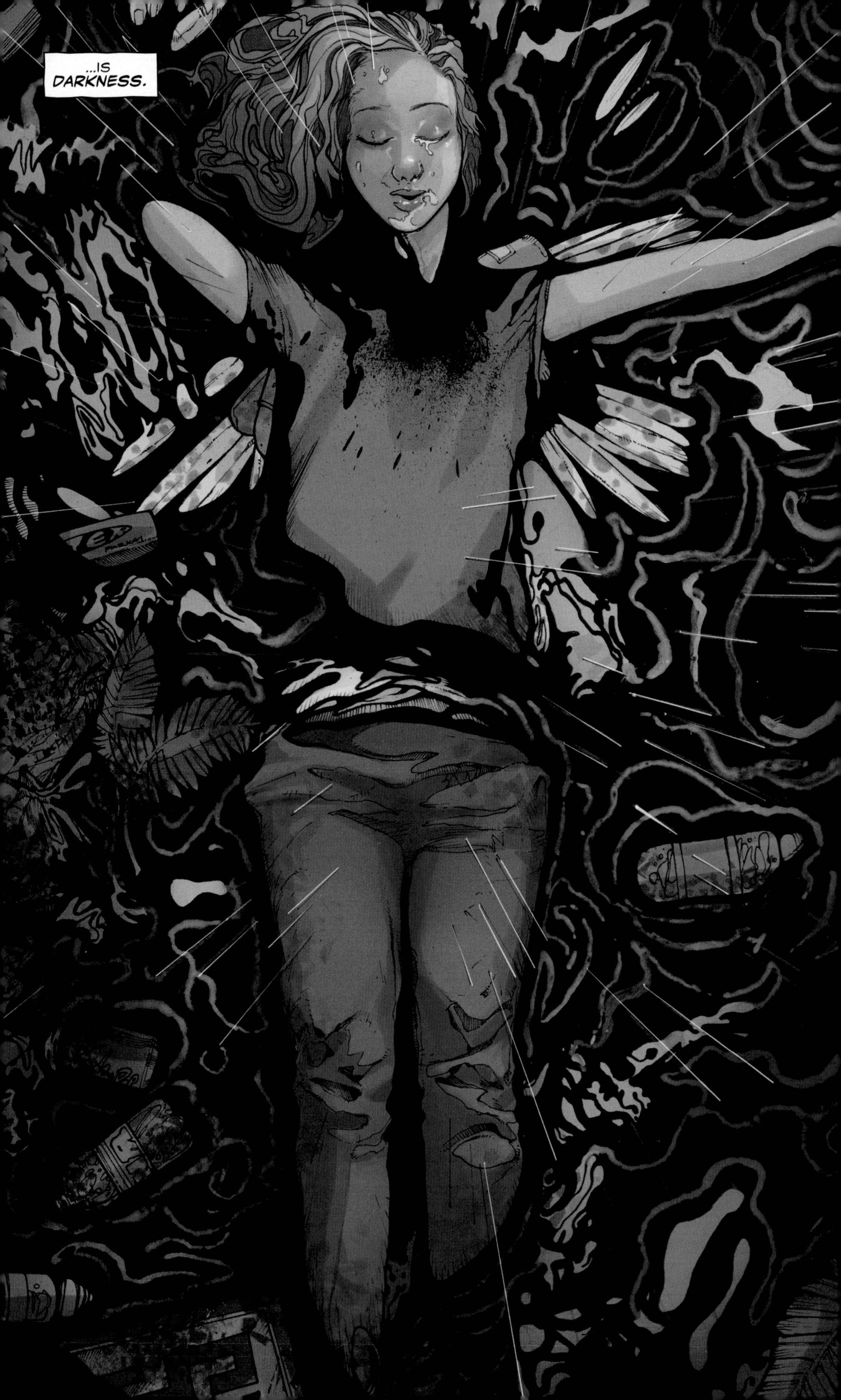
...IS
DARKNESS.

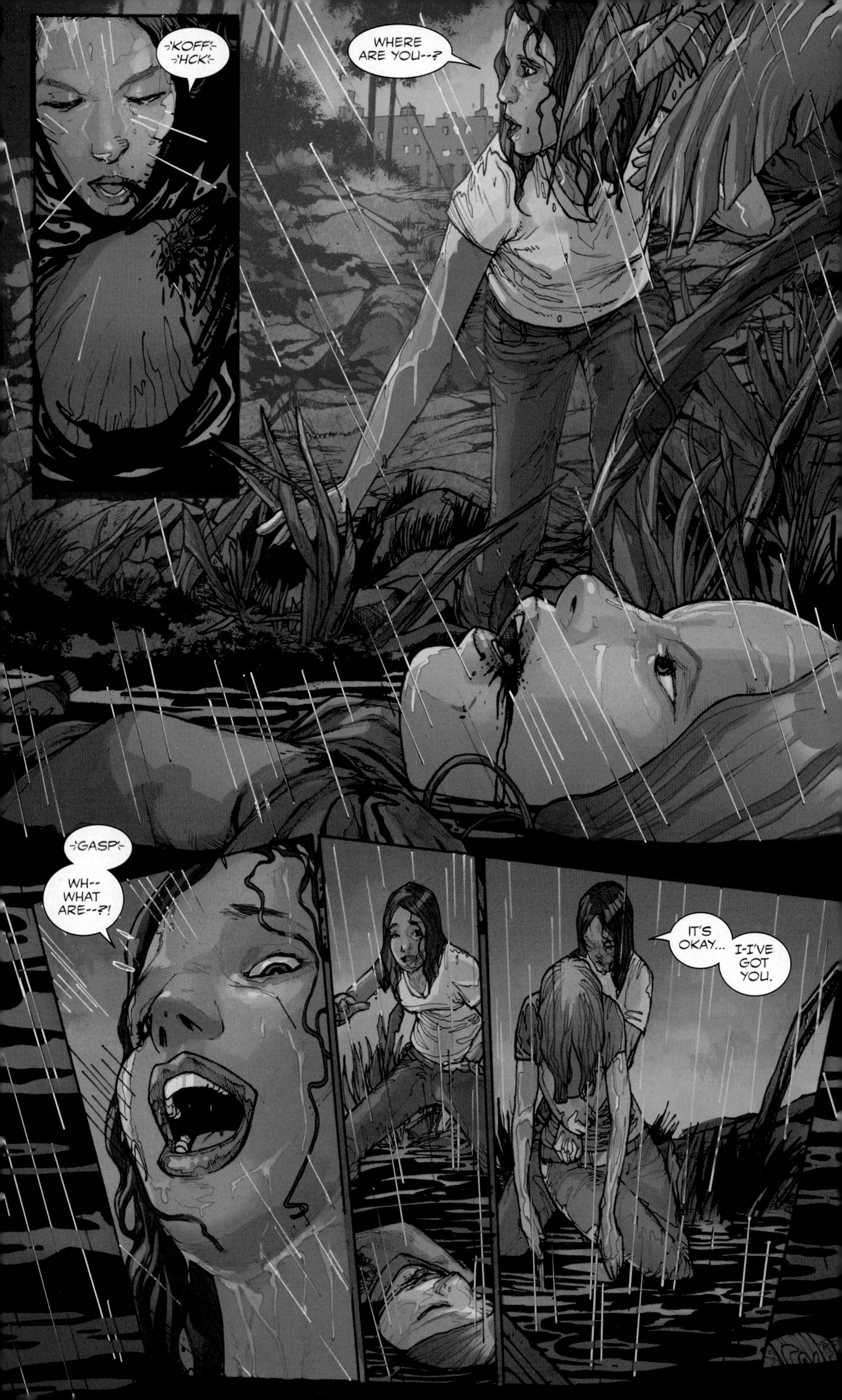
KOFF
HCK
WHERE ARE YOU--?
GASP
WH-- WHAT ARE--?!
IT'S OKAY... I-I'VE GOT YOU.

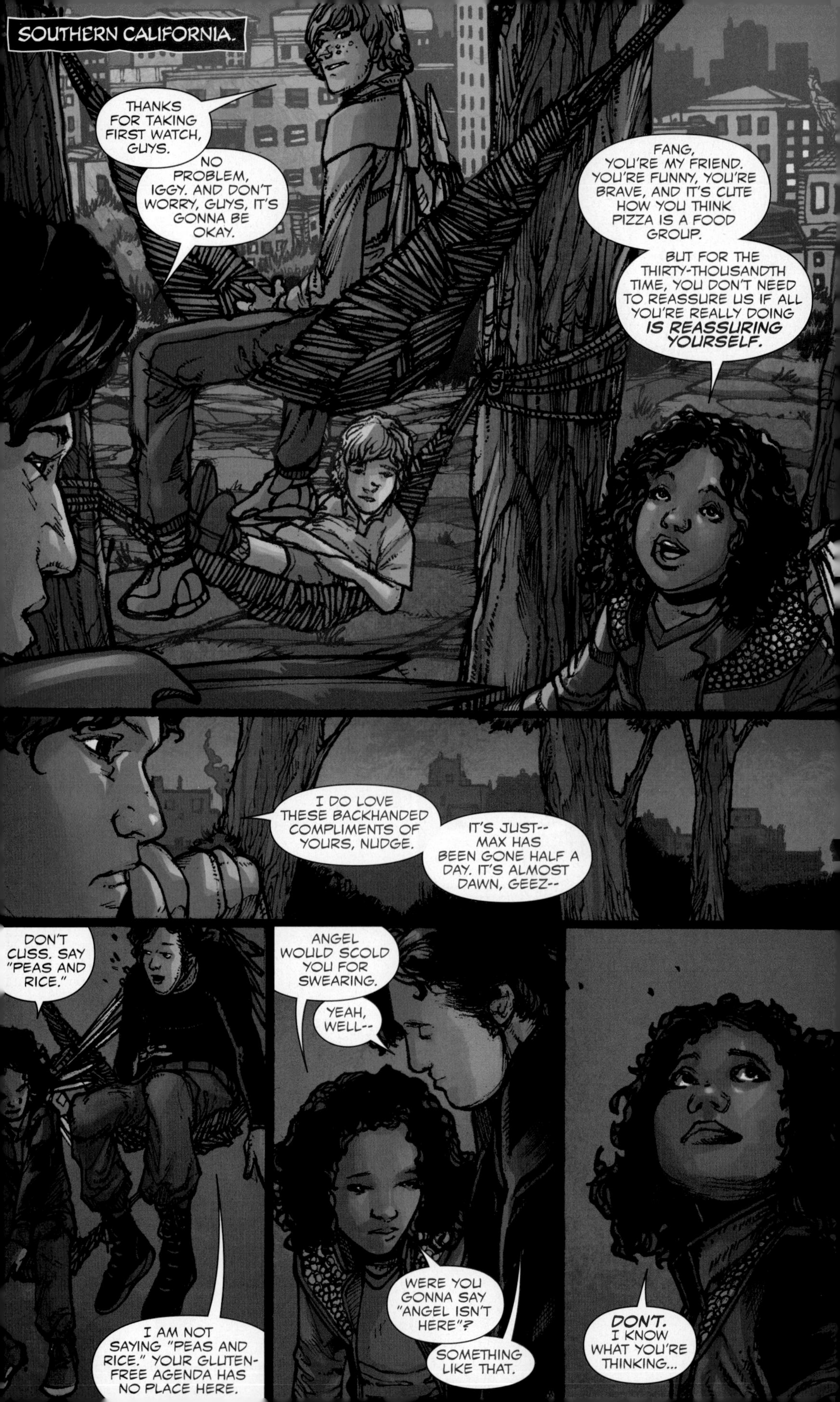
SOUTHERN CALIFORNIA.
THANKS FOR TAKING FIRST WATCH, GUYS.
NO PROBLEM, IGGY. AND DON'T WORRY, GUYS, IT'S GONNA BE OKAY.
FANG, YOU'RE MY FRIEND. YOU'RE FUNNY, YOU'RE BRAVE, AND IT'S CUTE HOW YOU THINK PIZZA IS A FOOD GROUP.
BUT FOR THE THIRTY-THOUSANDTH TIME, YOU DON'T NEED TO REASSURE US IF ALL YOU'RE REALLY DOING **IS REASSURING YOURSELF.**
I DO LOVE THESE BACKHANDED COMPLIMENTS OF YOURS, NUDGE.
IT'S JUST-- MAX HAS BEEN GONE HALF A DAY. IT'S ALMOST DAWN, GEEZ--
DON'T CUSS. SAY "PEAS AND RICE."
I AM NOT SAYING "PEAS AND RICE." YOUR GLUTEN-FREE AGENDA HAS NO PLACE HERE.
ANGEL WOULD SCOLD YOU FOR SWEARING.
YEAH, WELL--
WERE YOU GONNA SAY "ANGEL ISN'T HERE"?
SOMETHING LIKE THAT.
DON'T. I KNOW WHAT YOU'RE THINKING...

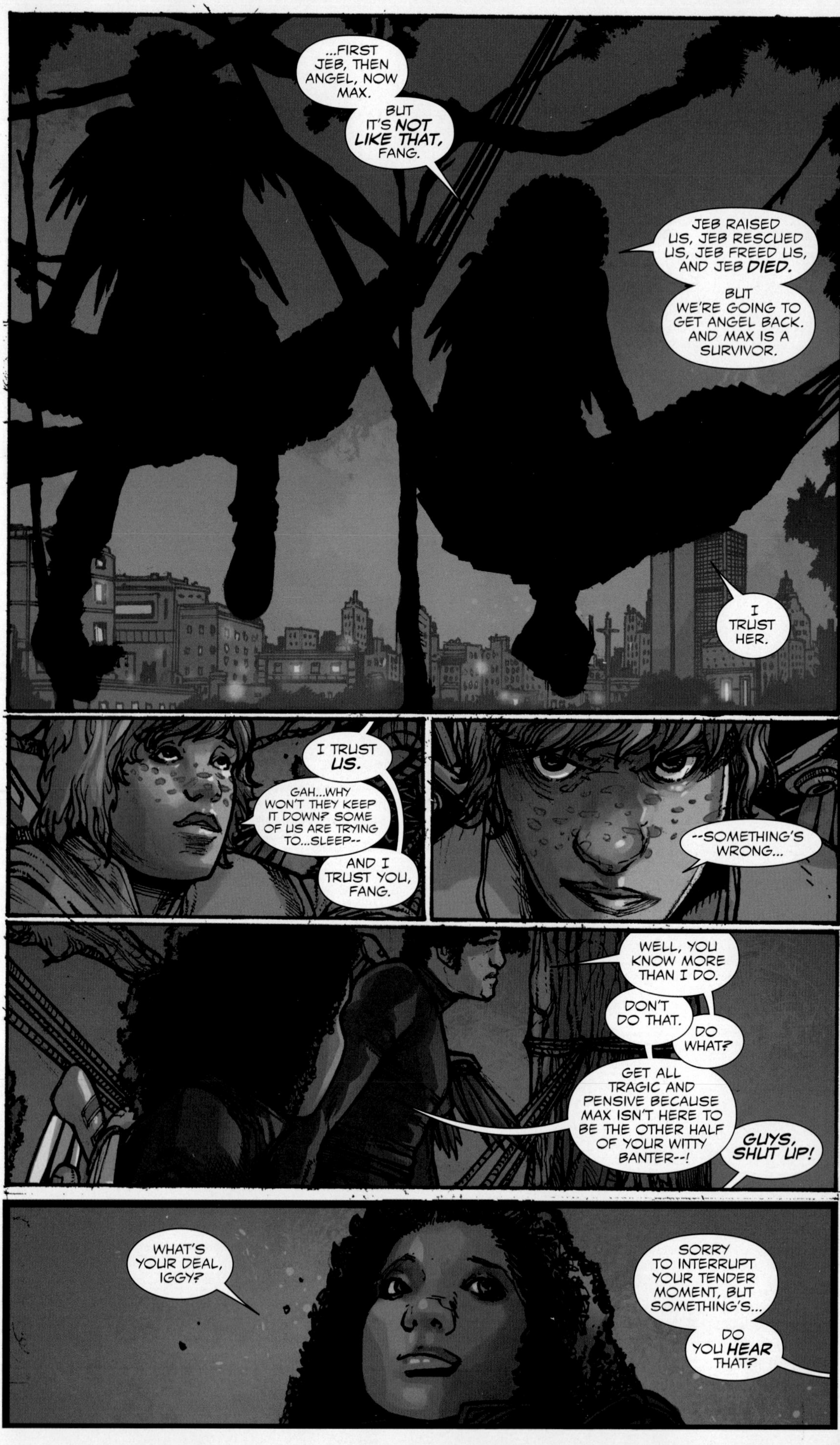
...FIRST JEB, THEN ANGEL, NOW MAX.
BUT IT'S **NOT LIKE THAT,** FANG.
JEB RAISED US, JEB RESCUED US, JEB FREED US, AND JEB **DIED.**
BUT WE'RE GOING TO GET ANGEL BACK. AND MAX IS A SURVIVOR.
I TRUST HER.
I TRUST **US.**
GAH...WHY WON'T THEY KEEP IT DOWN? SOME OF US ARE TRYING TO...SLEEP--
AND I TRUST YOU, FANG.
--SOMETHING'S WRONG...
WELL, YOU KNOW MORE THAN I DO.
DON'T DO THAT.
DO WHAT?
GET ALL TRAGIC AND PENSIVE BECAUSE MAX ISN'T HERE TO BE THE OTHER HALF OF YOUR WITTY BANTER--!
GUYS, SHUT UP!
WHAT'S YOUR DEAL, IGGY?
SORRY TO INTERRUPT YOUR TENDER MOMENT, BUT SOMETHING'S...
DO YOU **HEAR** THAT?

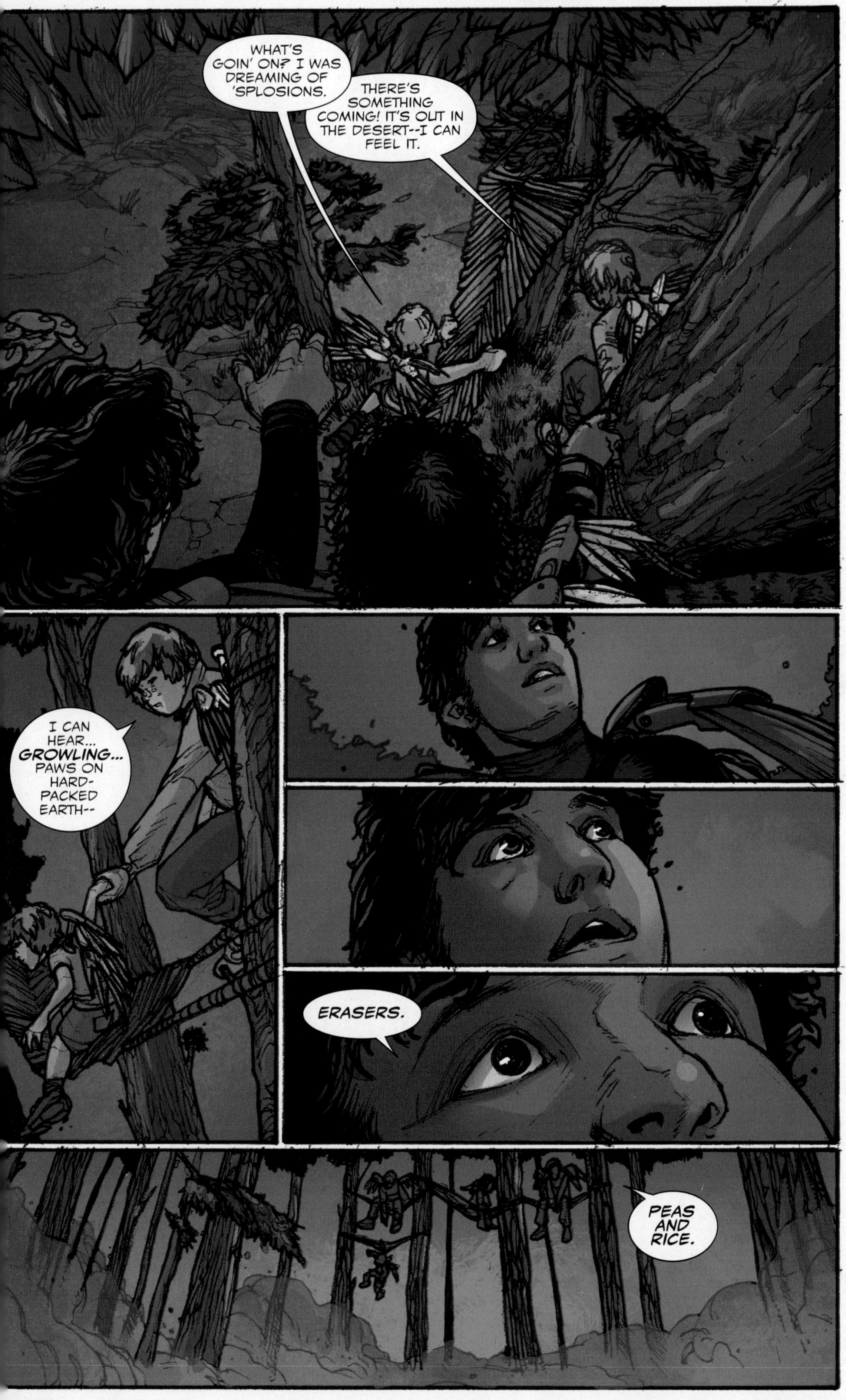
WHAT'S GOIN' ON? I WAS DREAMING OF 'SPLOSIONS.
THERE'S SOMETHING COMING! IT'S OUT IN THE DESERT--I CAN FEEL IT.
I CAN HEAR... GROWLING... PAWS ON HARD-PACKED EARTH--
ERASERS.
PEAS AND RICE.

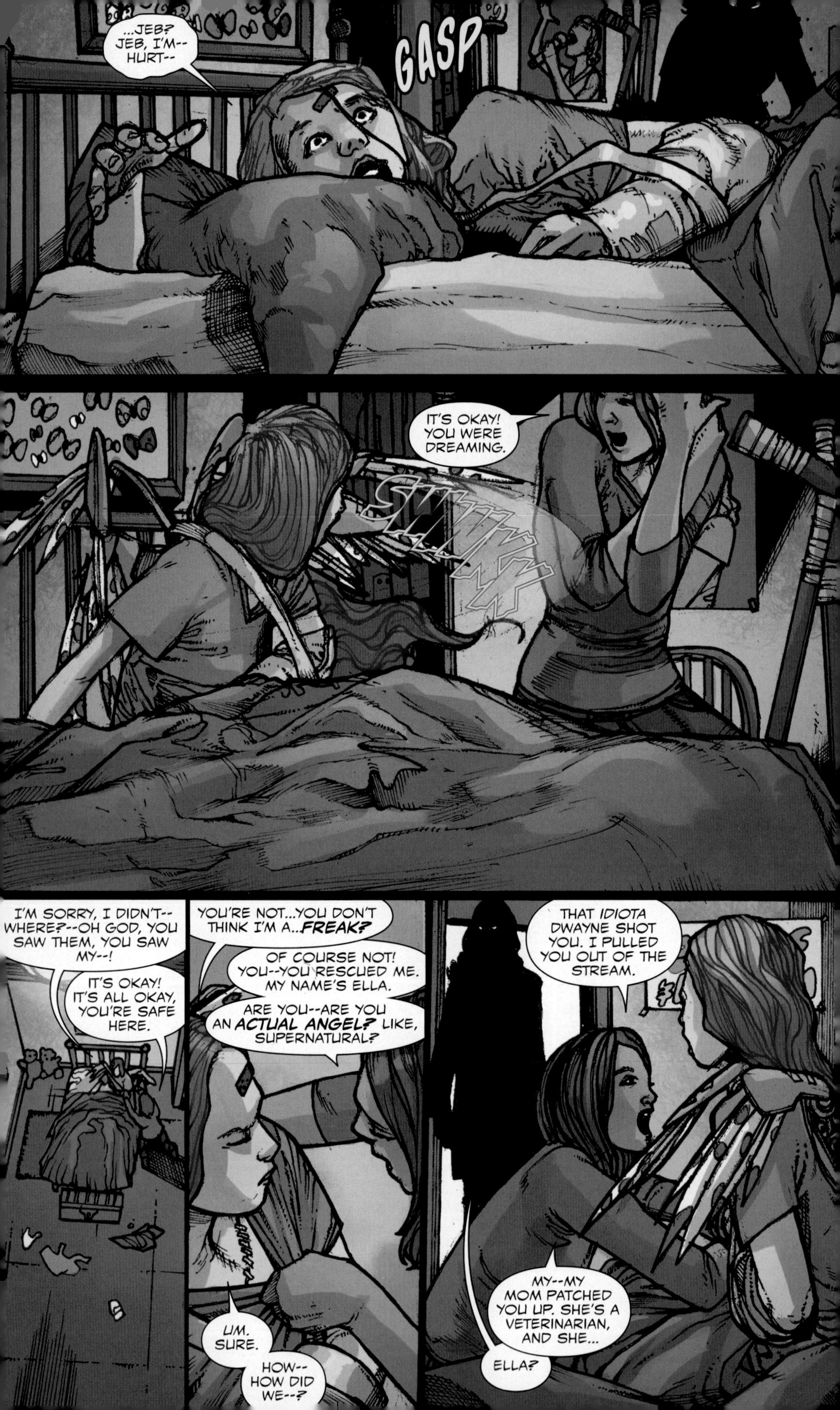
...JEB? JEB, I'M-- HURT--
GASP
IT'S OKAY! YOU WERE DREAMING.
SHHHNK
I'M SORRY, I DIDN'T-- WHERE?--OH GOD, YOU SAW THEM, YOU SAW MY--!
IT'S OKAY! IT'S ALL OKAY, YOU'RE SAFE HERE.
YOU'RE NOT...YOU DON'T THINK I'M A...FREAK?
OF COURSE NOT! YOU--YOU RESCUED ME. MY NAME'S ELLA.
ARE YOU--ARE YOU AN ACTUAL ANGEL? LIKE, SUPERNATURAL?
UM. SURE.
HOW-- HOW DID WE--?
THAT IDIOTA DWAYNE SHOT YOU. I PULLED YOU OUT OF THE STREAM.
MY--MY MOM PATCHED YOU UP. SHE'S A VETERINARIAN, AND SHE...
ELLA?

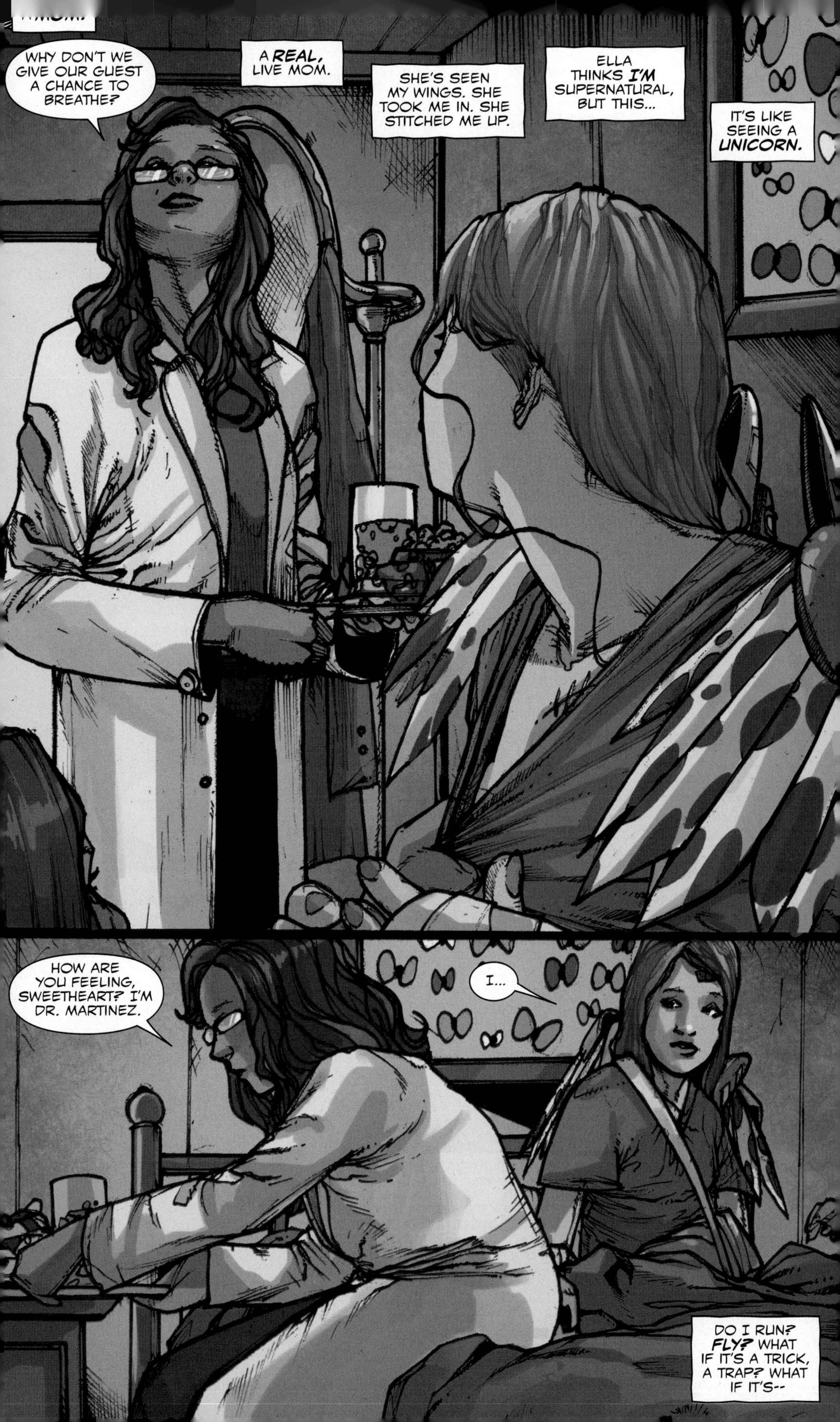
WHY DON'T WE GIVE OUR GUEST A CHANCE TO BREATHE?
A REAL, LIVE MOM.
SHE'S SEEN MY WINGS. SHE TOOK ME IN. SHE STITCHED ME UP.
ELLA THINKS I'M SUPERNATURAL, BUT THIS...
IT'S LIKE SEEING A UNICORN.
HOW ARE YOU FEELING, SWEETHEART? I'M DR. MARTINEZ.
I...
DO I RUN? FLY? WHAT IF IT'S A TRICK, A TRAP? WHAT IF IT'S--

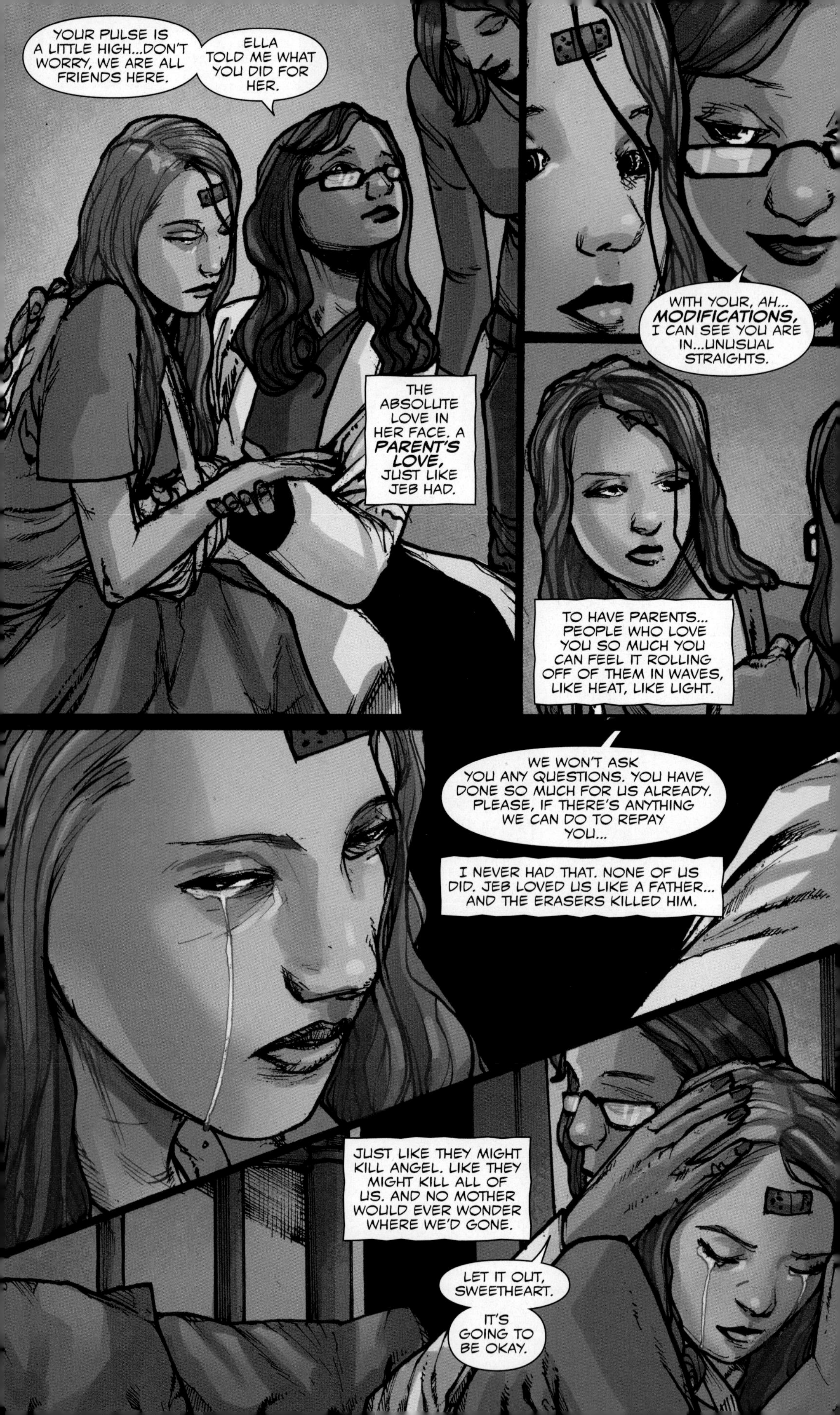

YOUR PULSE IS A LITTLE HIGH...DON'T WORRY, WE ARE ALL FRIENDS HERE.
ELLA TOLD ME WHAT YOU DID FOR HER.
WITH YOUR, AH... MODIFICATIONS, I CAN SEE YOU ARE IN...UNUSUAL STRAIGHTS.
THE ABSOLUTE LOVE IN HER FACE. A PARENT'S LOVE, JUST LIKE JEB HAD.
TO HAVE PARENTS... PEOPLE WHO LOVE YOU SO MUCH YOU CAN FEEL IT ROLLING OFF OF THEM IN WAVES, LIKE HEAT, LIKE LIGHT.
WE WON'T ASK YOU ANY QUESTIONS. YOU HAVE DONE SO MUCH FOR US ALREADY. PLEASE, IF THERE'S ANYTHING WE CAN DO TO REPAY YOU...
I NEVER HAD THAT. NONE OF US DID. JEB LOVED US LIKE A FATHER... AND THE ERASERS KILLED HIM.
JUST LIKE THEY MIGHT KILL ANGEL. LIKE THEY MIGHT KILL ALL OF US. AND NO MOTHER WOULD EVER WONDER WHERE WE'D GONE.
LET IT OUT, SWEETHEART.
IT'S GOING TO BE OKAY.

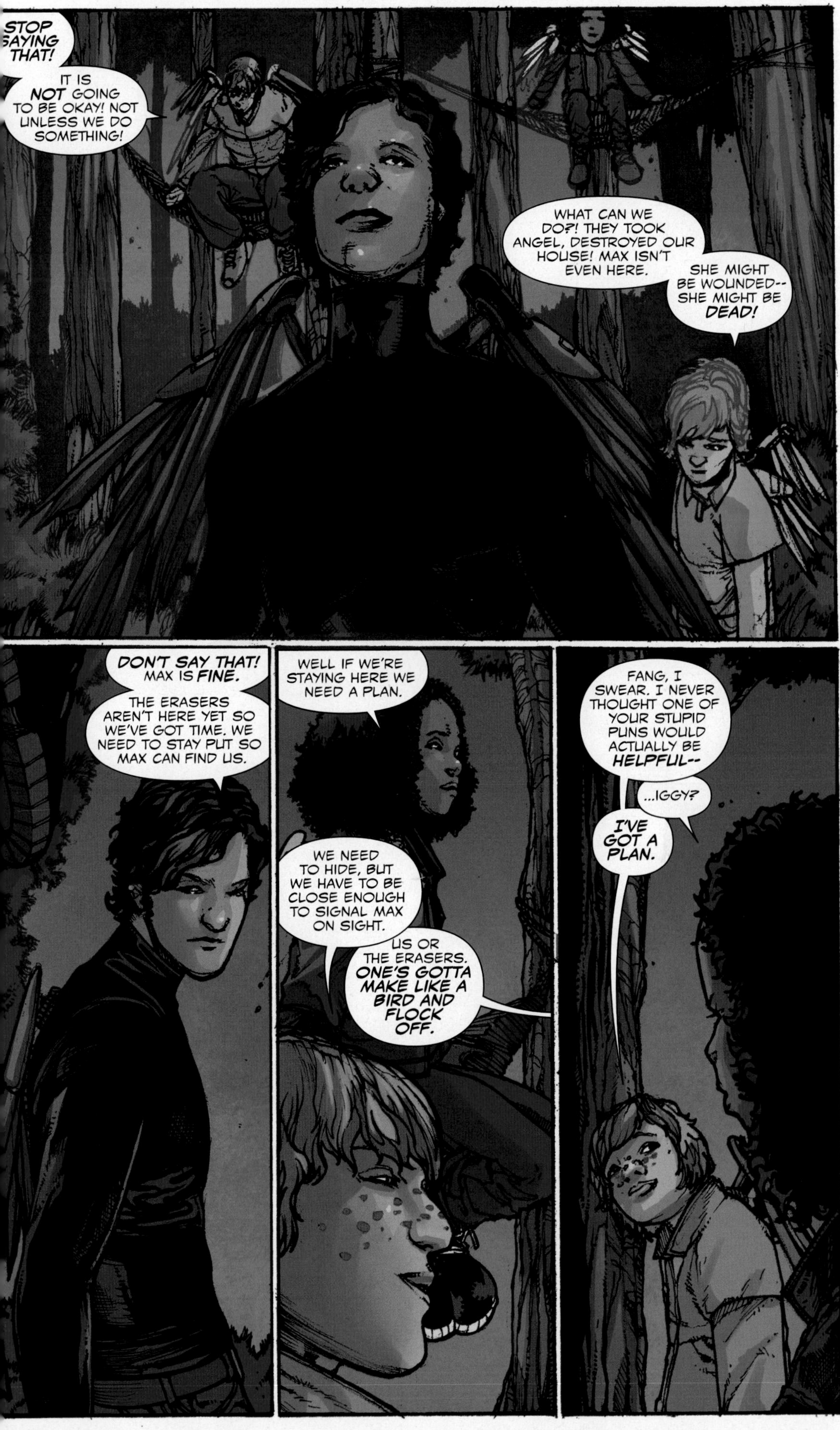
STOP SAYING THAT!
IT IS NOT GOING TO BE OKAY! NOT UNLESS WE DO SOMETHING!
WHAT CAN WE DO?! THEY TOOK ANGEL, DESTROYED OUR HOUSE! MAX ISN'T EVEN HERE.
SHE MIGHT BE WOUNDED-- SHE MIGHT BE DEAD!
DON'T SAY THAT! MAX IS FINE.
THE ERASERS AREN'T HERE YET SO WE'VE GOT TIME. WE NEED TO STAY PUT SO MAX CAN FIND US.
WELL IF WE'RE STAYING HERE WE NEED A PLAN.
WE NEED TO HIDE, BUT WE HAVE TO BE CLOSE ENOUGH TO SIGNAL MAX ON SIGHT.
US OR THE ERASERS. ONE'S GOTTA MAKE LIKE A BIRD AND FLOCK OFF.
FANG, I SWEAR. I NEVER THOUGHT ONE OF YOUR STUPID PUNS WOULD ACTUALLY BE HELPFUL--
...IGGY?
I'VE GOT A PLAN.

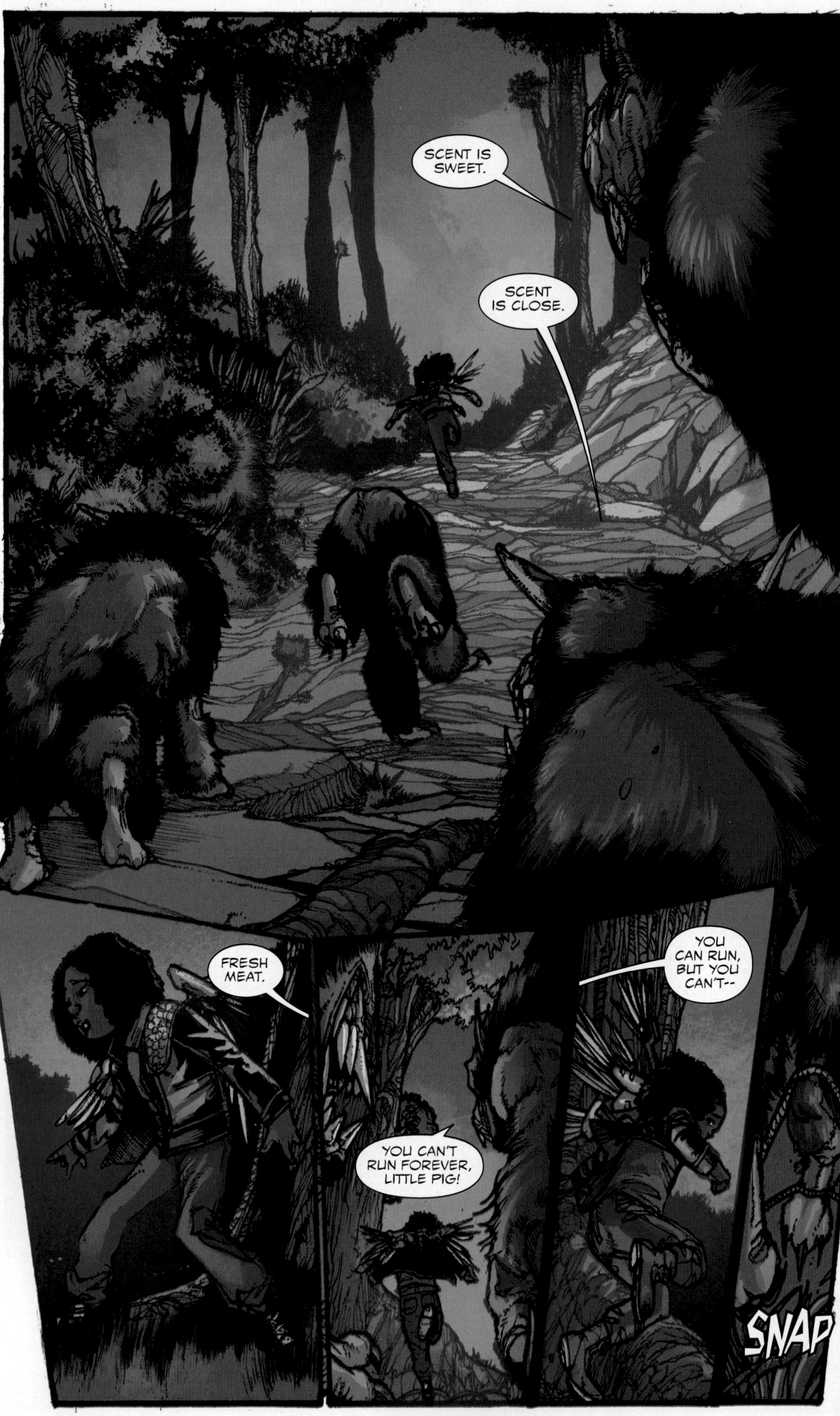
SCENT IS SWEET.
SCENT IS CLOSE.
FRESH MEAT.
YOU CAN'T RUN FOREVER, LITTLE PIG!
YOU CAN RUN, BUT YOU CAN'T--
SNAP

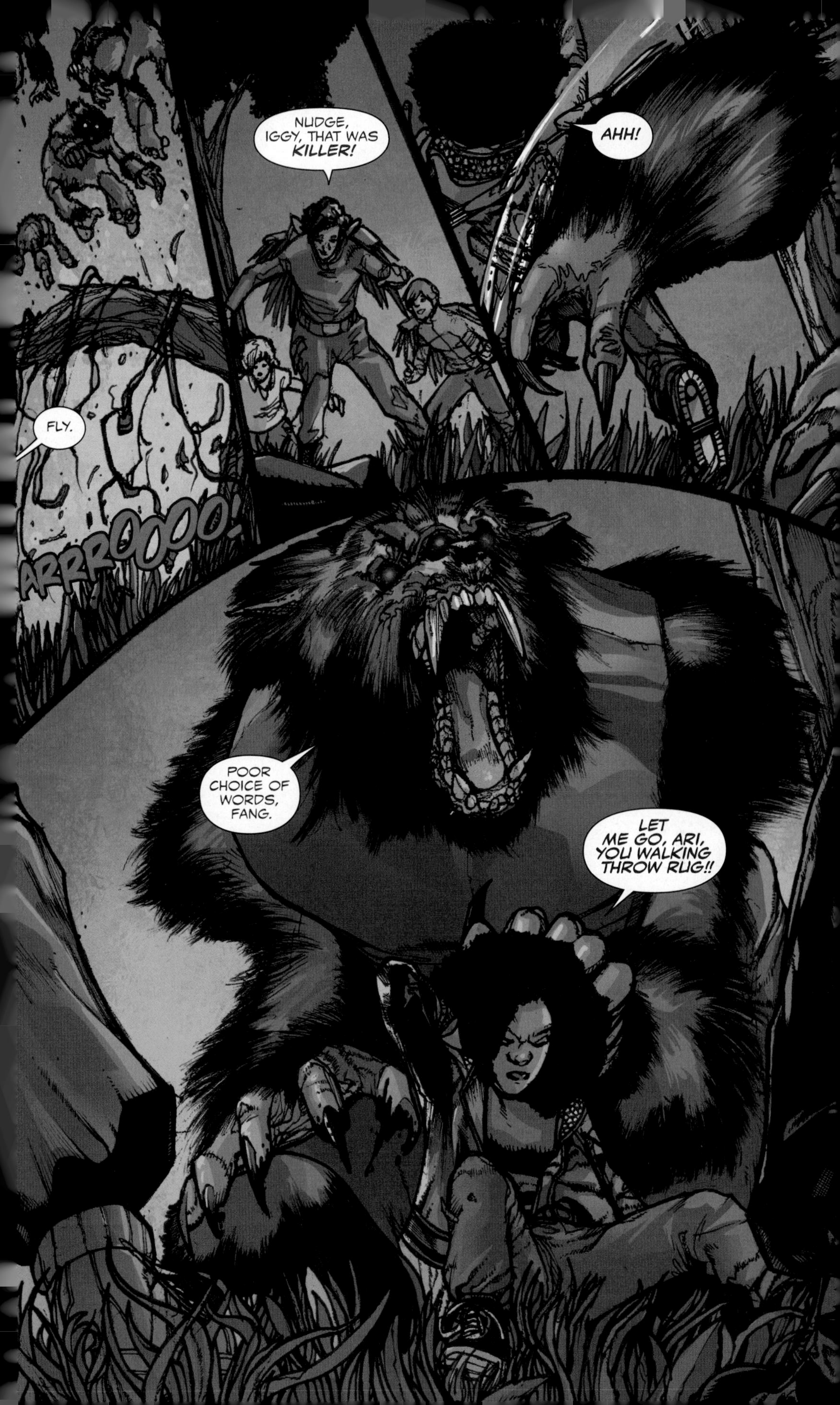
NUDGE, IGGY, THAT WAS KILLER!
AHH!
FLY.
ARRROOOO!
POOR CHOICE OF WORDS, FANG.
LET ME GO, ARI, YOU WALKING THROW RUG!!

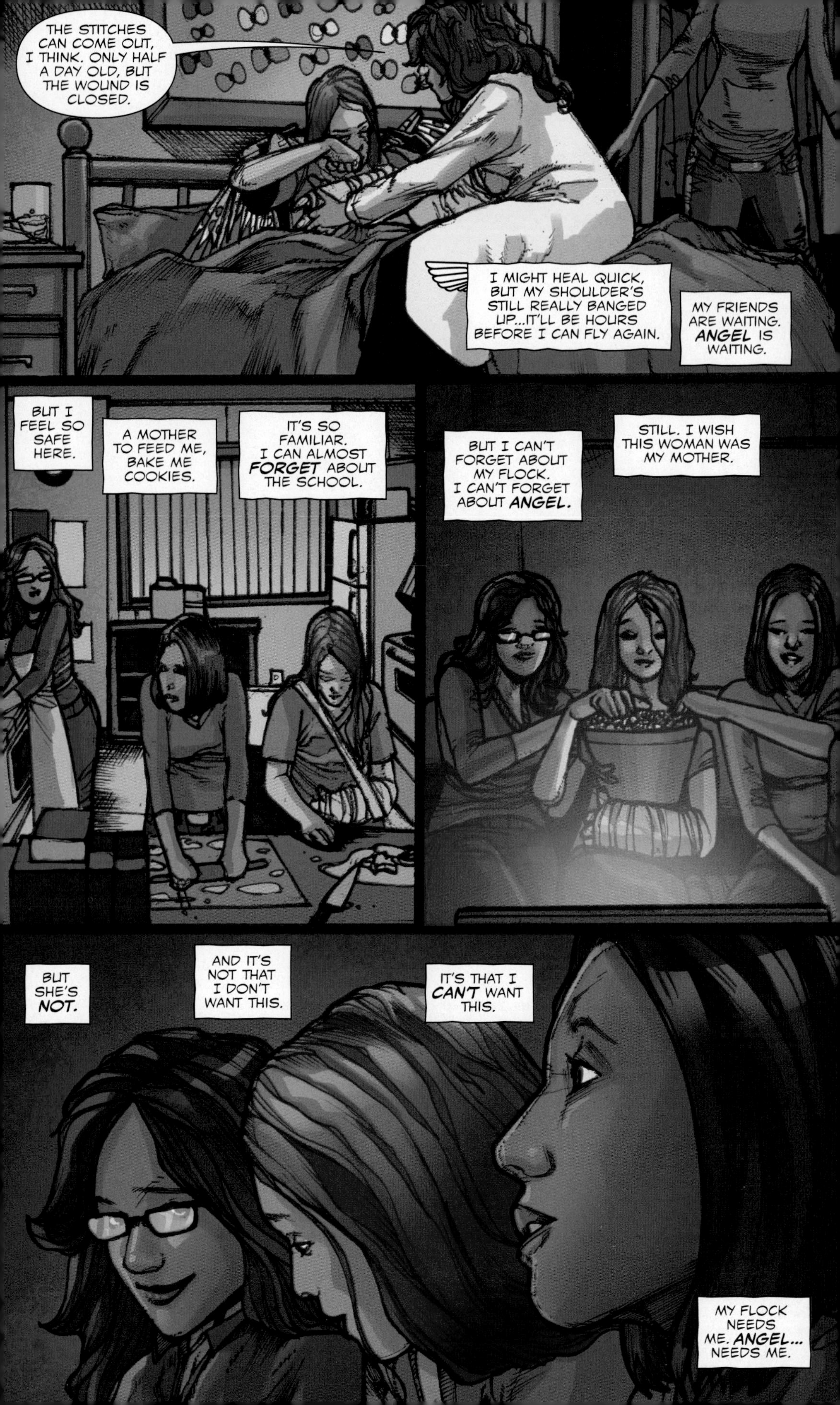
THE STITCHES CAN COME OUT, I THINK. ONLY HALF A DAY OLD, BUT THE WOUND IS CLOSED.
I MIGHT HEAL QUICK, BUT MY SHOULDER'S STILL REALLY BANGED UP...IT'LL BE HOURS BEFORE I CAN FLY AGAIN.
MY FRIENDS ARE WAITING. ANGEL IS WAITING.
BUT I FEEL SO SAFE HERE.
A MOTHER TO FEED ME, BAKE ME COOKIES.
IT'S SO FAMILIAR. I CAN ALMOST FORGET ABOUT THE SCHOOL.
BUT I CAN'T FORGET ABOUT MY FLOCK. I CAN'T FORGET ABOUT ANGEL.
STILL. I WISH THIS WOMAN WAS MY MOTHER.
BUT SHE'S NOT.
AND IT'S NOT THAT I DON'T WANT THIS.
IT'S THAT I CAN'T WANT THIS.
MY FLOCK NEEDS ME. ANGEL... NEEDS ME.

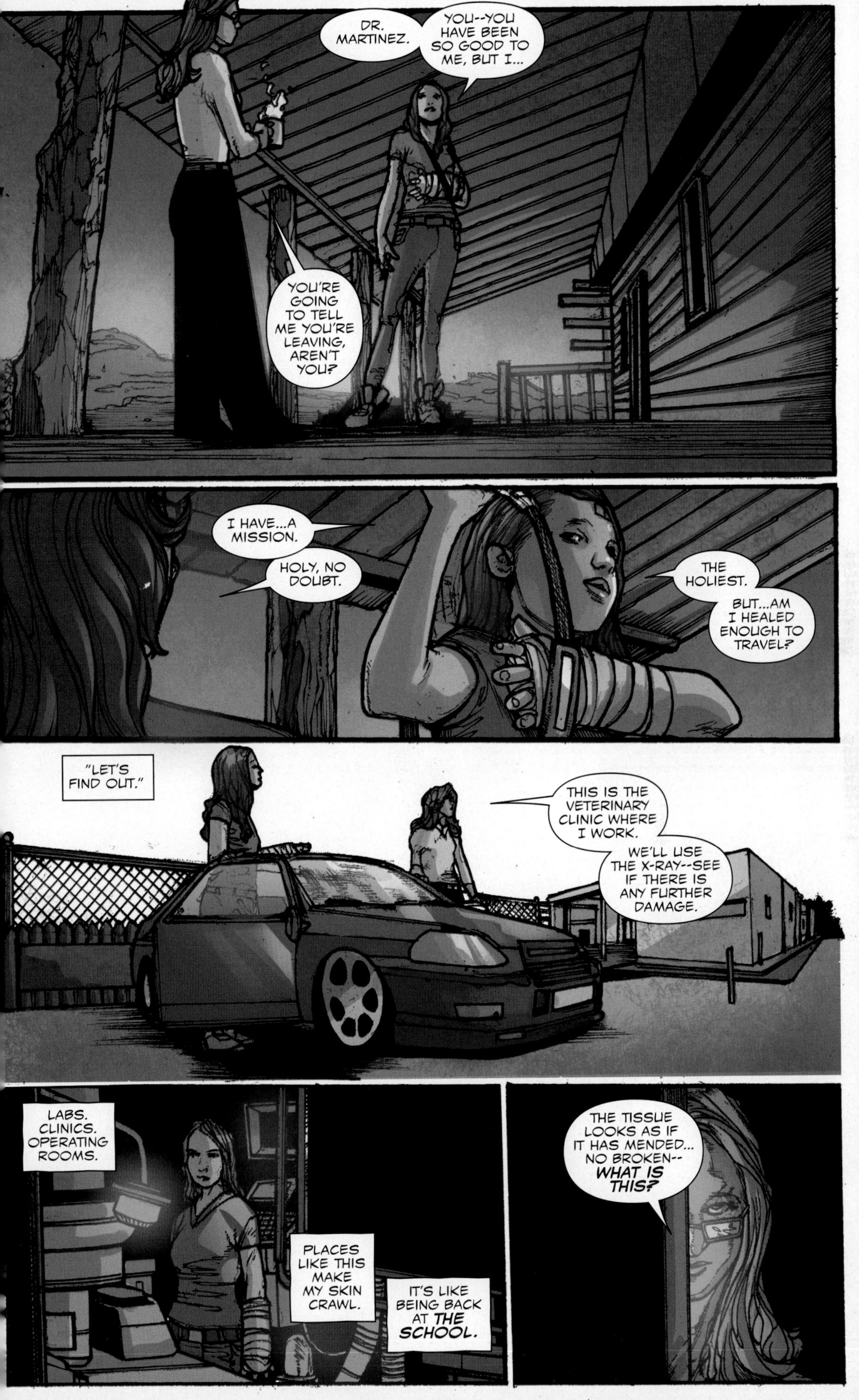
DR. MARTINEZ.
YOU--YOU HAVE BEEN SO GOOD TO ME, BUT I...
YOU'RE GOING TO TELL ME YOU'RE LEAVING, AREN'T YOU?
I HAVE...A MISSION.
HOLY, NO DOUBT.
THE HOLIEST.
BUT...AM I HEALED ENOUGH TO TRAVEL?
"LET'S FIND OUT."
THIS IS THE VETERINARY CLINIC WHERE I WORK.
WE'LL USE THE X-RAY--SEE IF THERE IS ANY FURTHER DAMAGE.
LABS. CLINICS. OPERATING ROOMS.
PLACES LIKE THIS MAKE MY SKIN CRAWL.
IT'S LIKE BEING BACK AT THE SCHOOL.
THE TISSUE LOOKS AS IF IT HAS MENDED... NO BROKEN-- WHAT IS THIS?

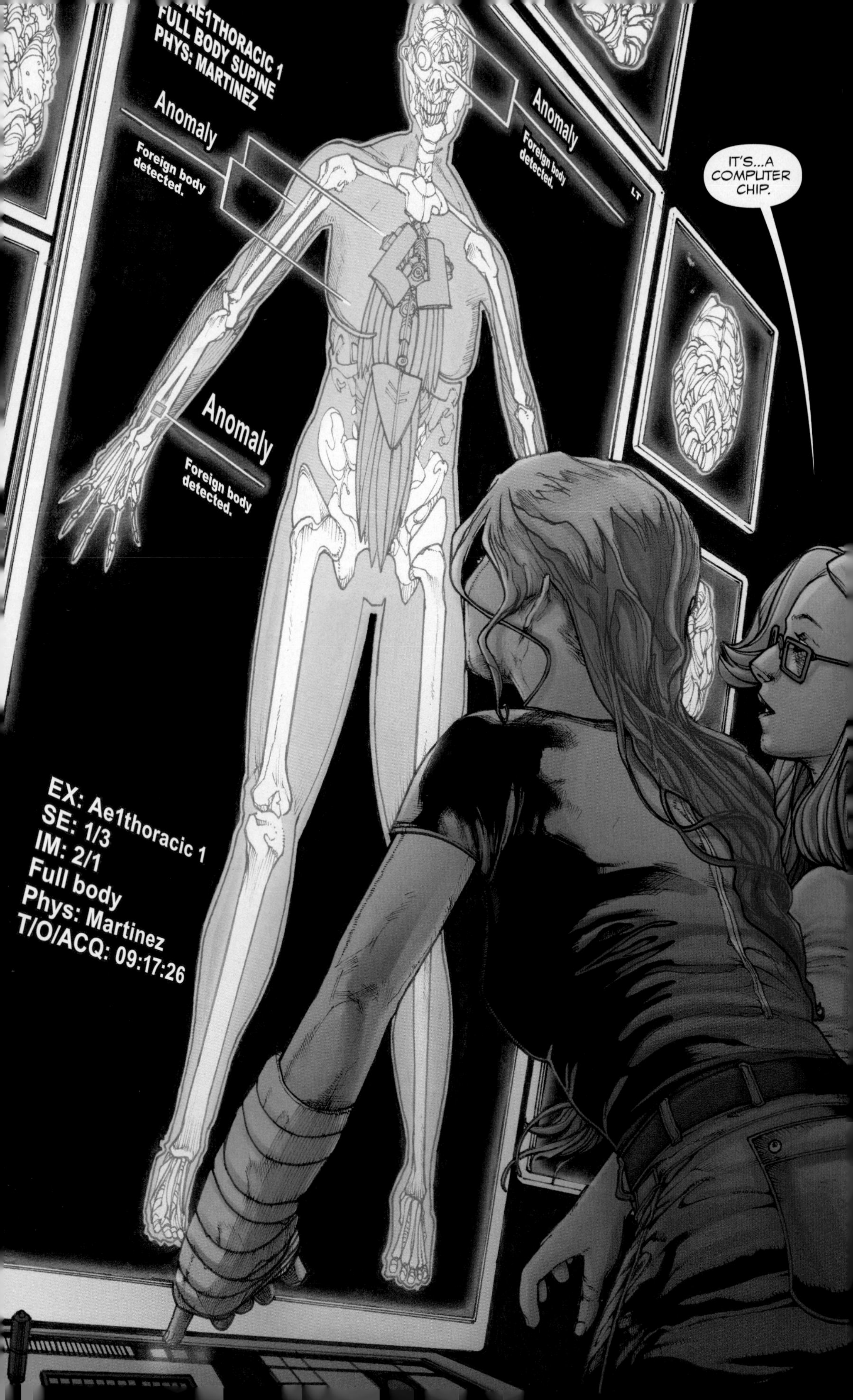
AE1THORACIC 1
FULL BODY SUPINE
PHYS: MARTINEZ
Anomaly
Foreign body detected.
Anomaly
Foreign body detected.
LT
IT'S...A COMPUTER CHIP.
Anomaly
Foreign body detected.
EX: Ae1thoracic 1
SE: 1/3
IM: 2/1
Full body
Phys: Martinez
T/O/ACQ: 09:17:26

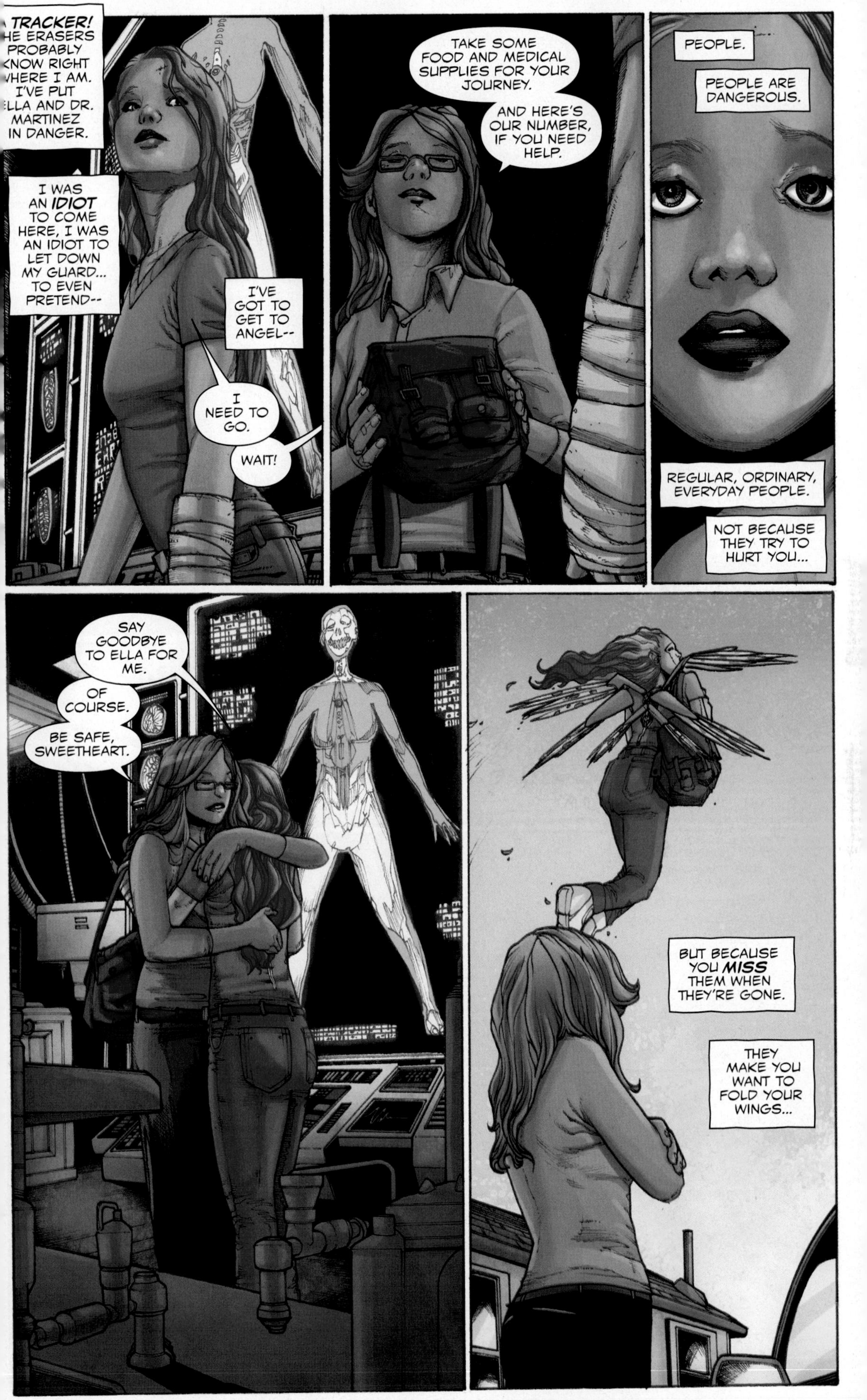

TRACKER! HE ERASERS PROBABLY KNOW RIGHT WHERE I AM. I'VE PUT ELLA AND DR. MARTINEZ IN DANGER.
I WAS AN IDIOT TO COME HERE, I WAS AN IDIOT TO LET DOWN MY GUARD... TO EVEN PRETEND--
I'VE GOT TO GET TO ANGEL--
I NEED TO GO.
WAIT!
TAKE SOME FOOD AND MEDICAL SUPPLIES FOR YOUR JOURNEY.
AND HERE'S OUR NUMBER, IF YOU NEED HELP.
PEOPLE.
PEOPLE ARE DANGEROUS.
REGULAR, ORDINARY, EVERYDAY PEOPLE.
NOT BECAUSE THEY TRY TO HURT YOU...
SAY GOODBYE TO ELLA FOR ME.
OF COURSE.
BE SAFE, SWEETHEART.
BUT BECAUSE YOU MISS THEM WHEN THEY'RE GONE.
THEY MAKE YOU WANT TO FOLD YOUR WINGS...

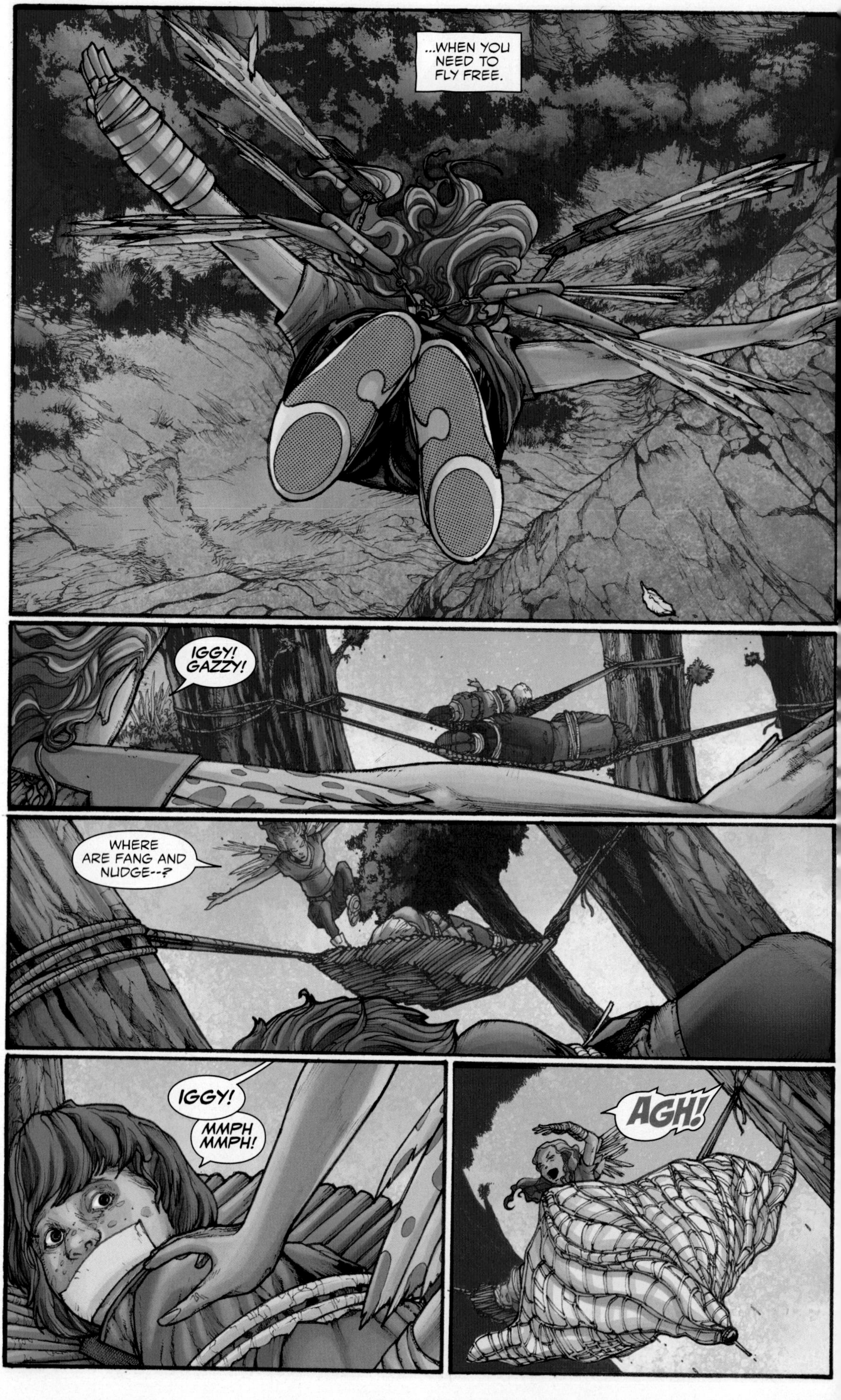
...WHEN YOU NEED TO FLY FREE.
IGGY! GAZZY!
WHERE ARE FANG AND NUDGE--?
IGGY!
MMPH MMPH!
AGH!

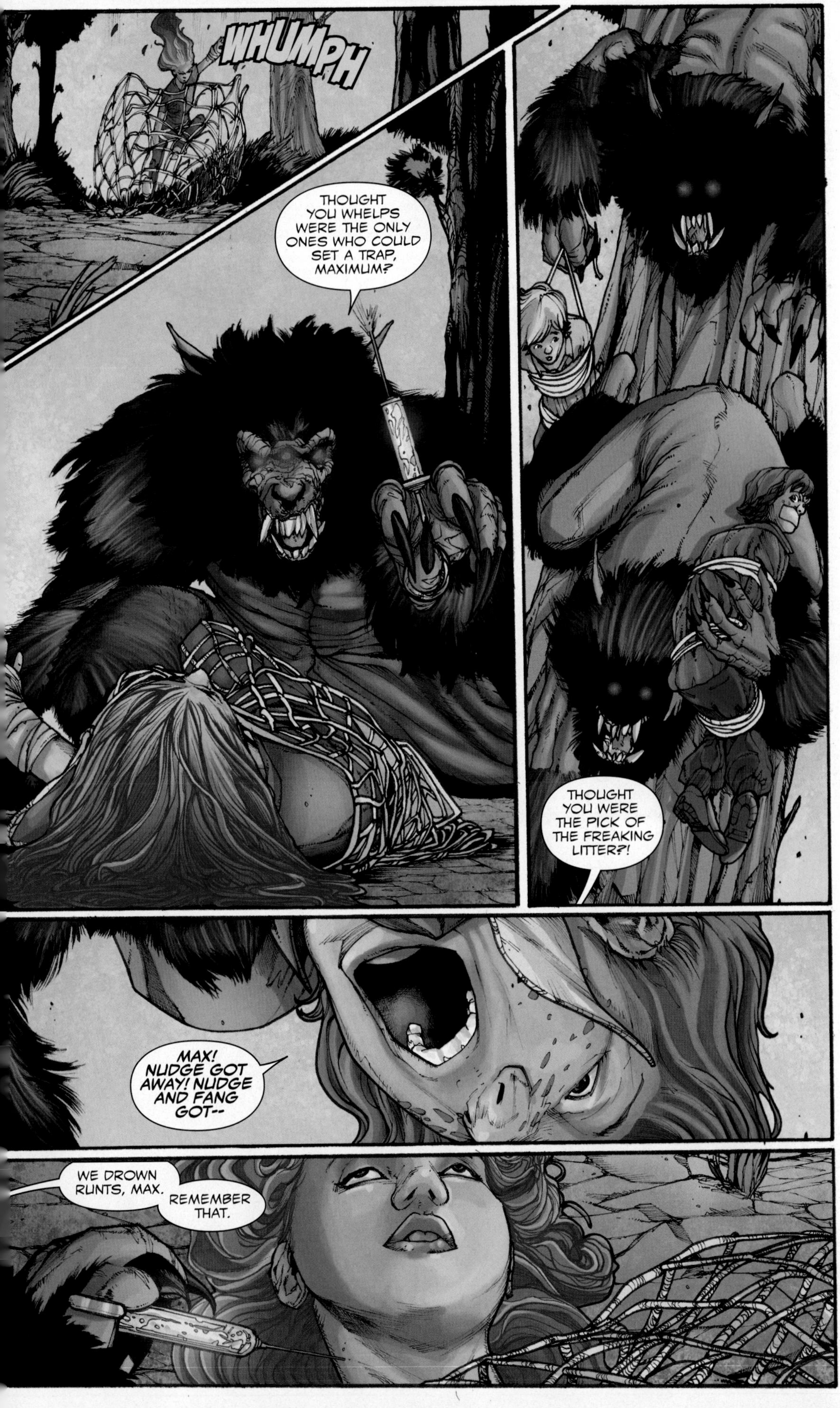
WHUMPH
THOUGHT YOU WHELPS WERE THE ONLY ONES WHO COULD SET A TRAP, MAXIMUM?
THOUGHT YOU WERE THE PICK OF THE FREAKING LITTER?!
MAX! NUDGE GOT AWAY! NUDGE AND FANG GOT--
WE DROWN RUNTS, MAX.
REMEMBER THAT.

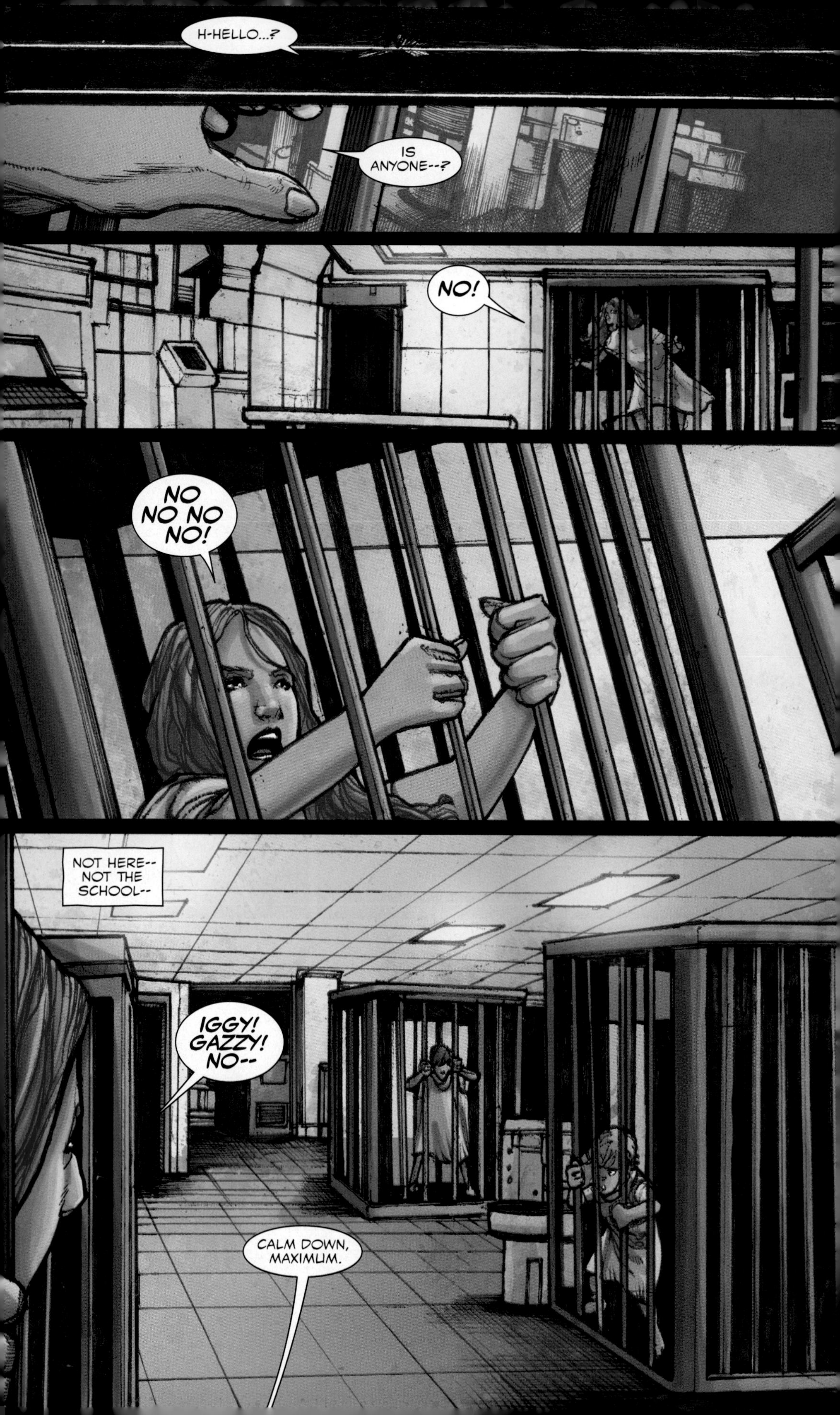
H-HELLO...?
IS ANYONE--?
NO!
NO NO NO NO!
NOT HERE-- NOT THE SCHOOL--
IGGY! GAZZY! NO--
CALM DOWN, MAXIMUM.

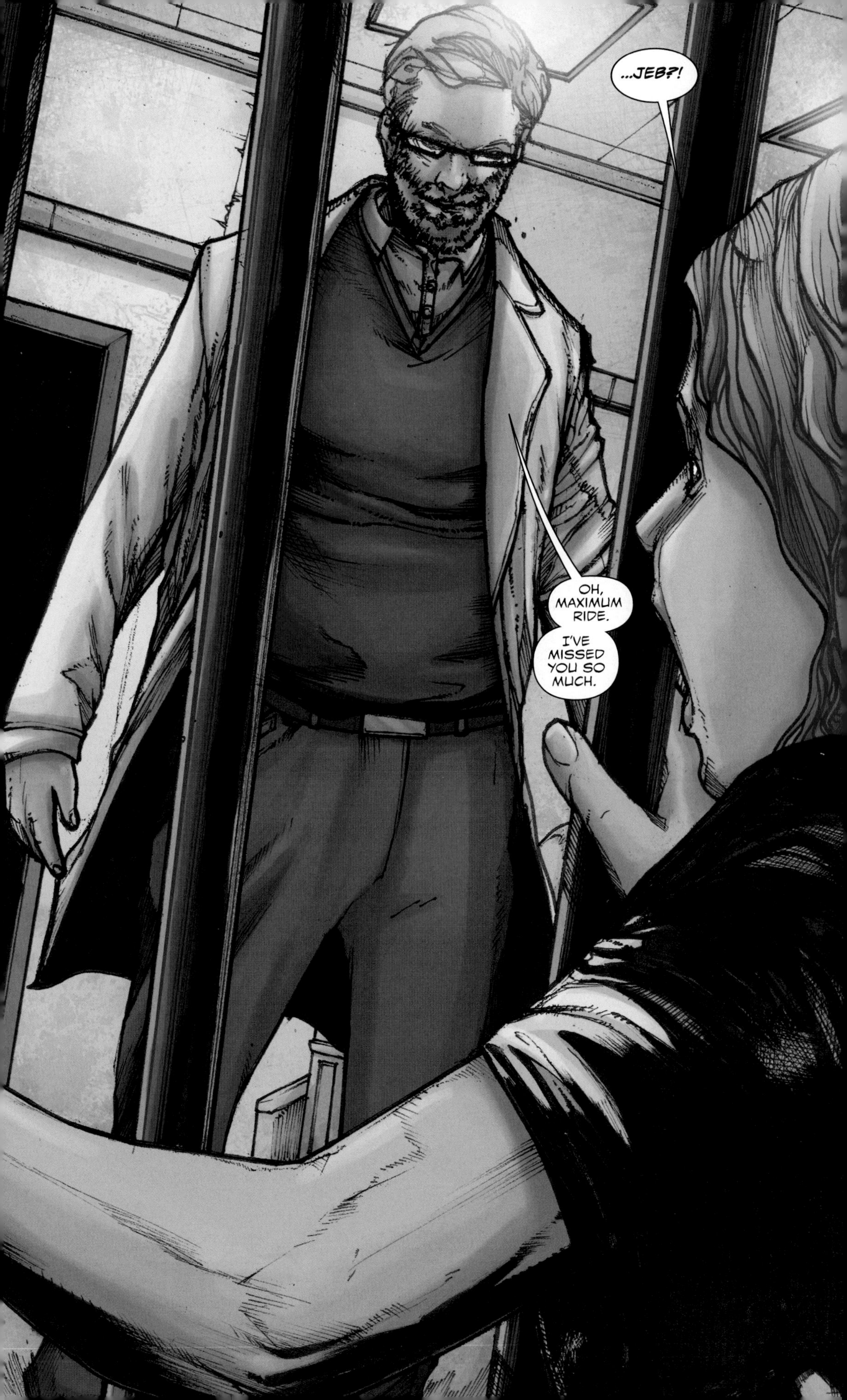
...JEB?!
OH, MAXIMUM RIDE.
I'VE MISSED YOU SO MUCH.

CHAPTER 3

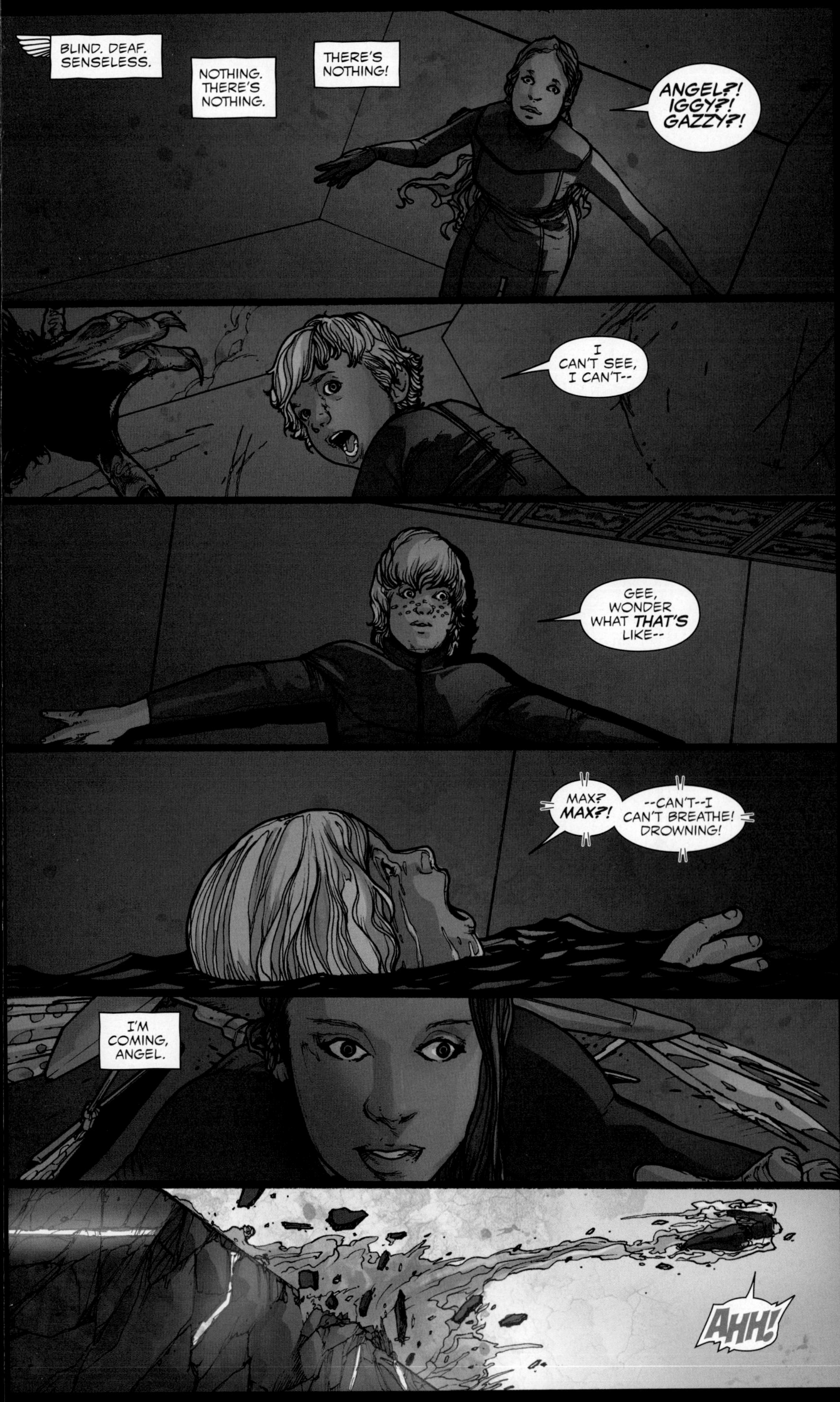
BLIND. DEAF. SENSELESS.
NOTHING. THERE'S NOTHING.
THERE'S NOTHING!
ANGEL?! IGGY?! GAZZY?!
I CAN'T SEE, I CAN'T--
GEE, WONDER WHAT THAT'S LIKE--
MAX? MAX?!
--CAN'T--I CAN'T BREATHE! DROWNING!
I'M COMING, ANGEL.
AHH!

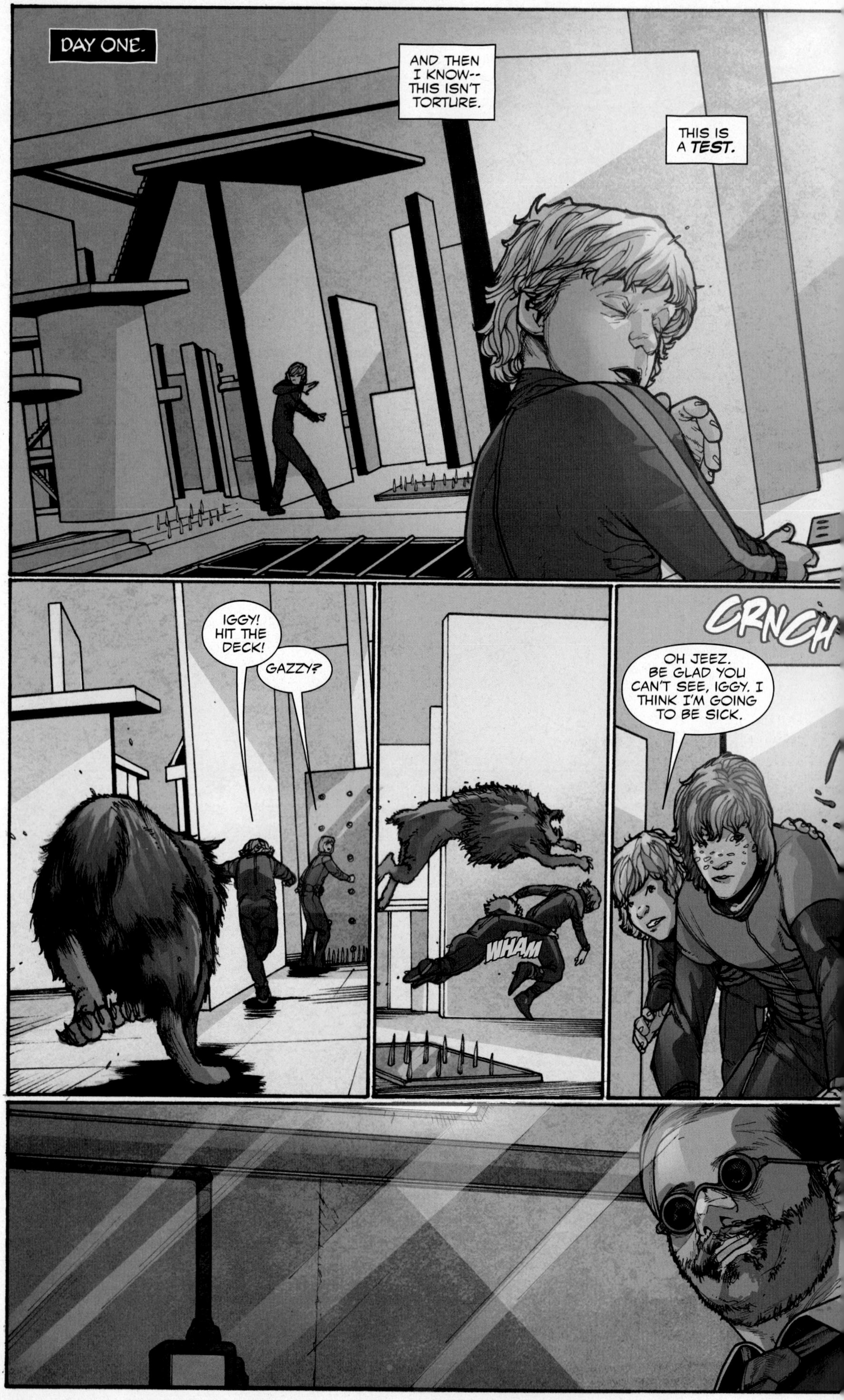
DAY ONE.
AND THEN I KNOW-- THIS ISN'T TORTURE.
THIS IS A TEST.
IGGY! HIT THE DECK!
GAZZY?
WHAM
CRNCH
OH JEEZ. BE GLAD YOU CAN'T SEE, IGGY. I THINK I'M GOING TO BE SICK.

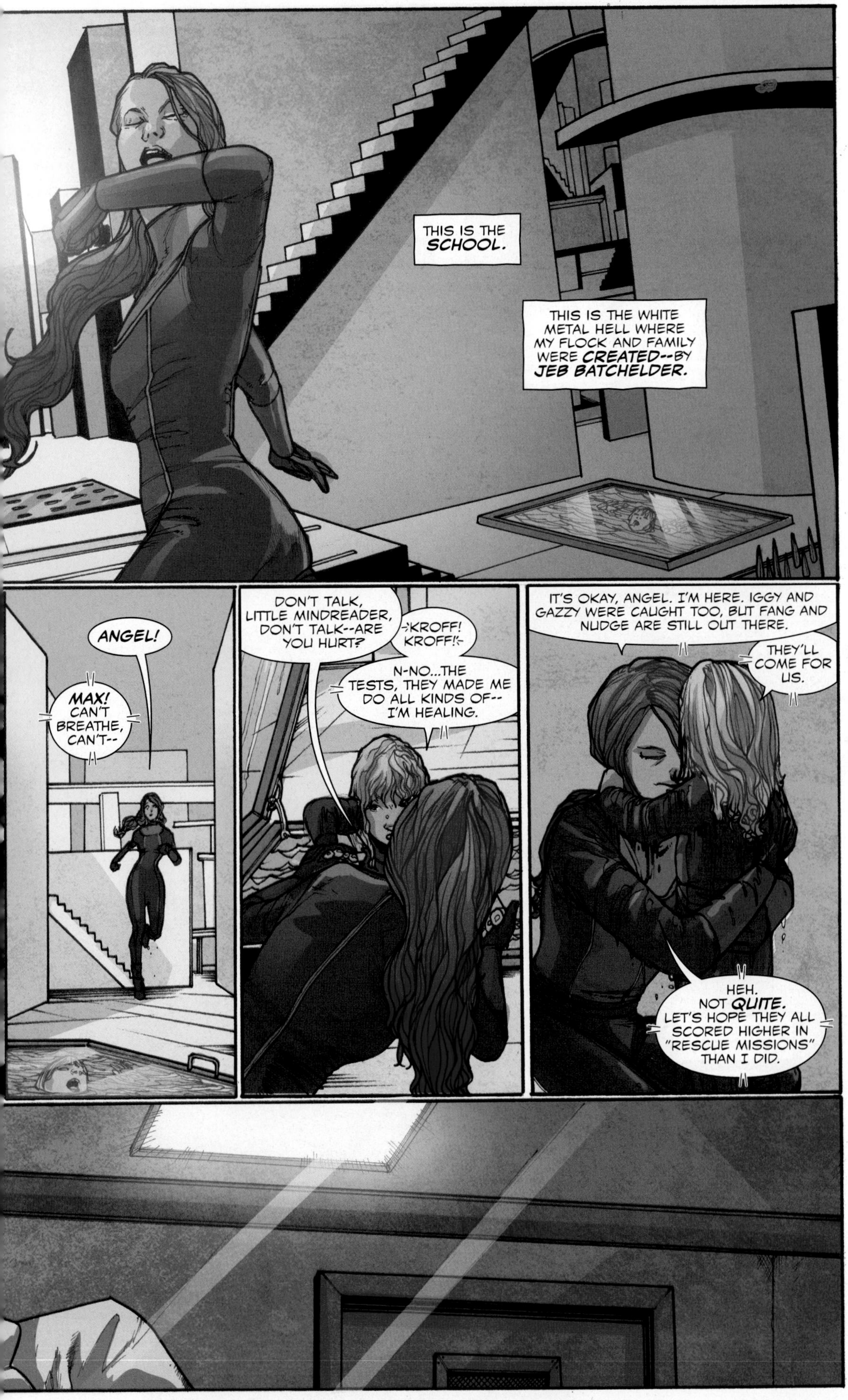
THIS IS THE SCHOOL.
THIS IS THE WHITE METAL HELL WHERE MY FLOCK AND FAMILY WERE CREATED--BY JEB BATCHELDER.
ANGEL!
MAX! CAN'T BREATHE, CAN'T--
DON'T TALK, LITTLE MINDREADER, DON'T TALK--ARE YOU HURT?
KROFF! KROFF!
N-NO...THE TESTS, THEY MADE ME DO ALL KINDS OF-- I'M HEALING.
IT'S OKAY, ANGEL. I'M HERE. IGGY AND GAZZY WERE CAUGHT TOO, BUT FANG AND NUDGE ARE STILL OUT THERE.
THEY'LL COME FOR US.
HEH. NOT QUITE. LET'S HOPE THEY ALL SCORED HIGHER IN "RESCUE MISSIONS" THAN I DID.

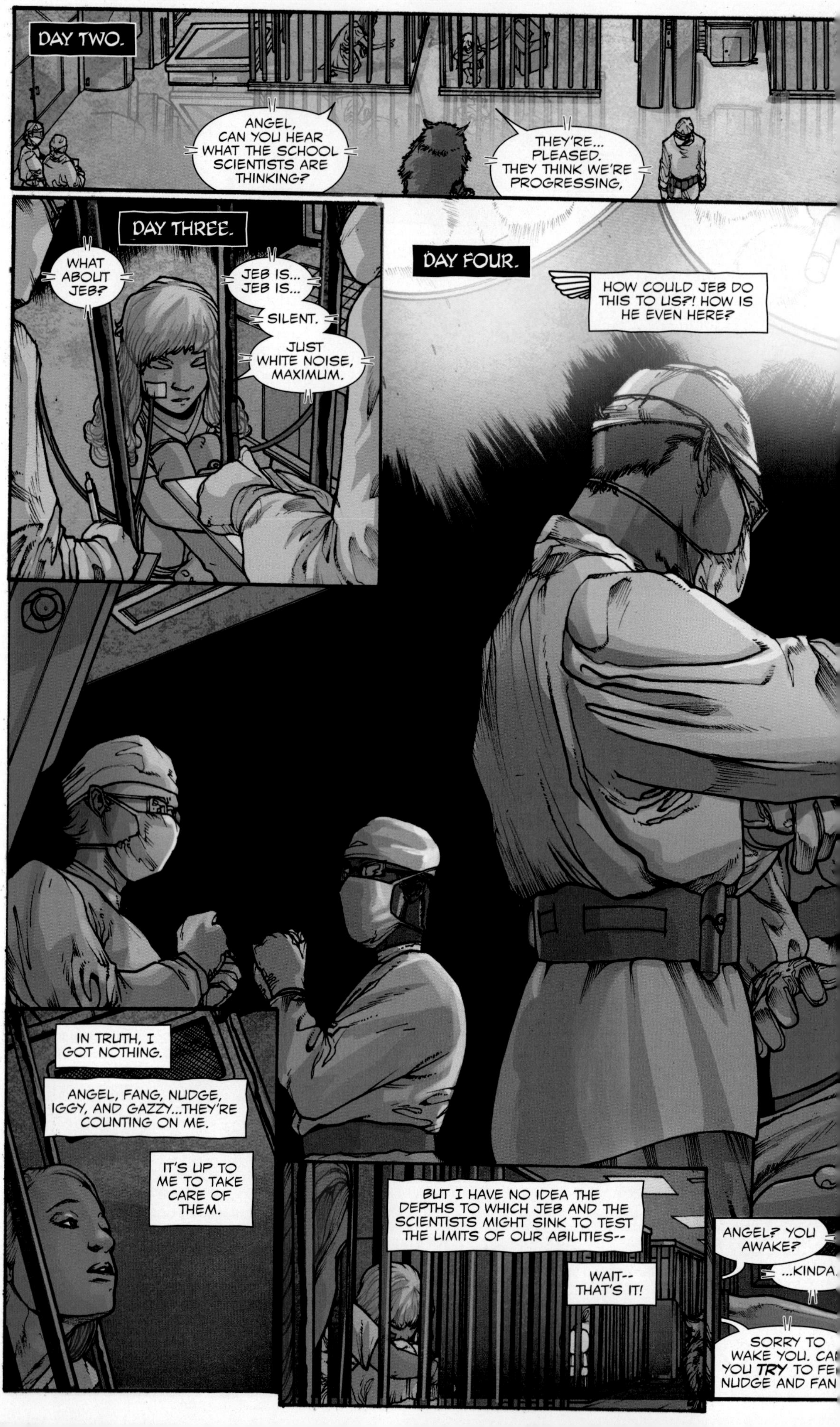
DAY TWO.
ANGEL, CAN YOU HEAR WHAT THE SCHOOL SCIENTISTS ARE THINKING?
THEY'RE... PLEASED. THEY THINK WE'RE PROGRESSING.
DAY THREE.
WHAT ABOUT JEB?
JEB IS... JEB IS...
SILENT.
JUST WHITE NOISE, MAXIMUM.
DAY FOUR.
HOW COULD JEB DO THIS TO US?! HOW IS HE EVEN HERE?
IN TRUTH, I GOT NOTHING.
ANGEL, FANG, NUDGE, IGGY, AND GAZZY...THEY'RE COUNTING ON ME.
IT'S UP TO ME TO TAKE CARE OF THEM.
BUT I HAVE NO IDEA THE DEPTHS TO WHICH JEB AND THE SCIENTISTS MIGHT SINK TO TEST THE LIMITS OF OUR ABILITIES--
WAIT-- THAT'S IT!
ANGEL? YOU AWAKE?
...KINDA.
SORRY TO WAKE YOU. CA YOU TRY TO FE NUDGE AND FAN

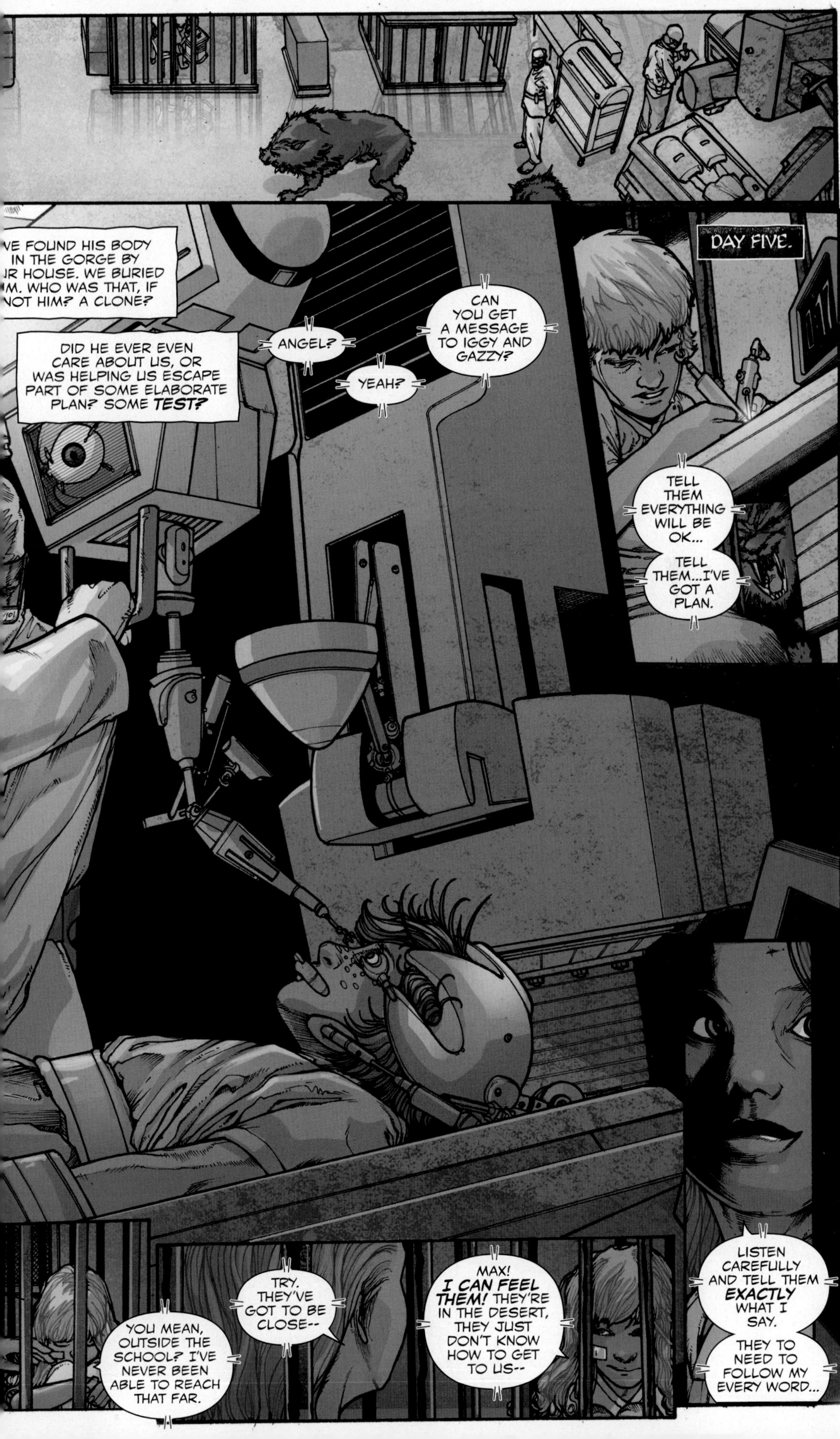

DAY FIVE.
VE FOUND HIS BODY IN THE GORGE BY IR HOUSE. WE BURIED IM. WHO WAS THAT, IF NOT HIM? A CLONE?
DID HE EVER EVEN CARE ABOUT US, OR WAS HELPING US ESCAPE PART OF SOME ELABORATE PLAN? SOME TEST?
ANGEL?
YEAH?
CAN YOU GET A MESSAGE TO IGGY AND GAZZY?
TELL THEM EVERYTHING WILL BE OK...
TELL THEM...I'VE GOT A PLAN.
YOU MEAN, OUTSIDE THE SCHOOL? I'VE NEVER BEEN ABLE TO REACH THAT FAR.
TRY. THEY'VE GOT TO BE CLOSE--
MAX! I CAN FEEL THEM! THEY'RE IN THE DESERT, THEY JUST DON'T KNOW HOW TO GET TO US--
LISTEN CAREFULLY AND TELL THEM EXACTLY WHAT I SAY.
THEY TO NEED TO FOLLOW MY EVERY WORD...

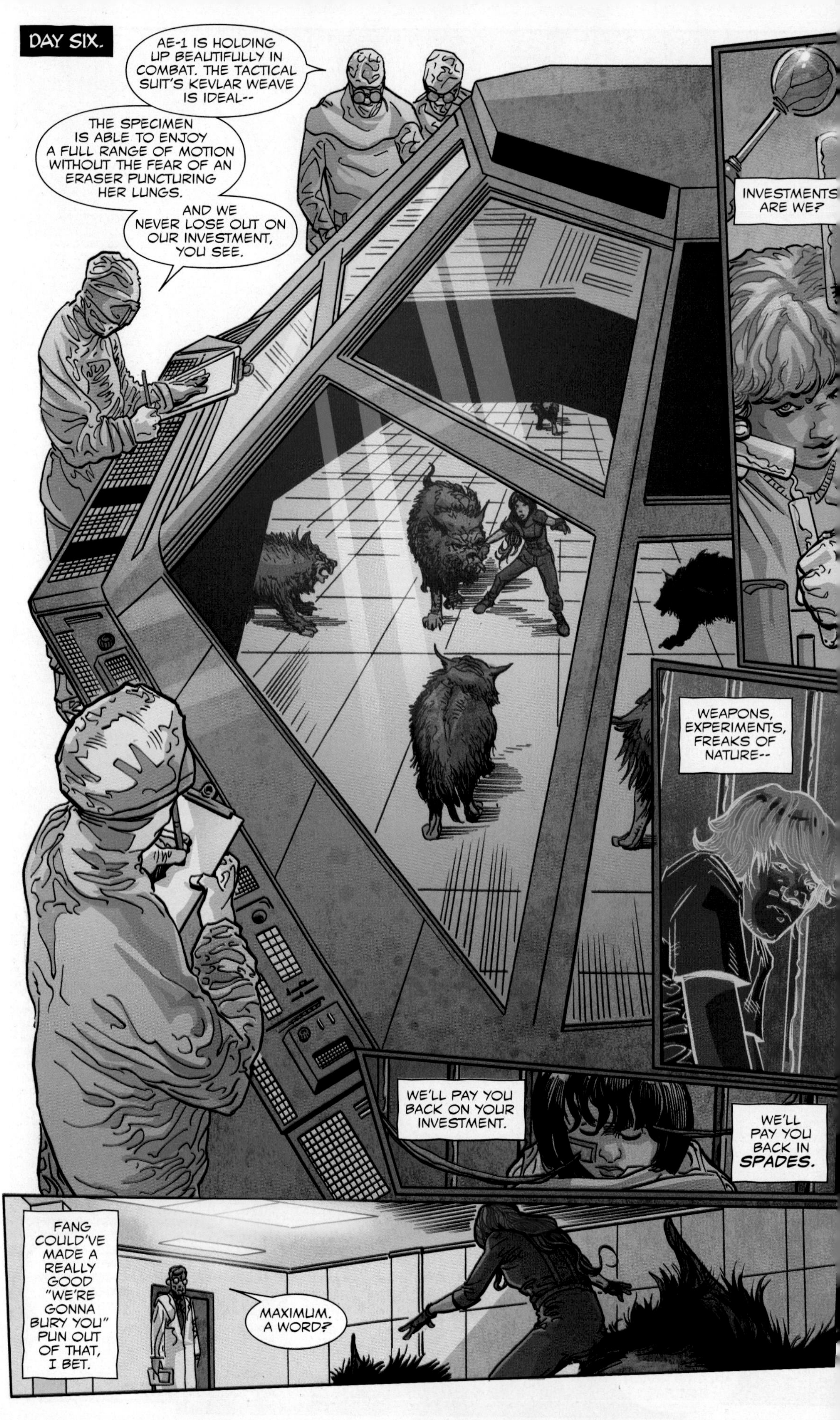
DAY SIX.
AE-1 IS HOLDING UP BEAUTIFULLY IN COMBAT. THE TACTICAL SUIT'S KEVLAR WEAVE IS IDEAL--
THE SPECIMEN IS ABLE TO ENJOY A FULL RANGE OF MOTION WITHOUT THE FEAR OF AN ERASER PUNCTURING HER LUNGS.
AND WE NEVER LOSE OUT ON OUR INVESTMENT, YOU SEE.
INVESTMENTS ARE WE?
WEAPONS, EXPERIMENTS, FREAKS OF NATURE--
WE'LL PAY YOU BACK ON YOUR INVESTMENT.
WE'LL PAY YOU BACK IN SPADES.
FANG COULD'VE MADE A REALLY GOOD "WE'RE GONNA BURY YOU" PUN OUT OF THAT, I BET.
MAXIMUM. A WORD?

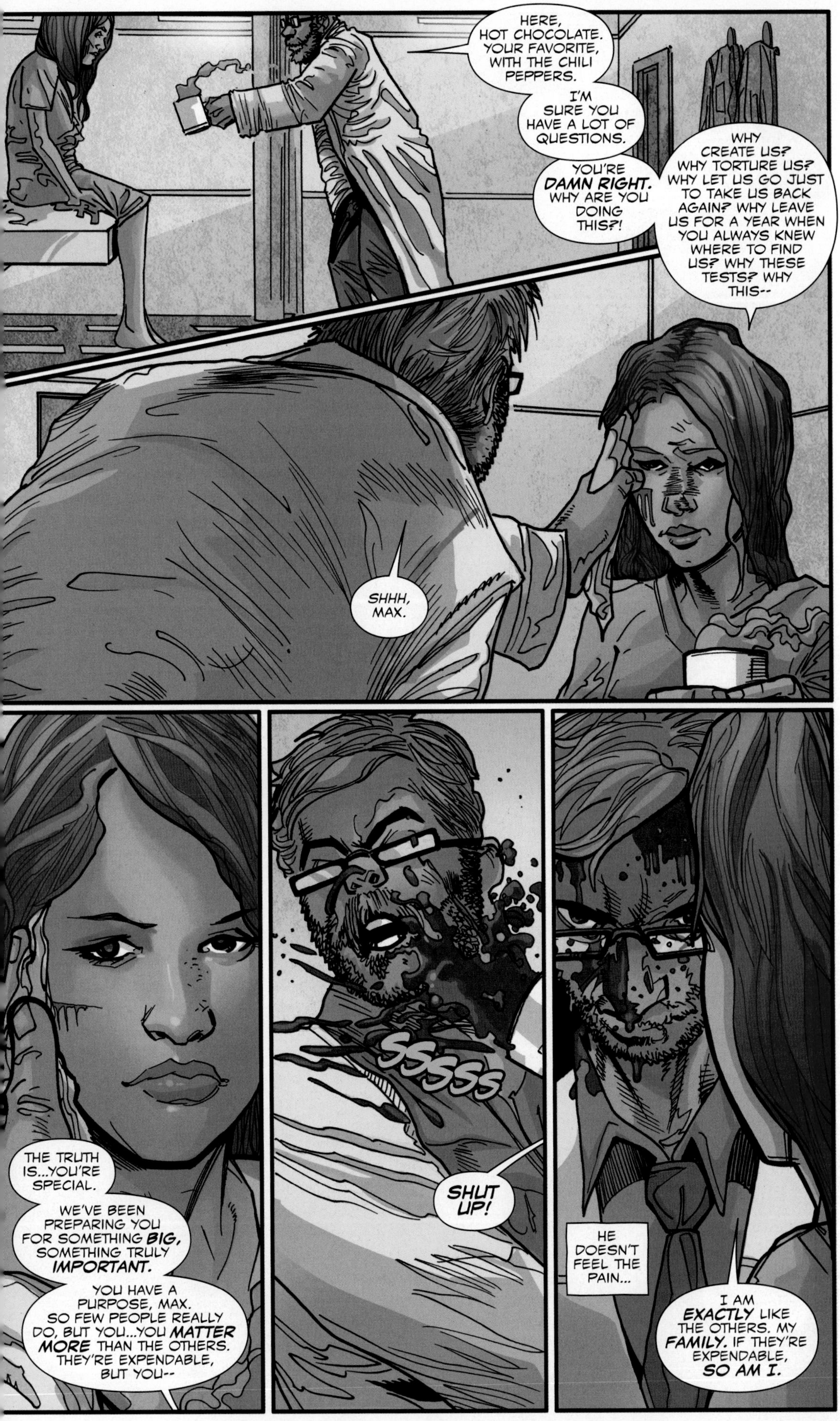
HERE, HOT CHOCOLATE. YOUR FAVORITE, WITH THE CHILI PEPPERS.
I'M SURE YOU HAVE A LOT OF QUESTIONS.
YOU'RE DAMN RIGHT. WHY ARE YOU DOING THIS?!
WHY CREATE US? WHY TORTURE US? WHY LET US GO JUST TO TAKE US BACK AGAIN? WHY LEAVE US FOR A YEAR WHEN YOU ALWAYS KNEW WHERE TO FIND US? WHY THESE TESTS? WHY THIS--
SHHH, MAX.
THE TRUTH IS...YOU'RE SPECIAL.
WE'VE BEEN PREPARING YOU FOR SOMETHING BIG, SOMETHING TRULY IMPORTANT.
YOU HAVE A PURPOSE, MAX. SO FEW PEOPLE REALLY DO, BUT YOU...YOU MATTER MORE THAN THE OTHERS. THEY'RE EXPENDABLE, BUT YOU--
SSSSS
SHUT UP!
HE DOESN'T FEEL THE PAIN...
I AM EXACTLY LIKE THE OTHERS. MY FAMILY. IF THEY'RE EXPENDABLE, SO AM I.

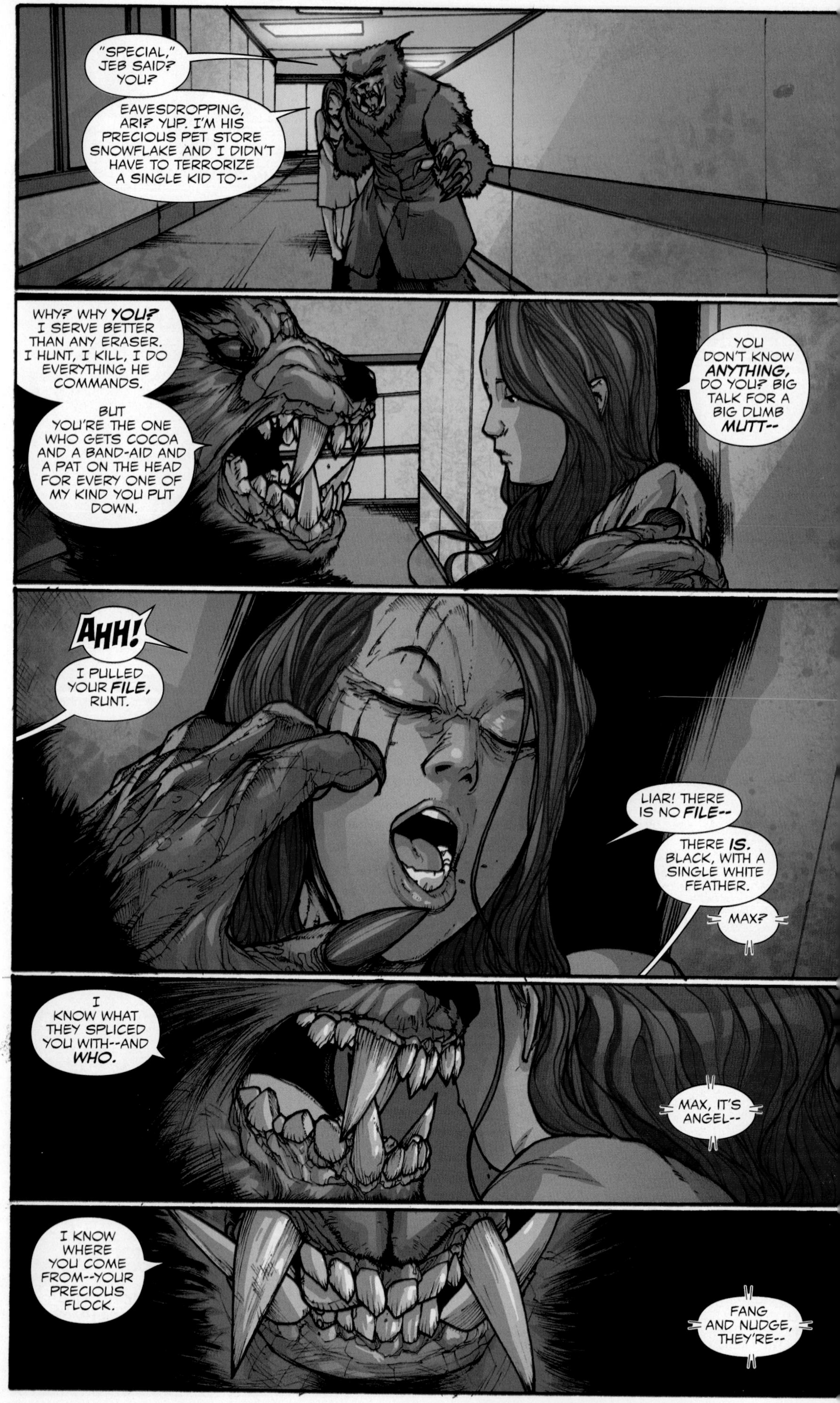
"SPECIAL," JEB SAID? YOU?
EAVESDROPPING, ARI? YUP. I'M HIS PRECIOUS PET STORE SNOWFLAKE AND I DIDN'T HAVE TO TERRORIZE A SINGLE KID TO--
WHY? WHY YOU? I SERVE BETTER THAN ANY ERASER. I HUNT, I KILL, I DO EVERYTHING HE COMMANDS.
BUT YOU'RE THE ONE WHO GETS COCOA AND A BAND-AID AND A PAT ON THE HEAD FOR EVERY ONE OF MY KIND YOU PUT DOWN.
YOU DON'T KNOW ANYTHING, DO YOU? BIG TALK FOR A BIG DUMB MUTT--
AHH!
I PULLED YOUR FILE, RUNT.
LIAR! THERE IS NO FILE--
THERE IS. BLACK, WITH A SINGLE WHITE FEATHER.
MAX?
I KNOW WHAT THEY SPLICED YOU WITH--AND WHO.
MAX, IT'S ANGEL--
I KNOW WHERE YOU COME FROM--YOUR PRECIOUS FLOCK.
FANG AND NUDGE, THEY'RE--

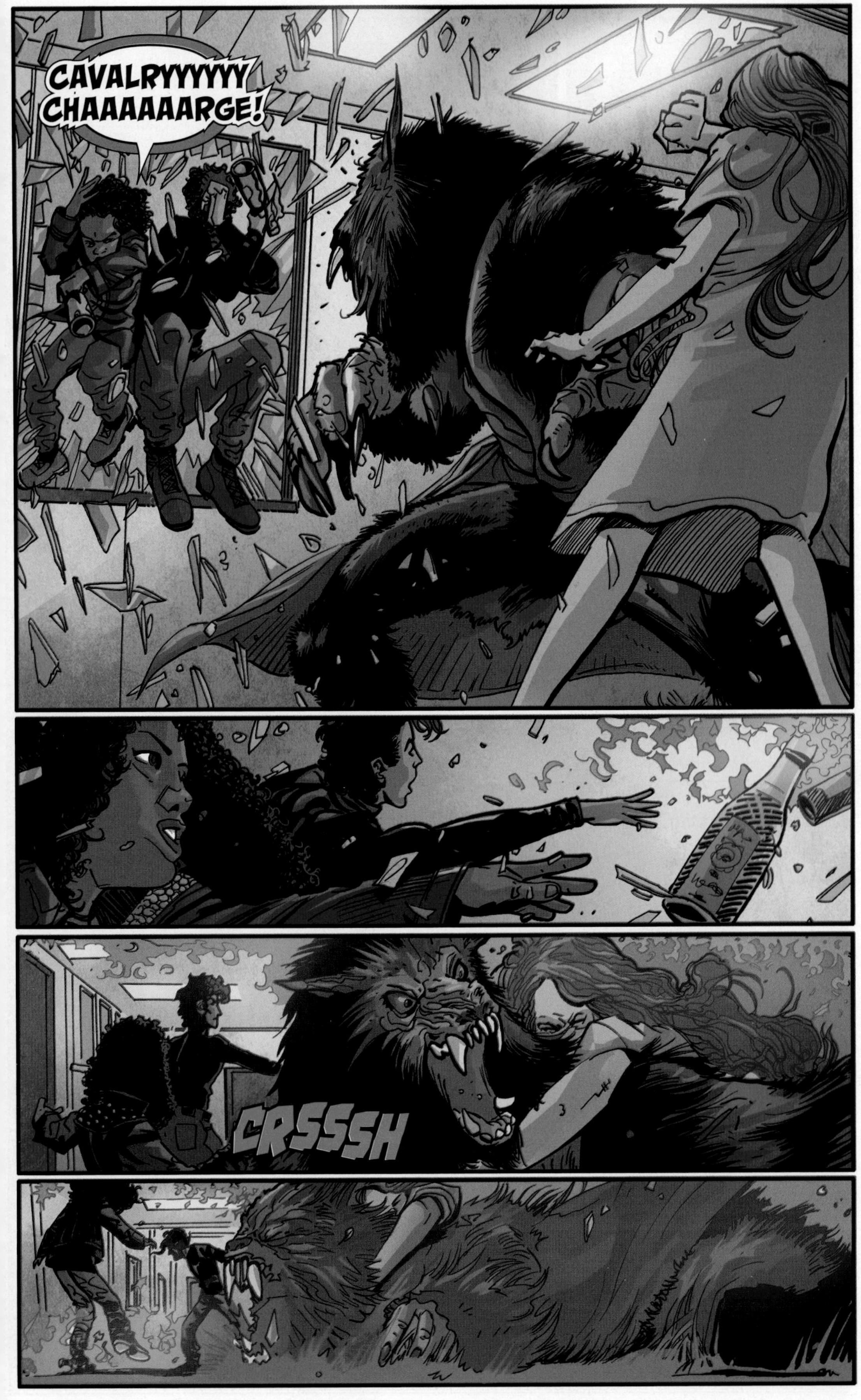
CAVALRYYYYYY CHAAAAAARGE!
CRSSSH

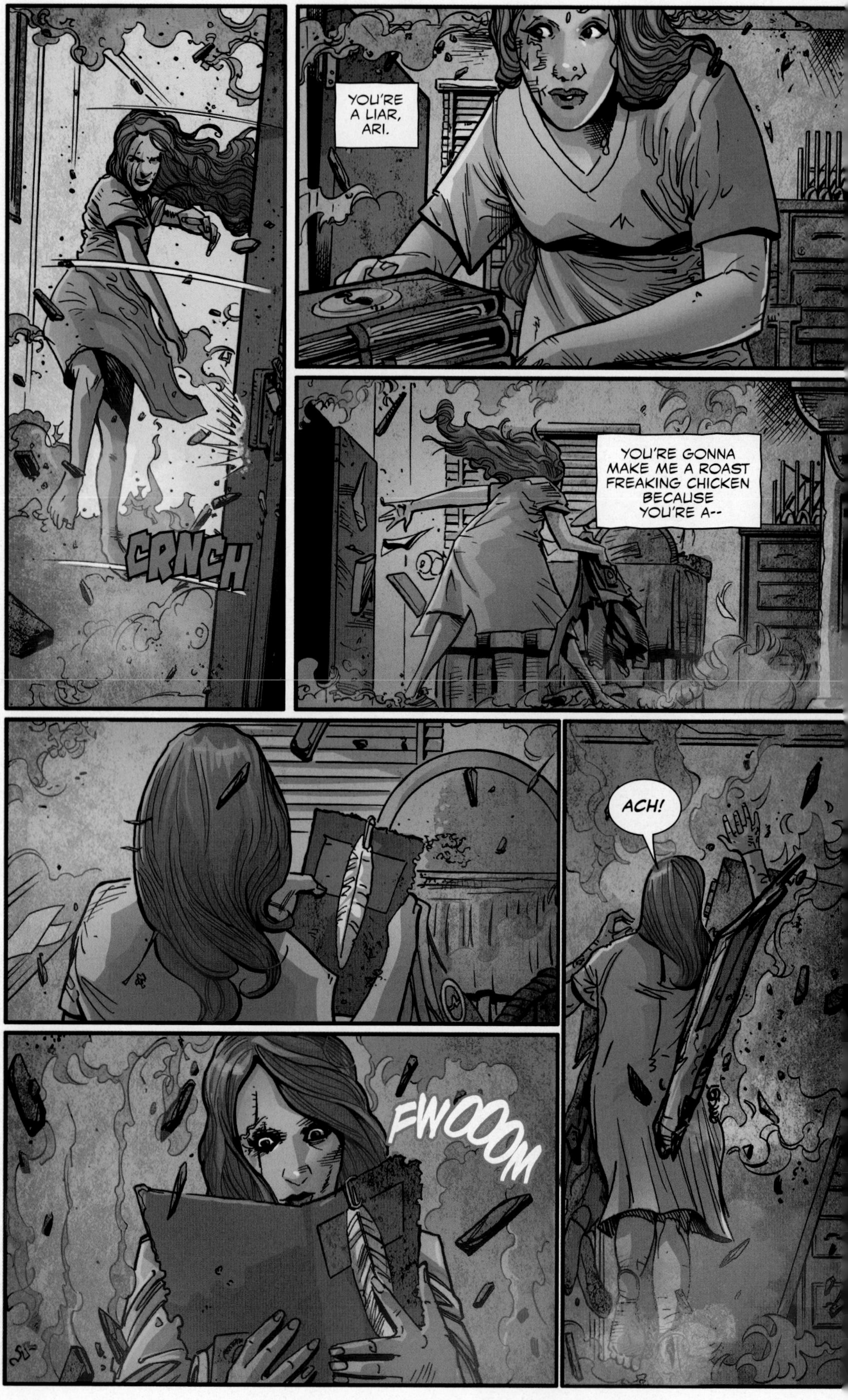
CRNCH
YOU'RE A LIAR, ARI.
YOU'RE GONNA MAKE ME A ROAST FREAKING CHICKEN BECAUSE YOU'RE A--
ACH!
FWOOOM

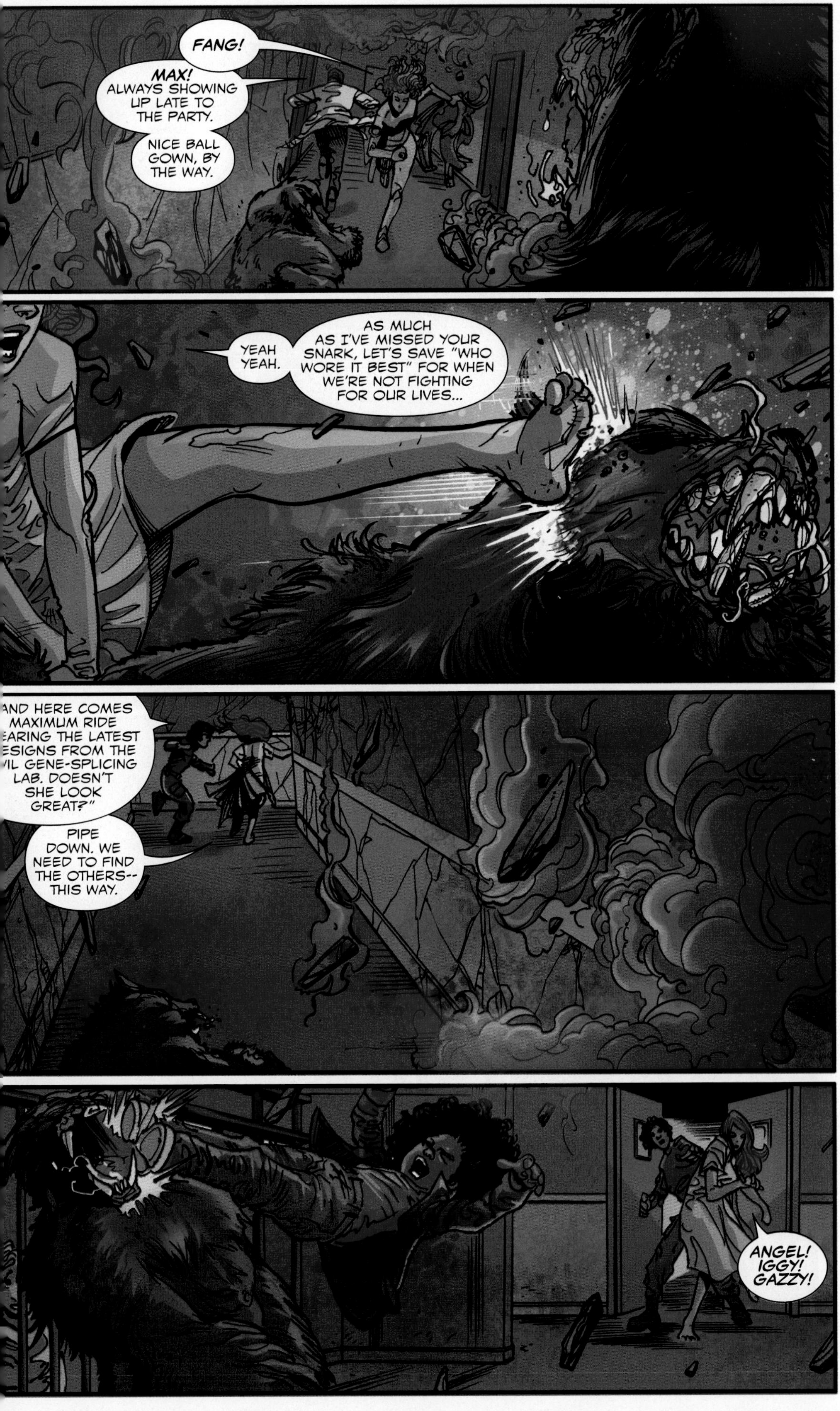
FANG!
MAX! ALWAYS SHOWING UP LATE TO THE PARTY.
NICE BALL GOWN, BY THE WAY.
YEAH YEAH.
AS MUCH AS I'VE MISSED YOUR SNARK, LET'S SAVE "WHO WORE IT BEST" FOR WHEN WE'RE NOT FIGHTING FOR OUR LIVES...
AND HERE COMES MAXIMUM RIDE EARING THE LATEST ESIGNS FROM THE VIL GENE-SPLICING LAB. DOESN'T SHE LOOK GREAT?"
PIPE DOWN. WE NEED TO FIND THE OTHERS-- THIS WAY.
ANGEL! IGGY! GAZZY!

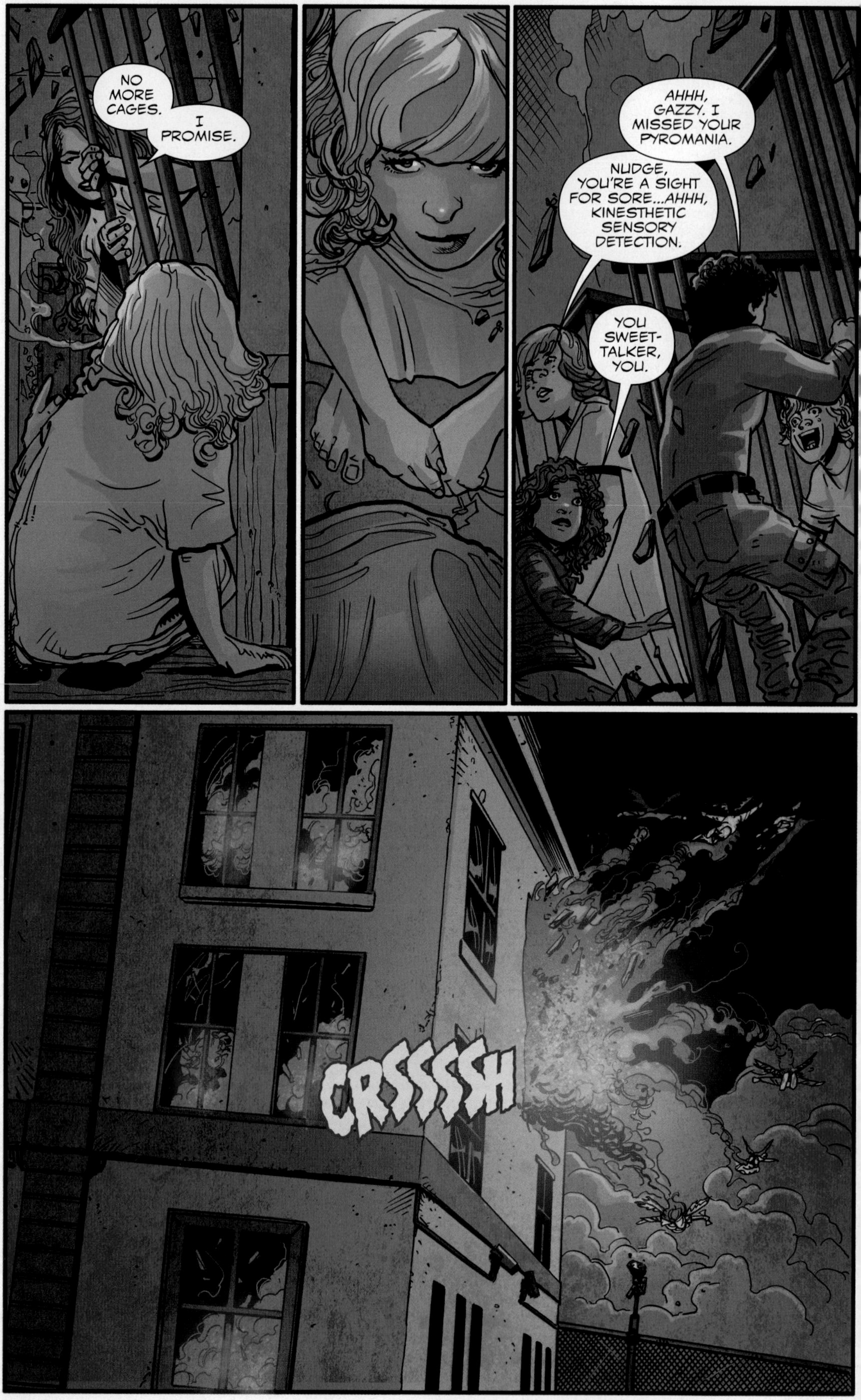
NO MORE CAGES.
I PROMISE.
AHHH, GAZZY. I MISSED YOUR PYROMANIA.
NUDGE, YOU'RE A SIGHT FOR SORE...AHHH, KINESTHETIC SENSORY DETECTION.
YOU SWEET-TALKER, YOU.
CRSSSSH

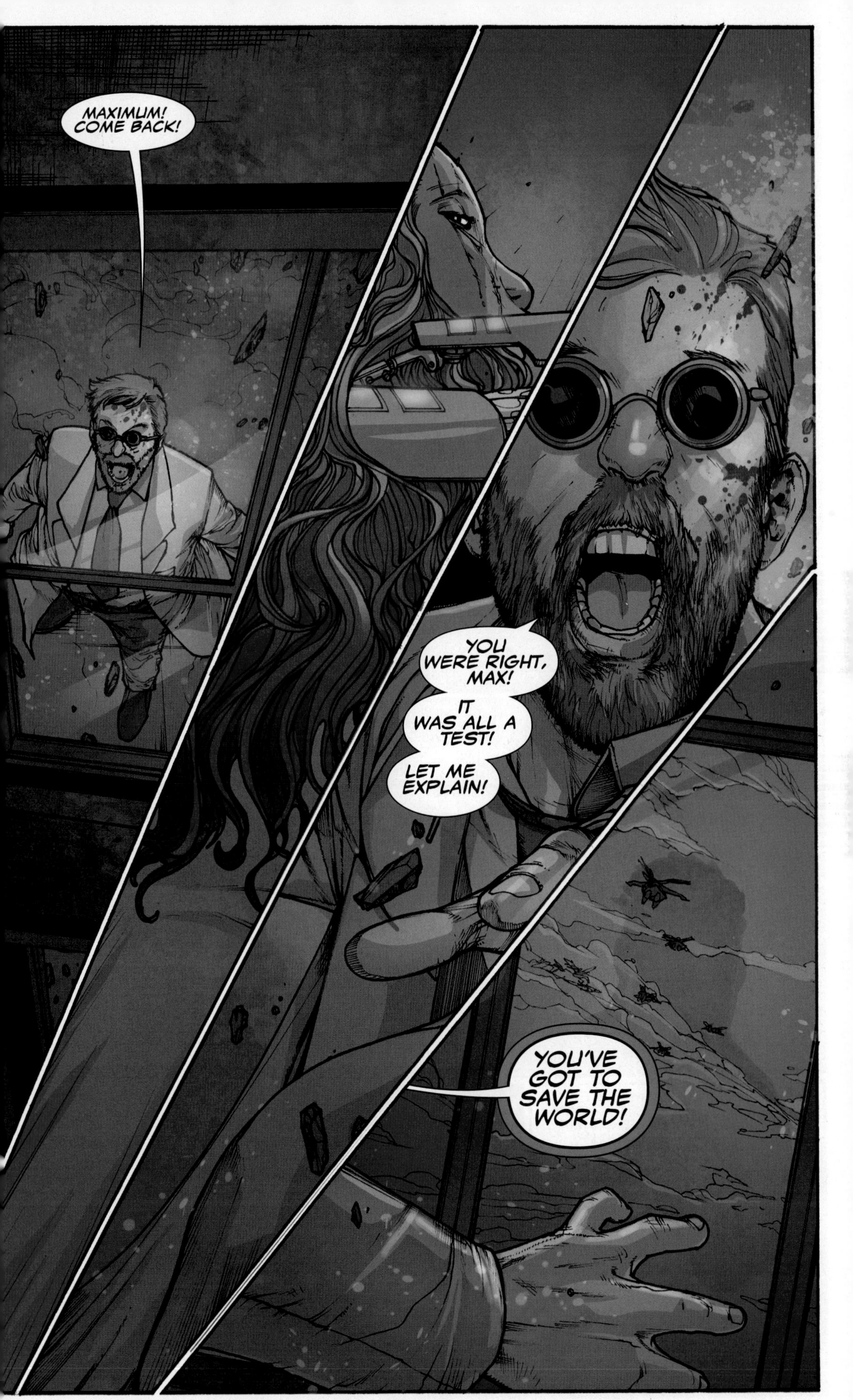

MAXIMUM! COME BACK!
YOU WERE RIGHT, MAX!
IT WAS ALL A TEST!
LET ME EXPLAIN!
YOU'VE GOT TO SAVE THE WORLD!

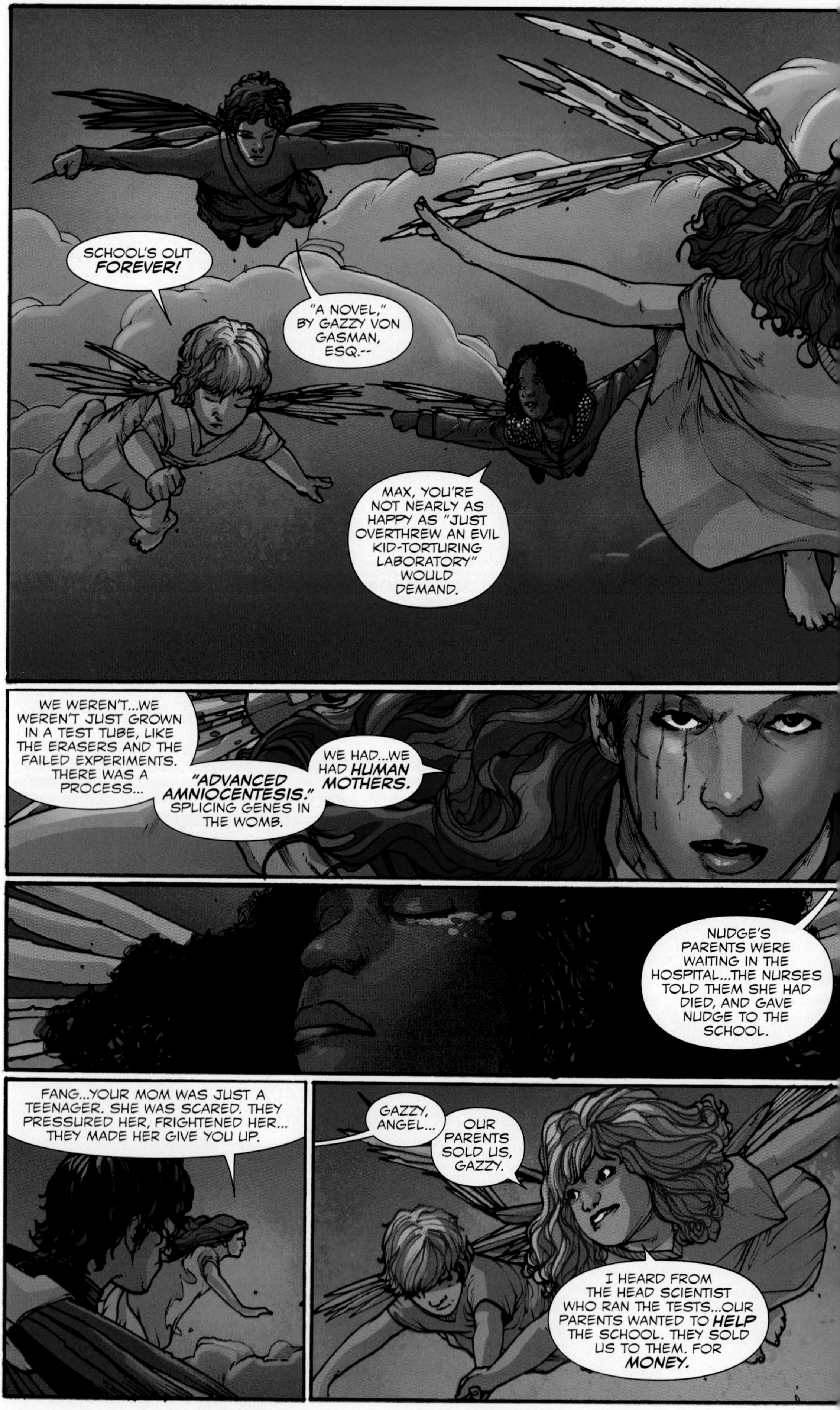

SCHOOL'S OUT FOREVER!
"A NOVEL," BY GAZZY VON GASMAN, ESQ.--
MAX, YOU'RE NOT NEARLY AS HAPPY AS "JUST OVERTHREW AN EVIL KID-TORTURING LABORATORY" WOULD DEMAND.
WE WEREN'T...WE WEREN'T JUST GROWN IN A TEST TUBE, LIKE THE ERASERS AND THE FAILED EXPERIMENTS. THERE WAS A PROCESS...
"ADVANCED AMNIOCENTESIS." SPLICING GENES IN THE WOMB.
WE HAD...WE HAD HUMAN MOTHERS.
NUDGE'S PARENTS WERE WAITING IN THE HOSPITAL...THE NURSES TOLD THEM SHE HAD DIED, AND GAVE NUDGE TO THE SCHOOL.
FANG...YOUR MOM WAS JUST A TEENAGER. SHE WAS SCARED. THEY PRESSURED HER, FRIGHTENED HER... THEY MADE HER GIVE YOU UP.
GAZZY, ANGEL...
OUR PARENTS SOLD US, GAZZY.
I HEARD FROM THE HEAD SCIENTIST WHO RAN THE TESTS...OUR PARENTS WANTED TO HELP THE SCHOOL. THEY SOLD US TO THEM. FOR MONEY.

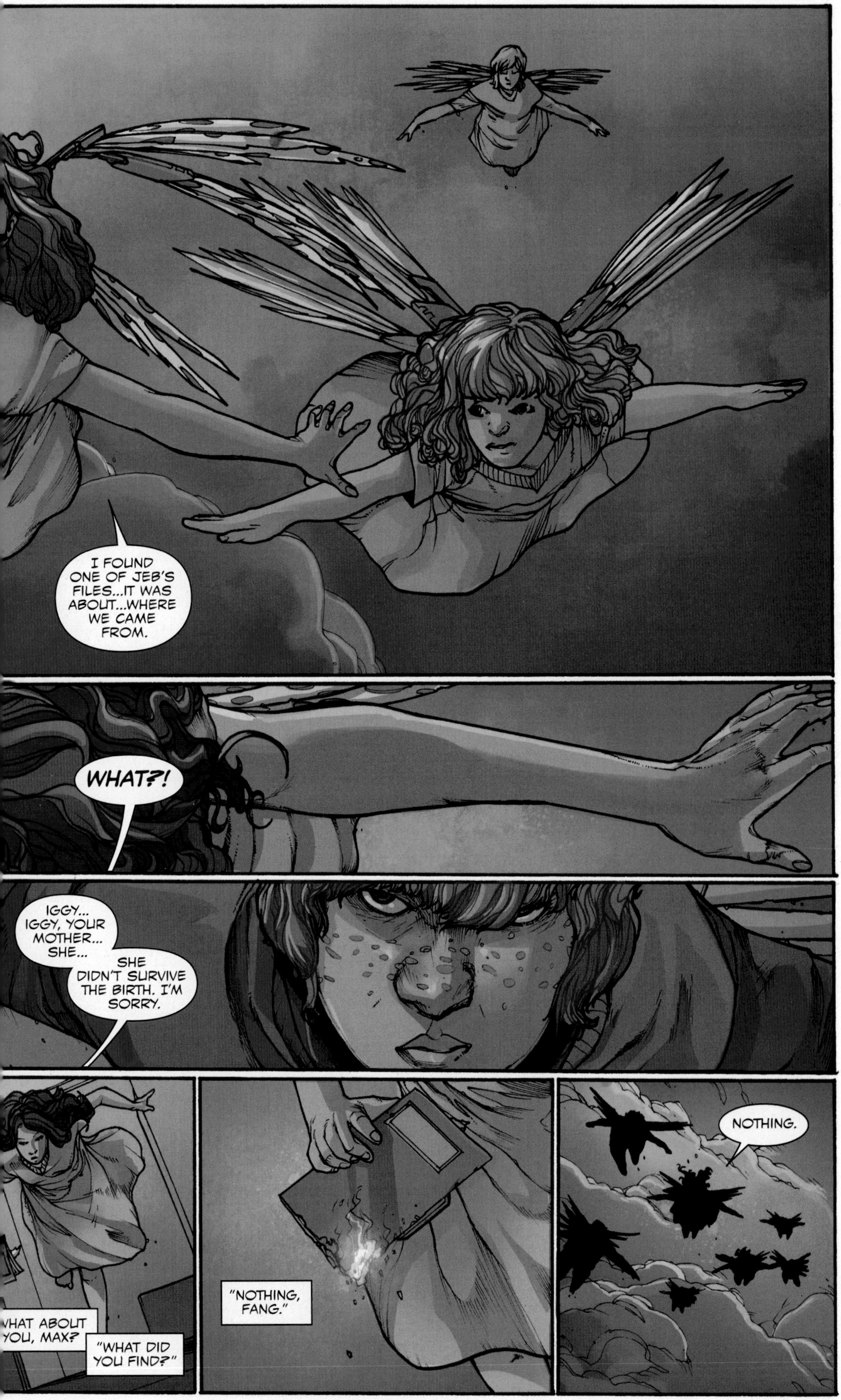
I FOUND ONE OF JEB'S FILES...IT WAS ABOUT...WHERE WE CAME FROM.
WHAT?!
IGGY... IGGY, YOUR MOTHER... SHE...
SHE DIDN'T SURVIVE THE BIRTH. I'M SORRY.
WHAT ABOUT YOU, MAX?
"WHAT DID YOU FIND?"
"NOTHING, FANG."
NOTHING.

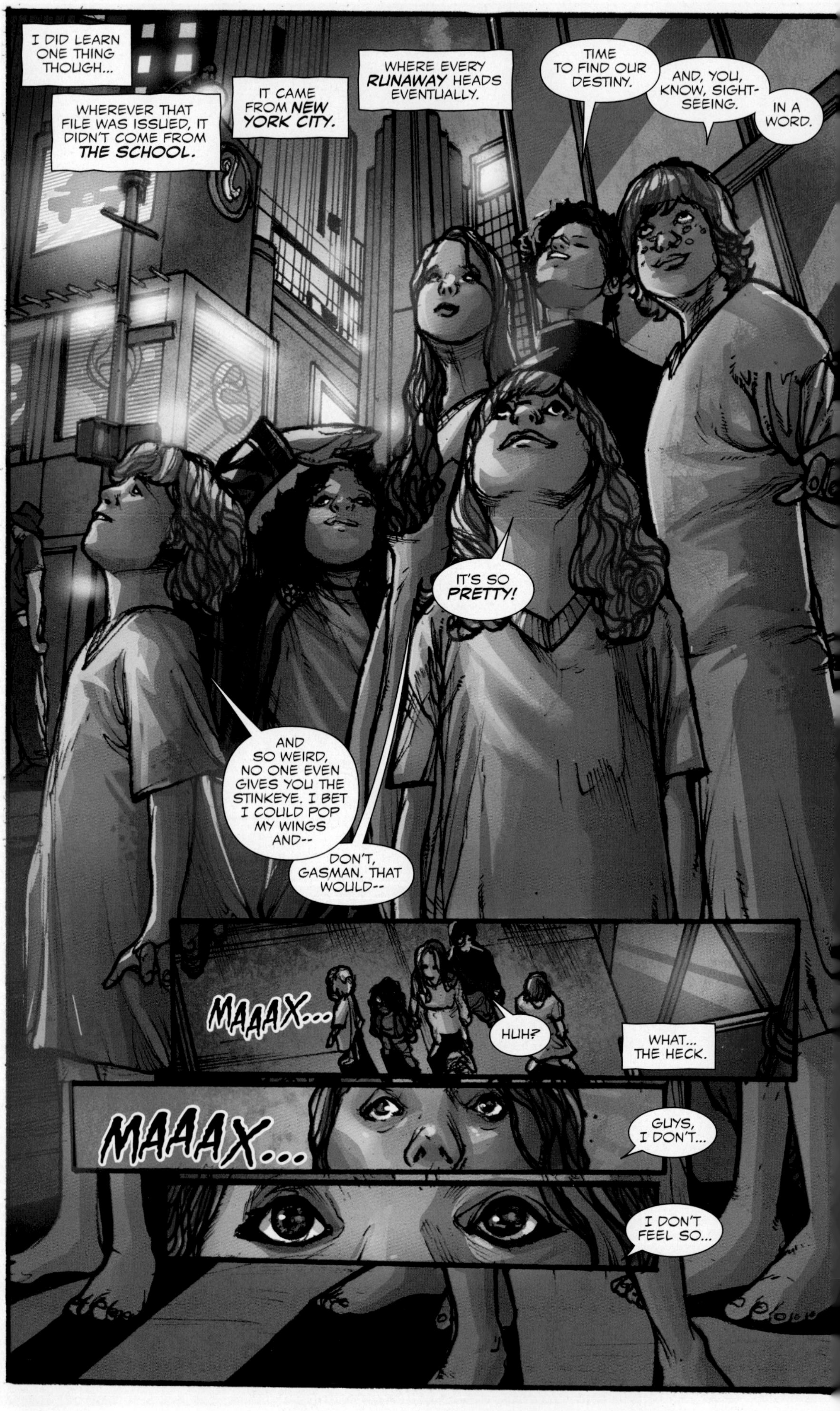
I DID LEARN ONE THING THOUGH...
WHEREVER THAT FILE WAS ISSUED, IT DIDN'T COME FROM **THE SCHOOL.**
IT CAME FROM **NEW YORK CITY.**
WHERE EVERY **RUNAWAY** HEADS EVENTUALLY.
TIME TO FIND OUR DESTINY.
AND, YOU, KNOW, SIGHT-SEEING.
IN A WORD.
IT'S SO **PRETTY!**
AND SO WEIRD, NO ONE EVEN GIVES YOU THE STINKEYE. I BET I COULD POP MY WINGS AND--
DON'T, GASMAN. THAT WOULD--
MAAAX...
HUH?
WHAT... THE HECK.
MAAAX...
GUYS, I DON'T...
I DON'T FEEL SO...

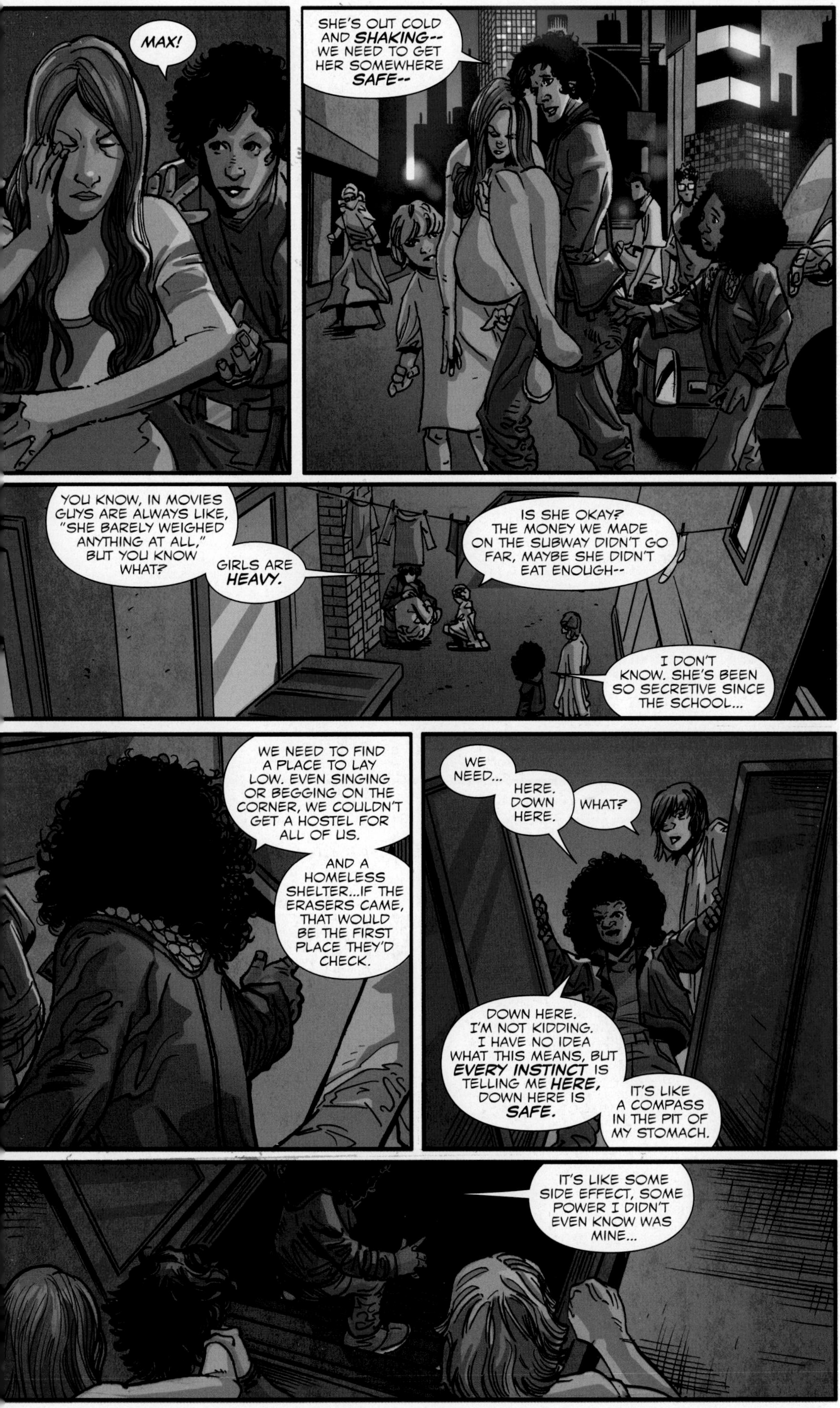
MAX!
SHE'S OUT COLD AND SHAKING-- WE NEED TO GET HER SOMEWHERE SAFE--
YOU KNOW, IN MOVIES GUYS ARE ALWAYS LIKE, "SHE BARELY WEIGHED ANYTHING AT ALL," BUT YOU KNOW WHAT?
GIRLS ARE HEAVY.
IS SHE OKAY? THE MONEY WE MADE ON THE SUBWAY DIDN'T GO FAR, MAYBE SHE DIDN'T EAT ENOUGH--
I DON'T KNOW. SHE'S BEEN SO SECRETIVE SINCE THE SCHOOL...
WE NEED TO FIND A PLACE TO LAY LOW. EVEN SINGING OR BEGGING ON THE CORNER, WE COULDN'T GET A HOSTEL FOR ALL OF US.
AND A HOMELESS SHELTER...IF THE ERASERS CAME, THAT WOULD BE THE FIRST PLACE THEY'D CHECK.
WE NEED...
HERE. DOWN HERE.
WHAT?
DOWN HERE. I'M NOT KIDDING. I HAVE NO IDEA WHAT THIS MEANS, BUT EVERY INSTINCT IS TELLING ME HERE, DOWN HERE IS SAFE.
IT'S LIKE A COMPASS IN THE PIT OF MY STOMACH.
IT'S LIKE SOME SIDE EFFECT, SOME POWER I DIDN'T EVEN KNOW WAS MINE...

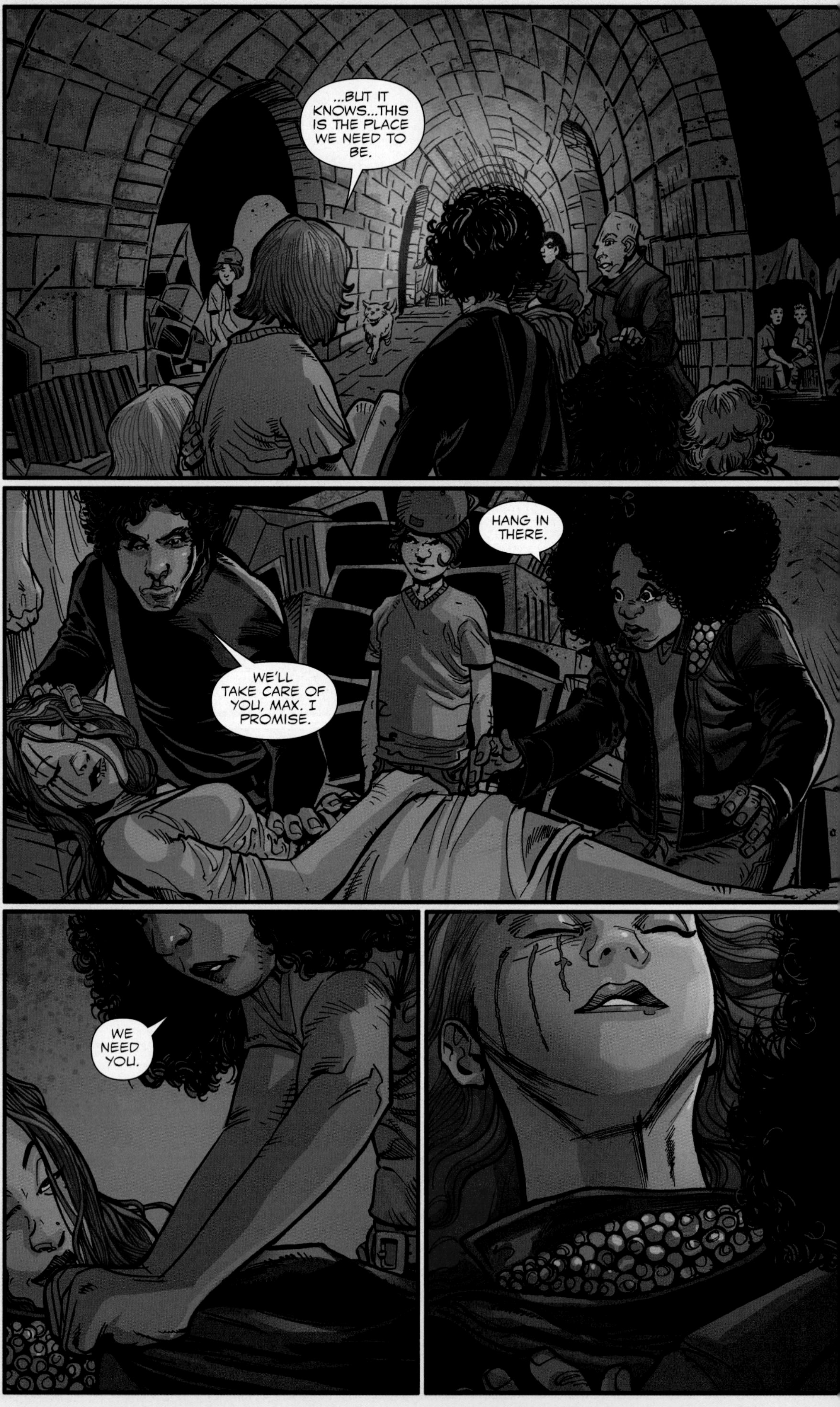
...BUT IT KNOWS...THIS IS THE PLACE WE NEED TO BE.
HANG IN THERE.
WE'LL TAKE CARE OF YOU, MAX. I PROMISE.
WE NEED YOU.

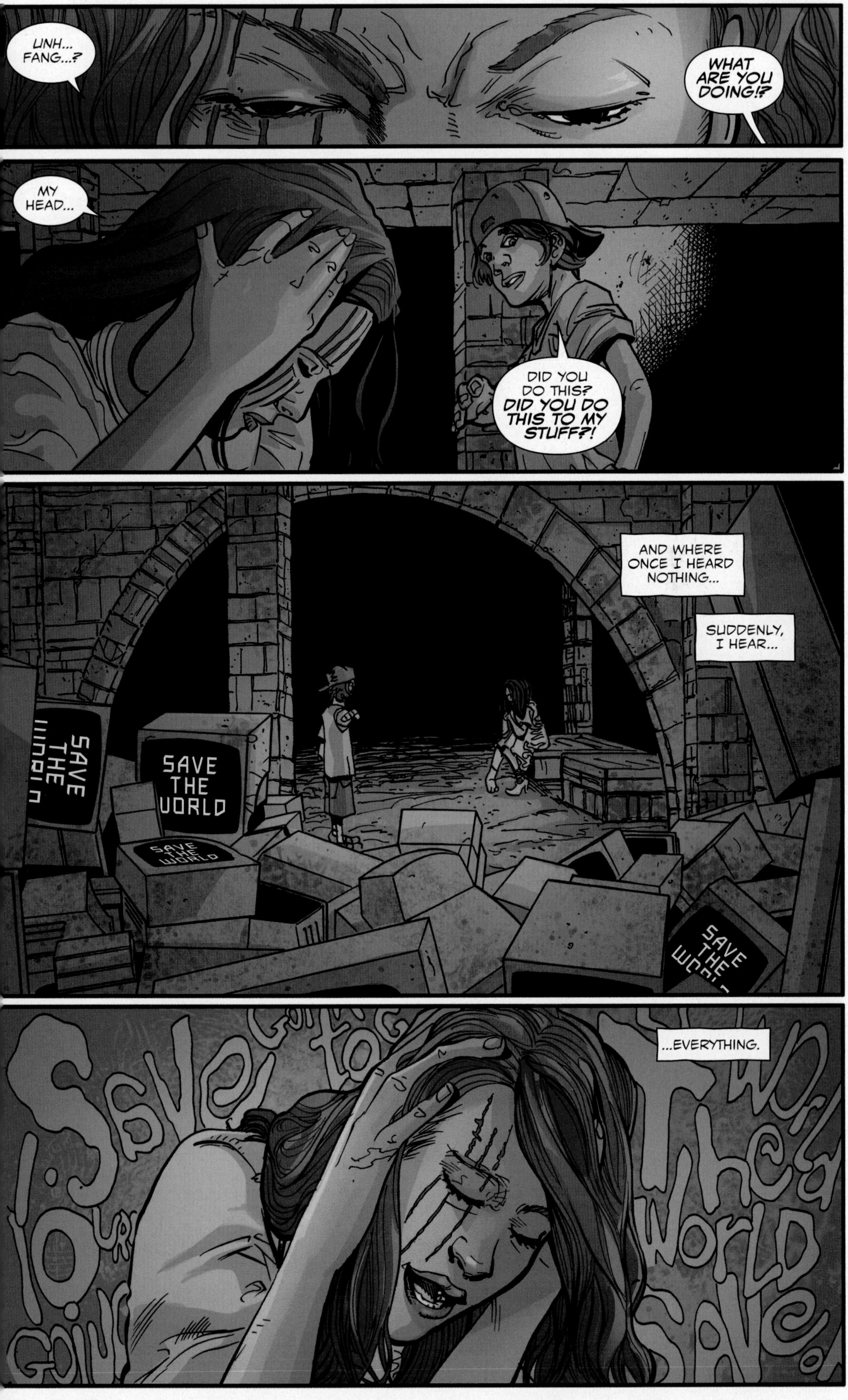
UNH... FANG...?
WHAT ARE YOU DOING!?
MY HEAD...
DID YOU DO THIS? DID YOU DO THIS TO MY STUFF?!
AND WHERE ONCE I HEARD NOTHING...
SUDDENLY, I HEAR...
SAVE THE WORLD
SAVE THE WORLD
...EVERYTHING.

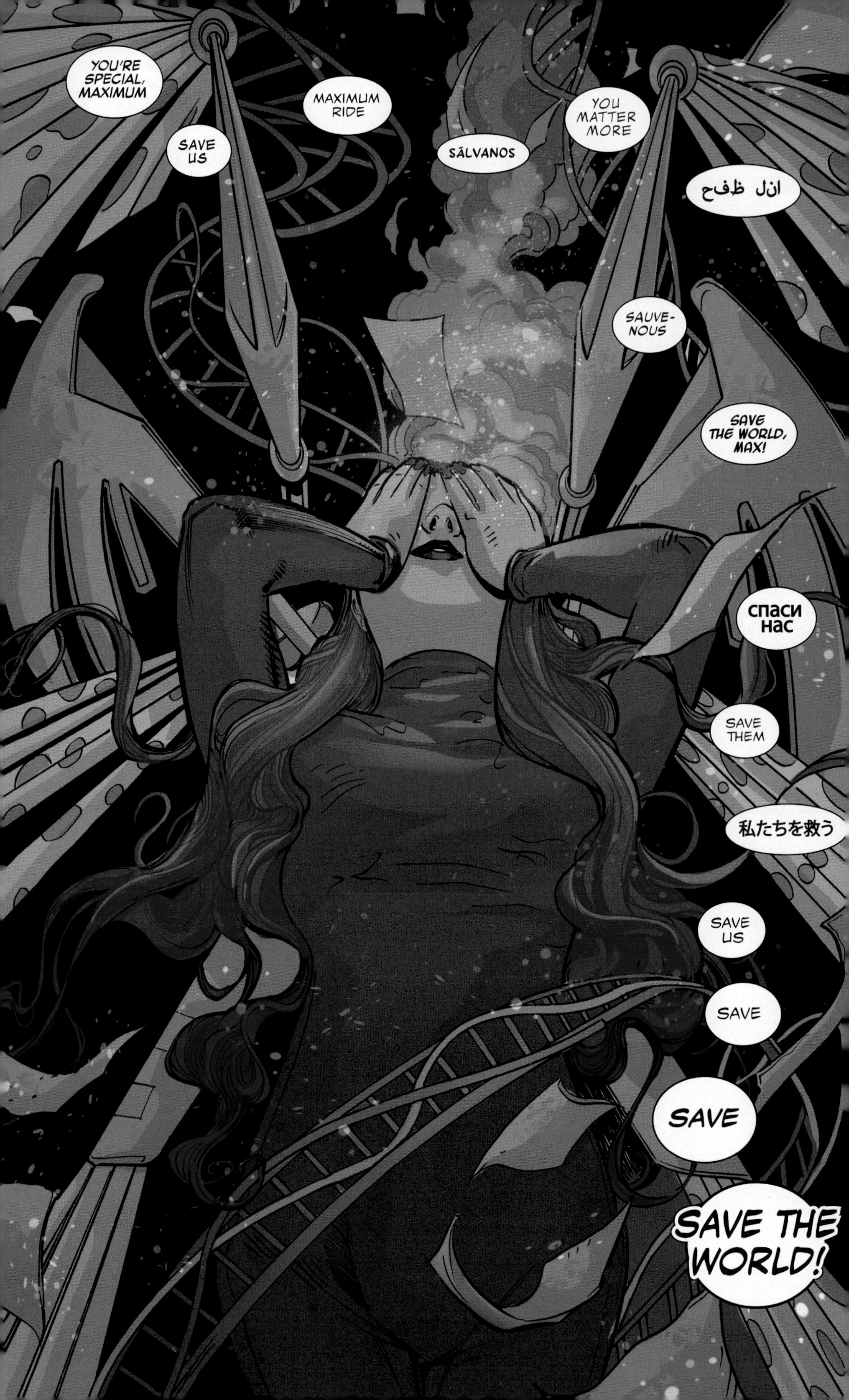
YOU'RE SPECIAL, MAXIMUM
SAVE US
MAXIMUM RIDE
SĀLVANOS
YOU MATTER MORE
انل ظفح
SAUVE-NOUS
SAVE THE WORLD, MAX!
спаси нас
SAVE THEM
私たちを救う
SAVE US
SAVE
SAVE
SAVE THE WORLD!

CHAPTER 6

CHAPTER 4

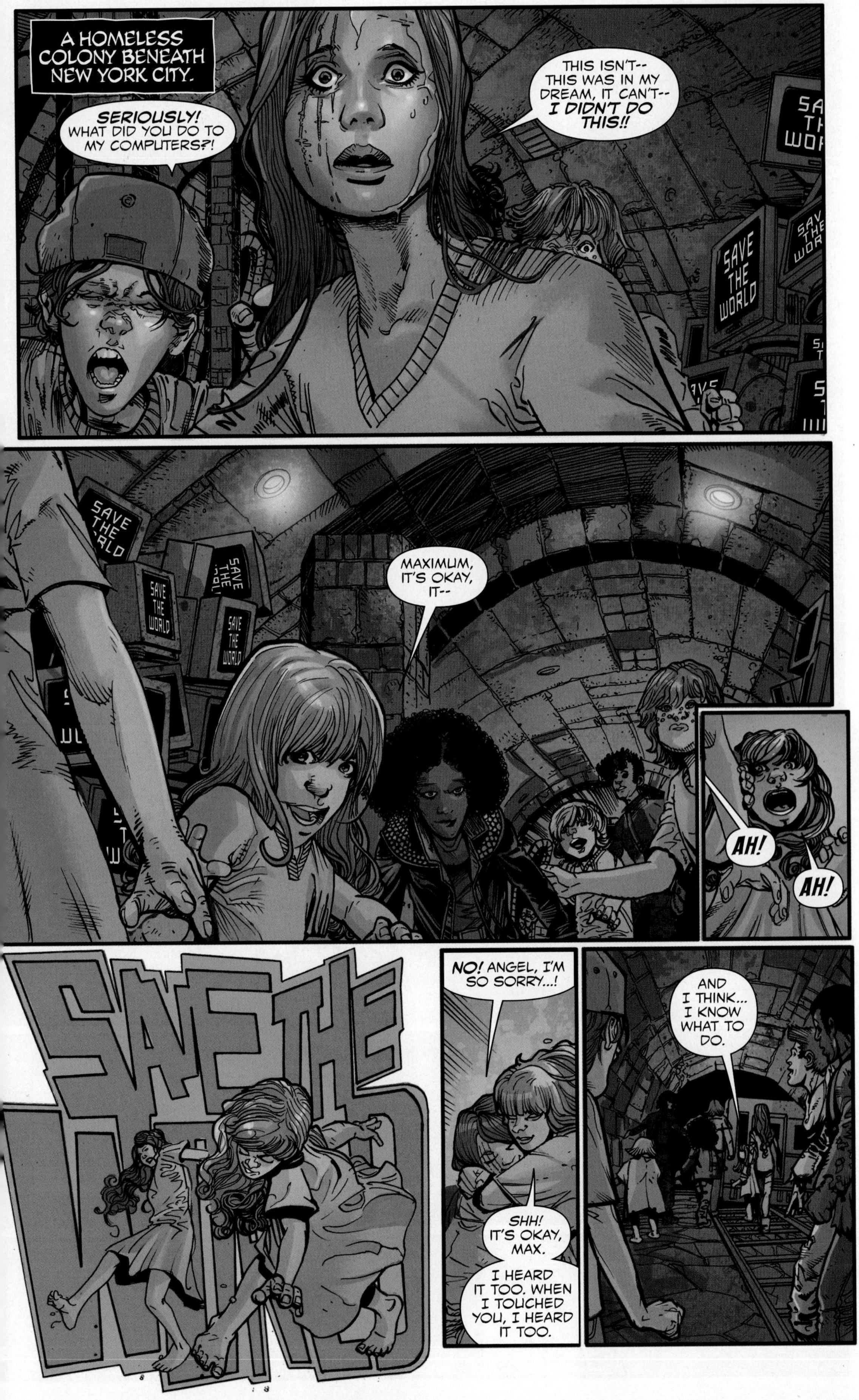

A HOMELESS COLONY BENEATH NEW YORK CITY.
SERIOUSLY! WHAT DID YOU DO TO MY COMPUTERS?!
THIS ISN'T-- THIS WAS IN MY DREAM, IT CAN'T-- I DIDN'T DO THIS!!
SAVE THE WORLD
MAXIMUM, IT'S OKAY, IT--
AH!
AH!
SAVE THE
NO! ANGEL, I'M SO SORRY...!
SHH! IT'S OKAY, MAX.
I HEARD IT TOO. WHEN I TOUCHED YOU, I HEARD IT TOO.
AND I THINK... I KNOW WHAT TO DO.

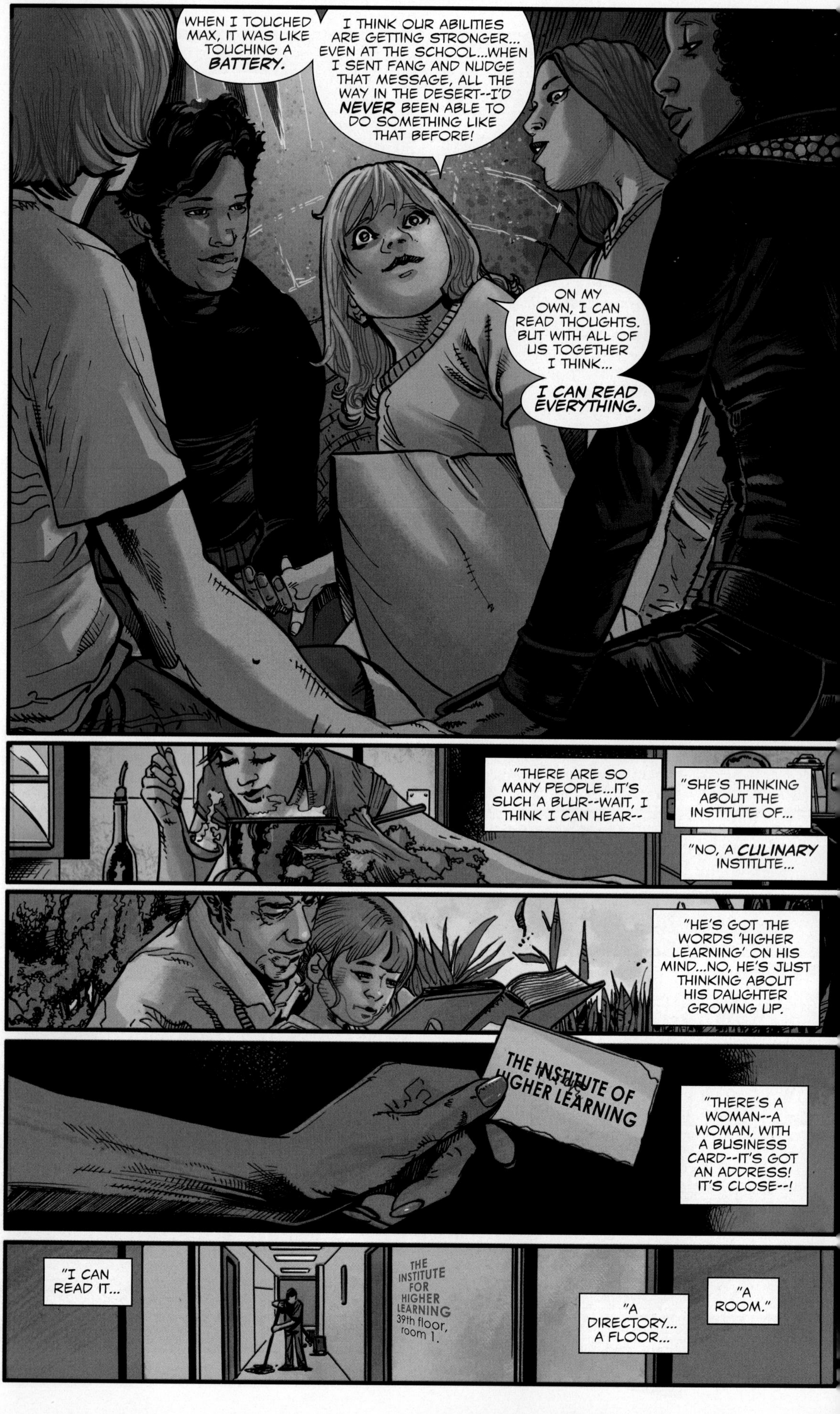

WHEN I TOUCHED MAX, IT WAS LIKE TOUCHING A BATTERY.
I THINK OUR ABILITIES ARE GETTING STRONGER... EVEN AT THE SCHOOL...WHEN I SENT FANG AND NUDGE THAT MESSAGE, ALL THE WAY IN THE DESERT--I'D NEVER BEEN ABLE TO DO SOMETHING LIKE THAT BEFORE!
ON MY OWN, I CAN READ THOUGHTS. BUT WITH ALL OF US TOGETHER I THINK...
I CAN READ EVERYTHING.
"THERE ARE SO MANY PEOPLE...IT'S SUCH A BLUR--WAIT, I THINK I CAN HEAR--
"SHE'S THINKING ABOUT THE INSTITUTE OF...
"NO, A CULINARY INSTITUTE...
"HE'S GOT THE WORDS 'HIGHER LEARNING' ON HIS MIND...NO, HE'S JUST THINKING ABOUT HIS DAUGHTER GROWING UP.
THE INSTITUTE OF HIGHER LEARNING
"THERE'S A WOMAN--A WOMAN, WITH A BUSINESS CARD--IT'S GOT AN ADDRESS! IT'S CLOSE--!
"I CAN READ IT...
THE INSTITUTE FOR HIGHER LEARNING 39th floor, room 1.
"A DIRECTORY... A FLOOR...
"A ROOM."

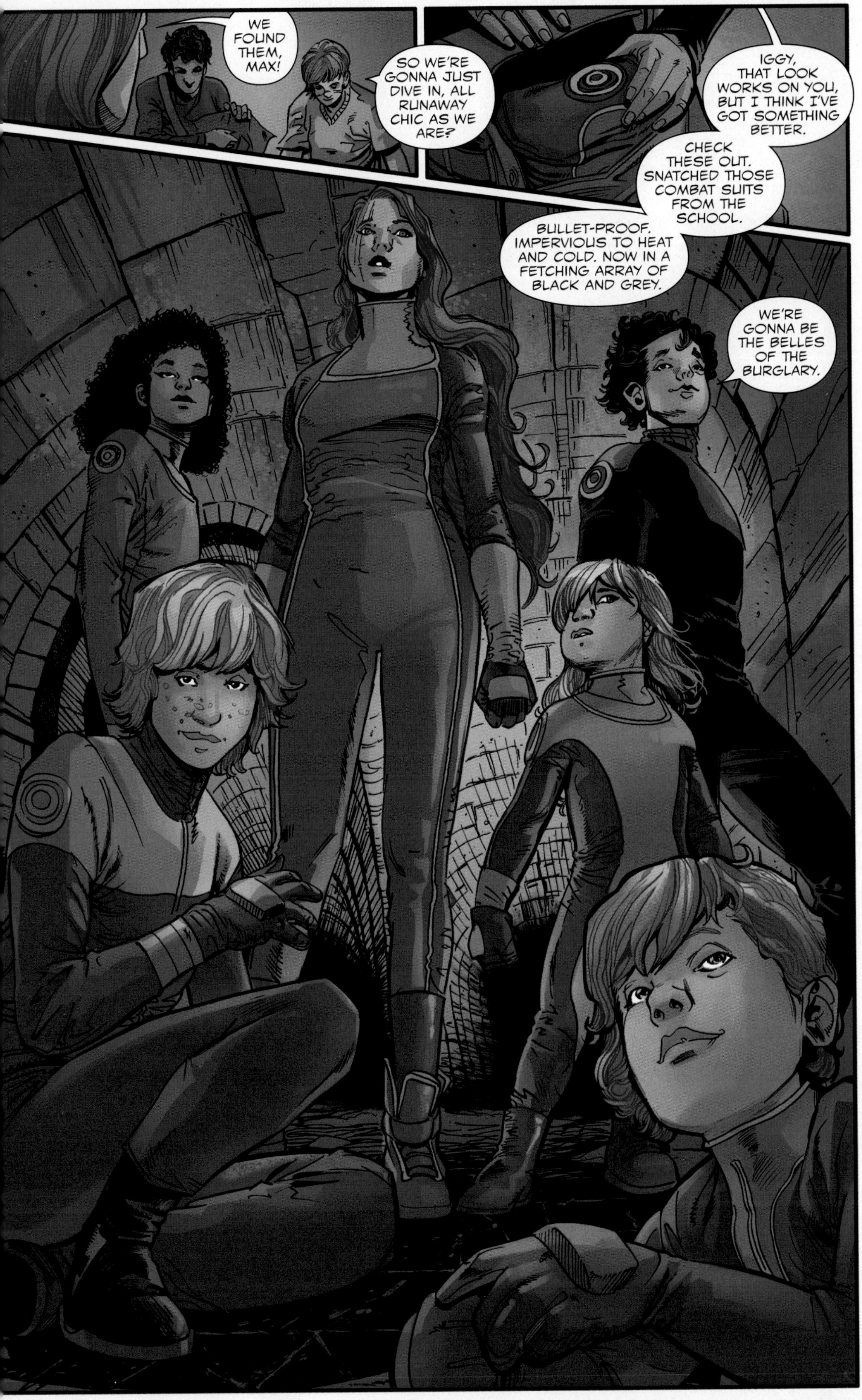

WE FOUND THEM, MAX!
SO WE'RE GONNA JUST DIVE IN, ALL RUNAWAY CHIC AS WE ARE?
IGGY, THAT LOOK WORKS ON YOU, BUT I THINK I'VE GOT SOMETHING BETTER.
CHECK THESE OUT. SNATCHED THOSE COMBAT SUITS FROM THE SCHOOL.
BULLET-PROOF. IMPERVIOUS TO HEAT AND COLD. NOW IN A FETCHING ARRAY OF BLACK AND GREY.
WE'RE GONNA BE THE BELLES OF THE BURGLARY.

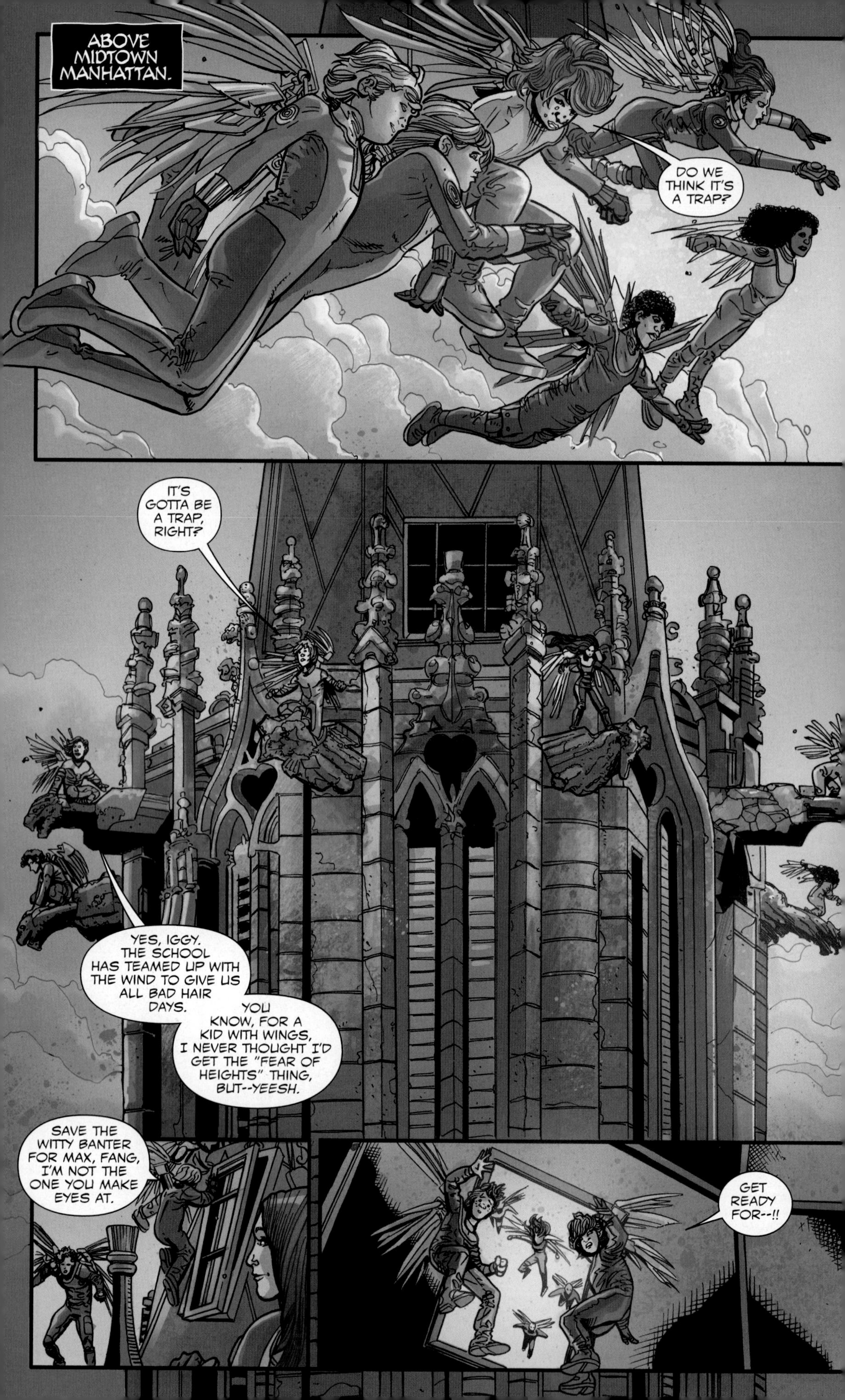
ABOVE MIDTOWN MANHATTAN.
DO WE THINK IT'S A TRAP?
IT'S GOTTA BE A TRAP, RIGHT?
YES, IGGY. THE SCHOOL HAS TEAMED UP WITH THE WIND TO GIVE US ALL BAD HAIR DAYS.
YOU KNOW, FOR A KID WITH WINGS, I NEVER THOUGHT I'D GET THE "FEAR OF HEIGHTS" THING, BUT--YEESH.
SAVE THE WITTY BANTER FOR MAX, FANG, I'M NOT THE ONE YOU MAKE EYES AT.
GET READY FOR--!!

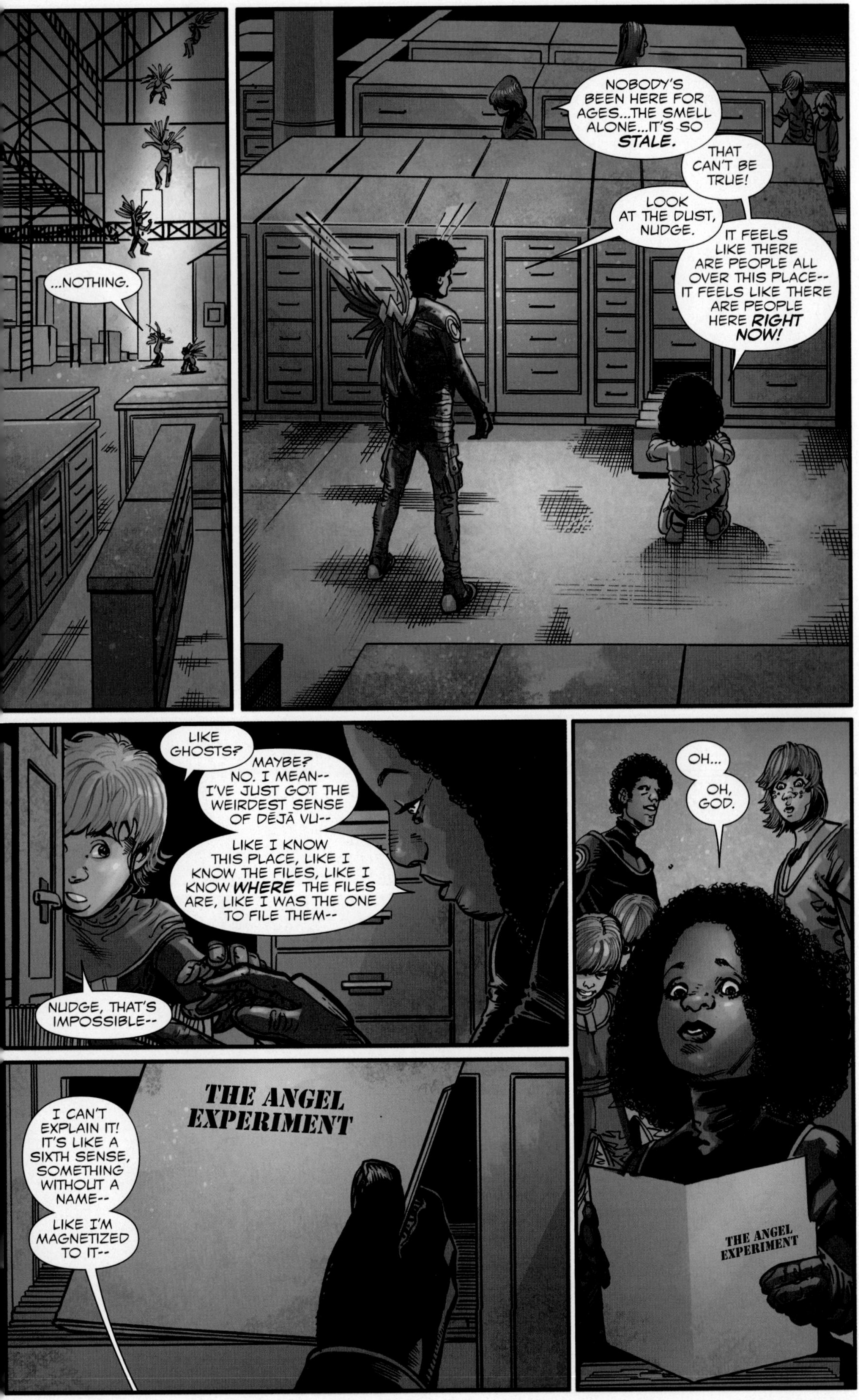
...NOTHING.
NOBODY'S BEEN HERE FOR AGES...THE SMELL ALONE...IT'S SO STALE.
THAT CAN'T BE TRUE!
LOOK AT THE DUST, NUDGE.
IT FEELS LIKE THERE ARE PEOPLE ALL OVER THIS PLACE-- IT FEELS LIKE THERE ARE PEOPLE HERE RIGHT NOW!
LIKE GHOSTS?
MAYBE? NO. I MEAN-- I'VE JUST GOT THE WEIRDEST SENSE OF DÉJÀ VU--
LIKE I KNOW THIS PLACE, LIKE I KNOW THE FILES, LIKE I KNOW WHERE THE FILES ARE, LIKE I WAS THE ONE TO FILE THEM--
NUDGE, THAT'S IMPOSSIBLE--
OH...
OH, GOD.
THE ANGEL EXPERIMENT
I CAN'T EXPLAIN IT! IT'S LIKE A SIXTH SENSE, SOMETHING WITHOUT A NAME--
LIKE I'M MAGNETIZED TO IT--
THE ANGEL EXPERIMENT

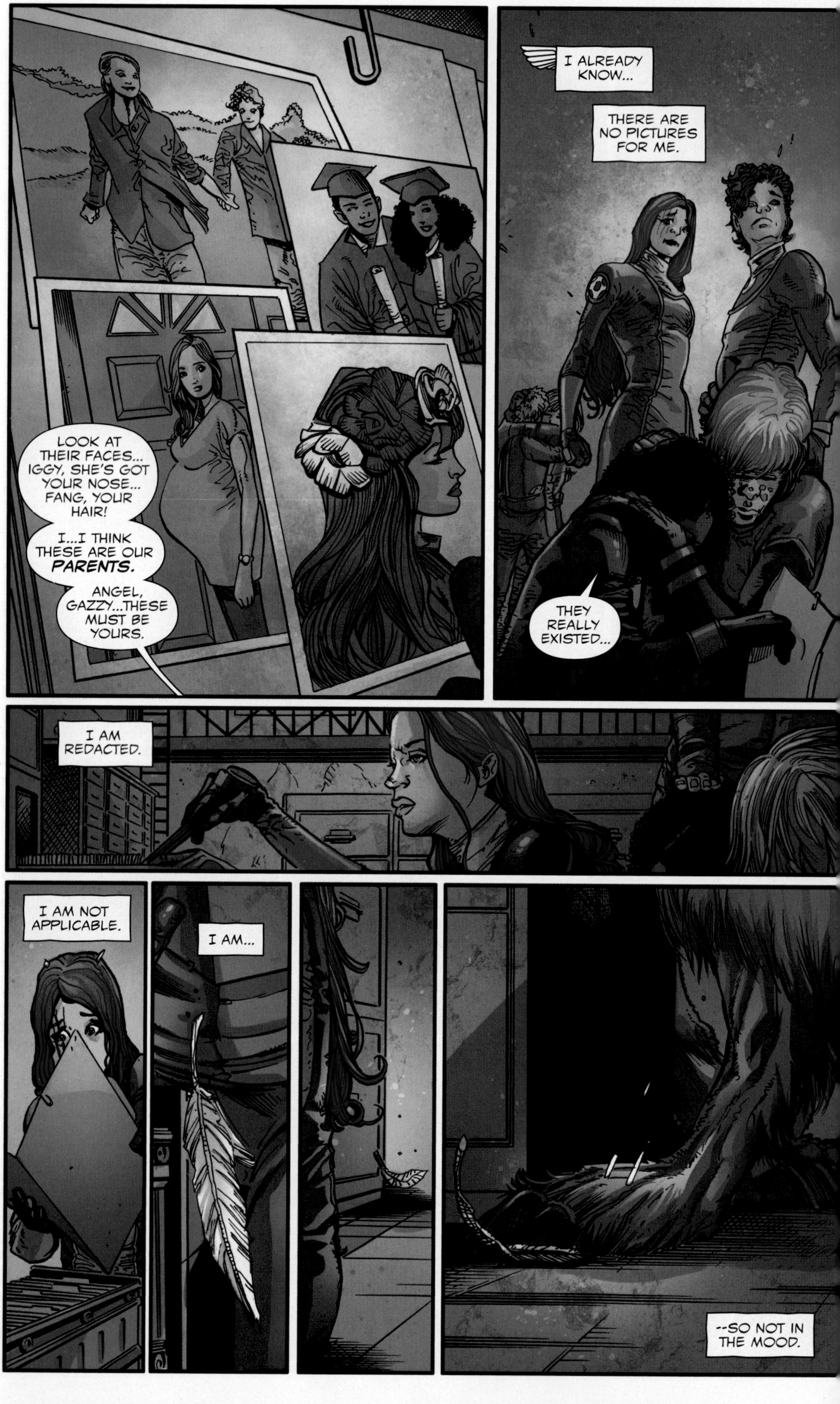
LOOK AT THEIR FACES... IGGY, SHE'S GOT YOUR NOSE... FANG, YOUR HAIR!
I...I THINK THESE ARE OUR PARENTS.
ANGEL, GAZZY...THESE MUST BE YOURS.
I ALREADY KNOW...
THERE ARE NO PICTURES FOR ME.
THEY REALLY EXISTED...
I AM REDACTED.
I AM NOT APPLICABLE.
I AM...
--SO NOT IN THE MOOD.

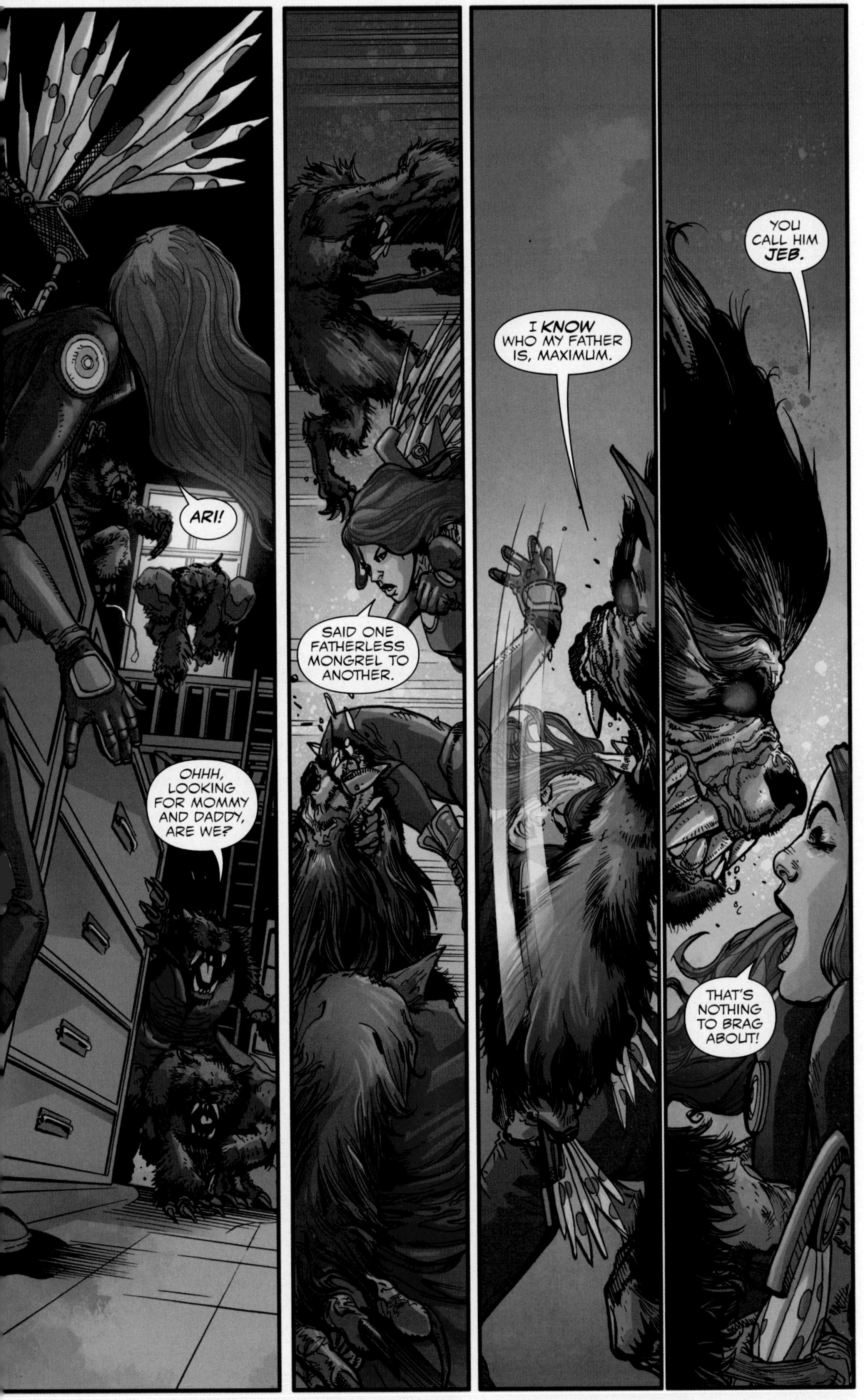
ARI!
OHHH, LOOKING FOR MOMMY AND DADDY, ARE WE?
SAID ONE FATHERLESS MONGREL TO ANOTHER.
I KNOW WHO MY FATHER IS, MAXIMUM.
YOU CALL HIM JEB.
THAT'S NOTHING TO BRAG ABOUT!

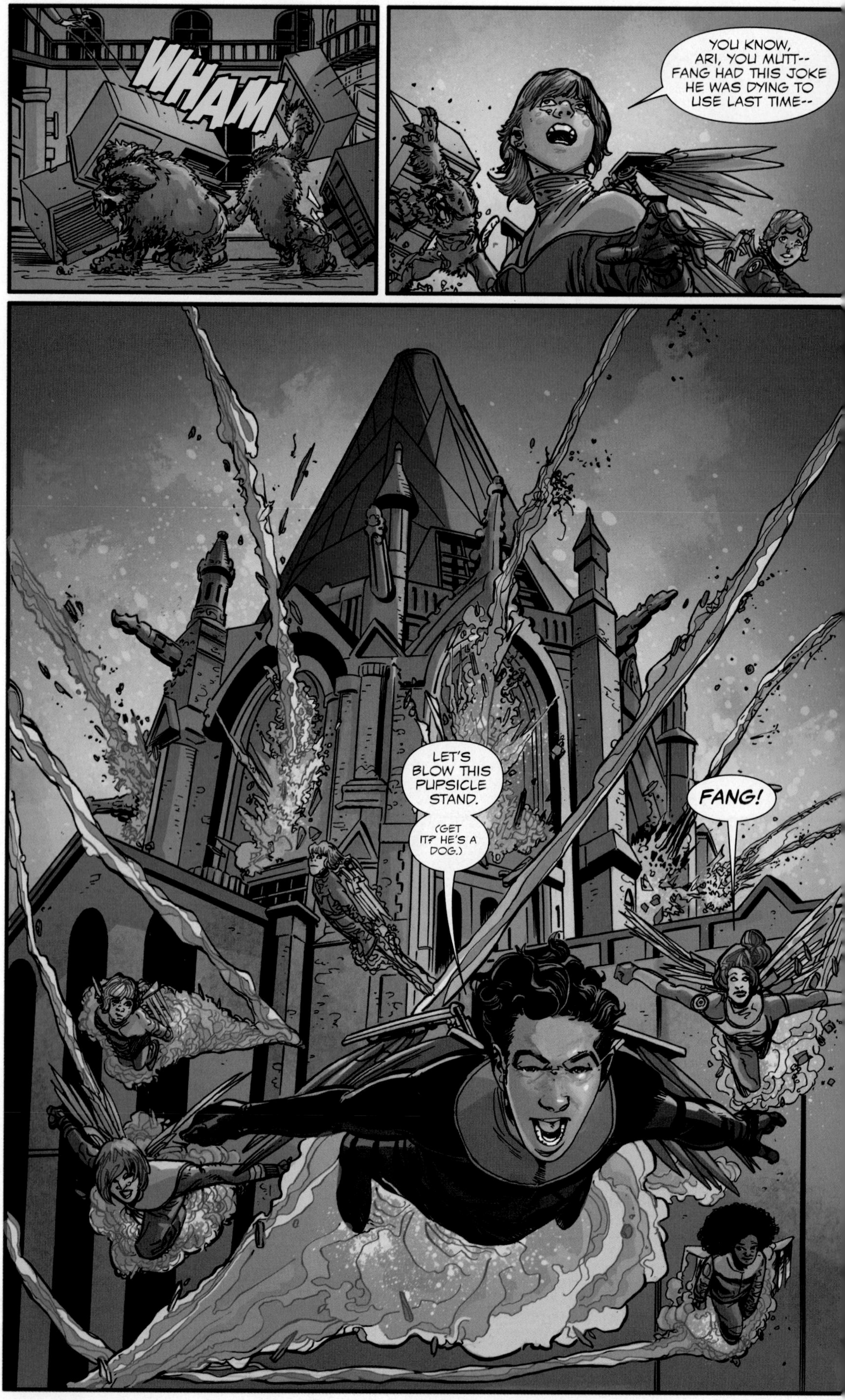
WHAM
YOU KNOW, ARI, YOU MUTT-- FANG HAD THIS JOKE HE WAS DYING TO USE LAST TIME--
LET'S BLOW THIS PUPSICLE STAND.
(GET IT? HE'S A DOG.)
FANG!

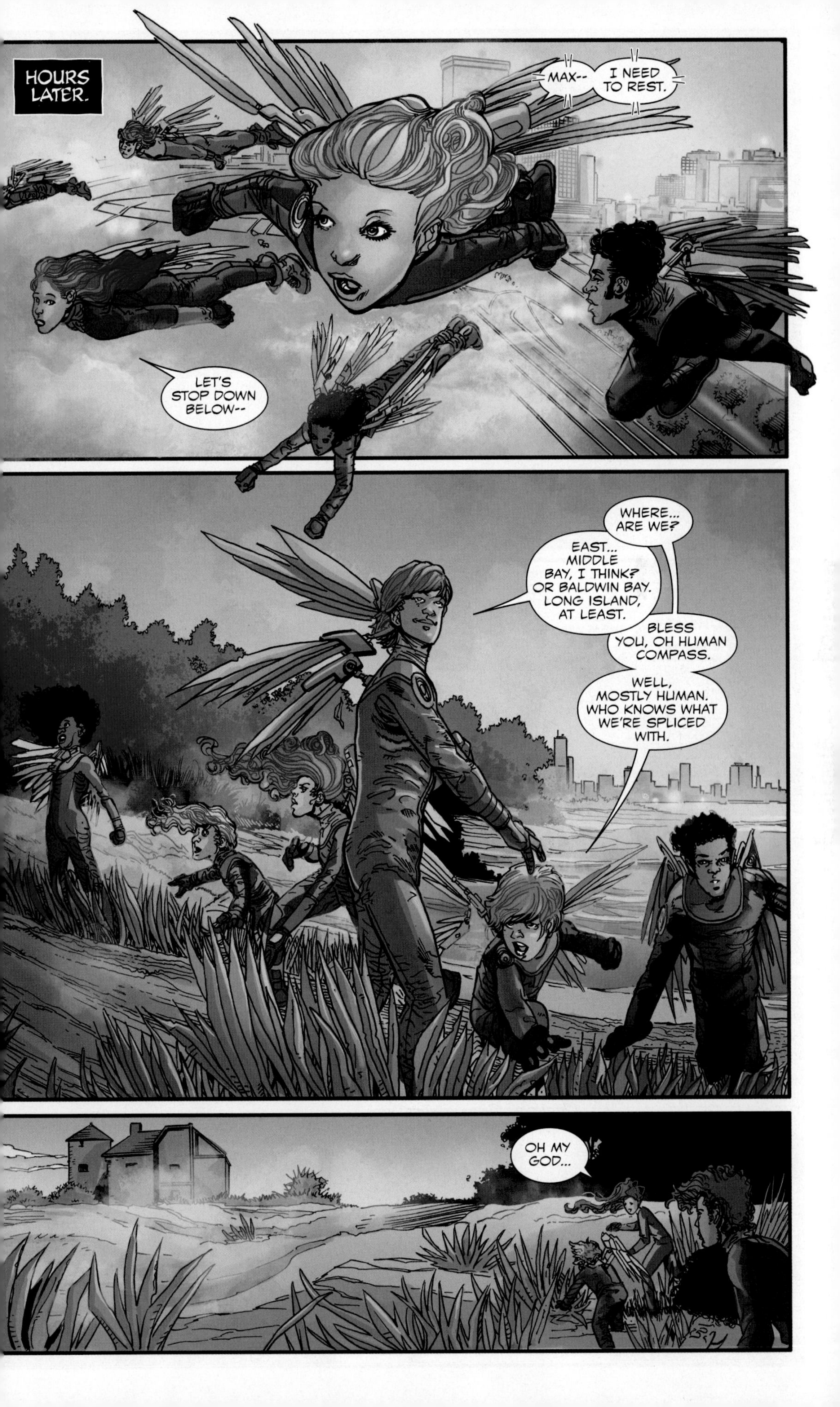
HOURS LATER.
MAX--
I NEED TO REST.
LET'S STOP DOWN BELOW--
WHERE... ARE WE?
EAST... MIDDLE BAY, I THINK? OR BALDWIN BAY. LONG ISLAND, AT LEAST.
BLESS YOU, OH HUMAN COMPASS.
WELL, MOSTLY HUMAN. WHO KNOWS WHAT WE'RE SPLICED WITH.
OH MY GOD...

...THIS IS PERFECT.

IT'S A...BAY HOUSE!

A WHAT?

THESE OLD FISHING COTTAGES IN THE MARSHES. THEY'RE ABANDONED BUT PEOPLE ARE TOO SCARED THAT DESTROYING THEM WILL HARM THE LOCAL ECOSYSTEM--

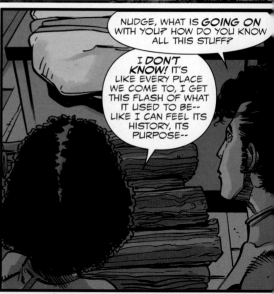

NUDGE, WHAT IS GOING ON WITH YOU? HOW DO YOU KNOW ALL THIS STUFF?

I DON'T KNOW! IT'S LIKE EVERY PLACE WE COME TO, I GET THIS FLASH OF WHAT IT USED TO BE-- LIKE I CAN FEEL ITS HISTORY, ITS PURPOSE--

THE BOTTOM LINE IS, IT SOUNDS LIKE WE'RE SAFE HERE. NO ONE'S GOING TO COME SNOOPING AROUND A PLACE THIS DILAPIDATED.

MAX, THIS BLANKET SMELLS LIKE FISH.

SHH.

WE'VE BEEN RUNNING, GUNNING, OVERWHELMED...AND EVERY CLUE WE FIND ABOUT WHERE WE CAME FROM SEEMS TO BE BOOBY-TRAPPED.

WE'VE GOT TO REST...

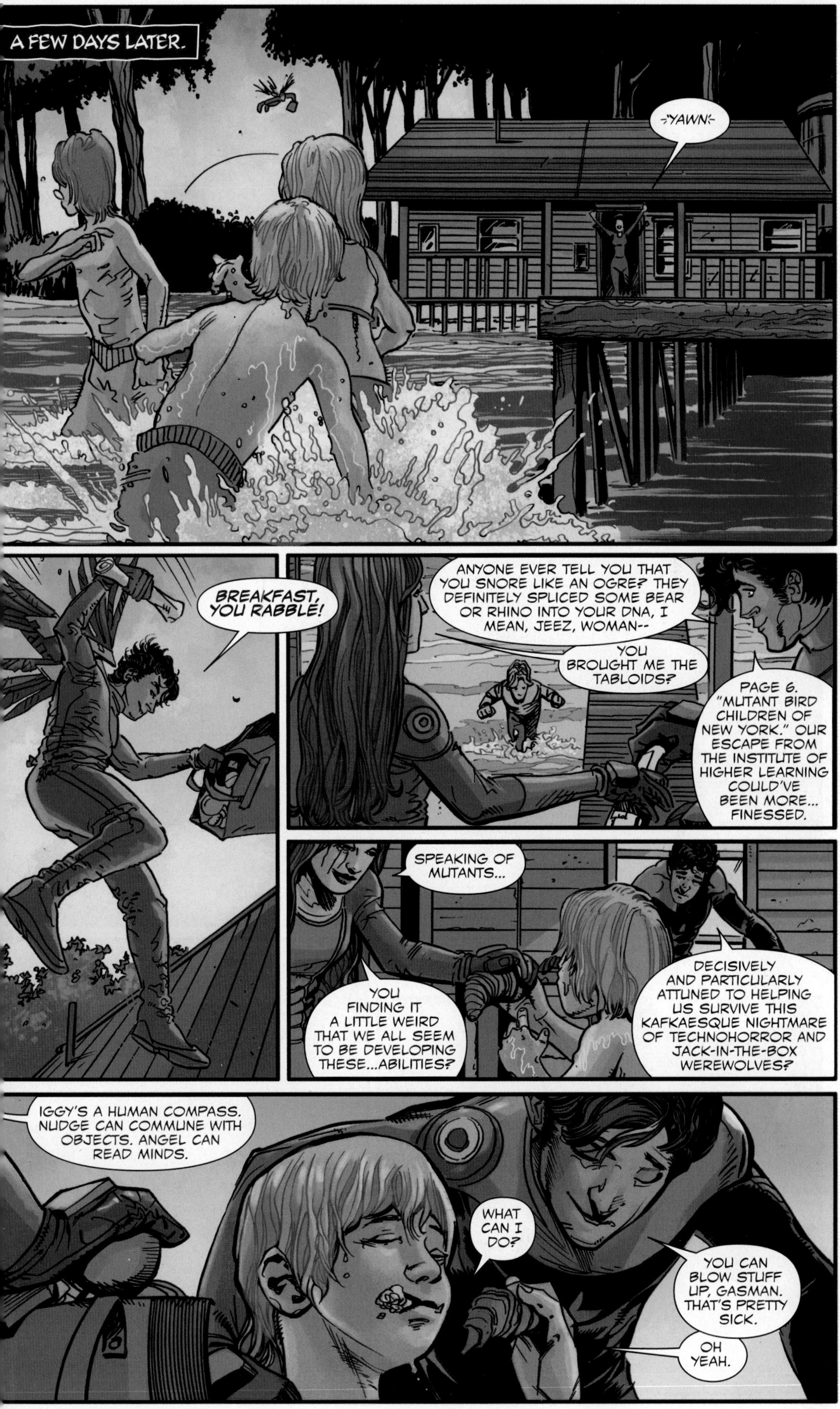
A FEW DAYS LATER.
-YAWN-
BREAKFAST, YOU RABBLE!
ANYONE EVER TELL YOU THAT YOU SNORE LIKE AN OGRE? THEY DEFINITELY SPLICED SOME BEAR OR RHINO INTO YOUR DNA, I MEAN, JEEZ, WOMAN--
YOU BROUGHT ME THE TABLOIDS?
PAGE 6. "MUTANT BIRD CHILDREN OF NEW YORK." OUR ESCAPE FROM THE INSTITUTE OF HIGHER LEARNING COULD'VE BEEN MORE... FINESSED.
SPEAKING OF MUTANTS...
YOU FINDING IT A LITTLE WEIRD THAT WE ALL SEEM TO BE DEVELOPING THESE...ABILITIES?
DECISIVELY AND PARTICULARLY ATTUNED TO HELPING US SURVIVE THIS KAFKAESQUE NIGHTMARE OF TECHNOHORROR AND JACK-IN-THE-BOX WEREWOLVES?
IGGY'S A HUMAN COMPASS. NUDGE CAN COMMUNE WITH OBJECTS. ANGEL CAN READ MINDS.
WHAT CAN I DO?
YOU CAN BLOW STUFF UP, GASMAN. THAT'S PRETTY SICK.
OH YEAH.

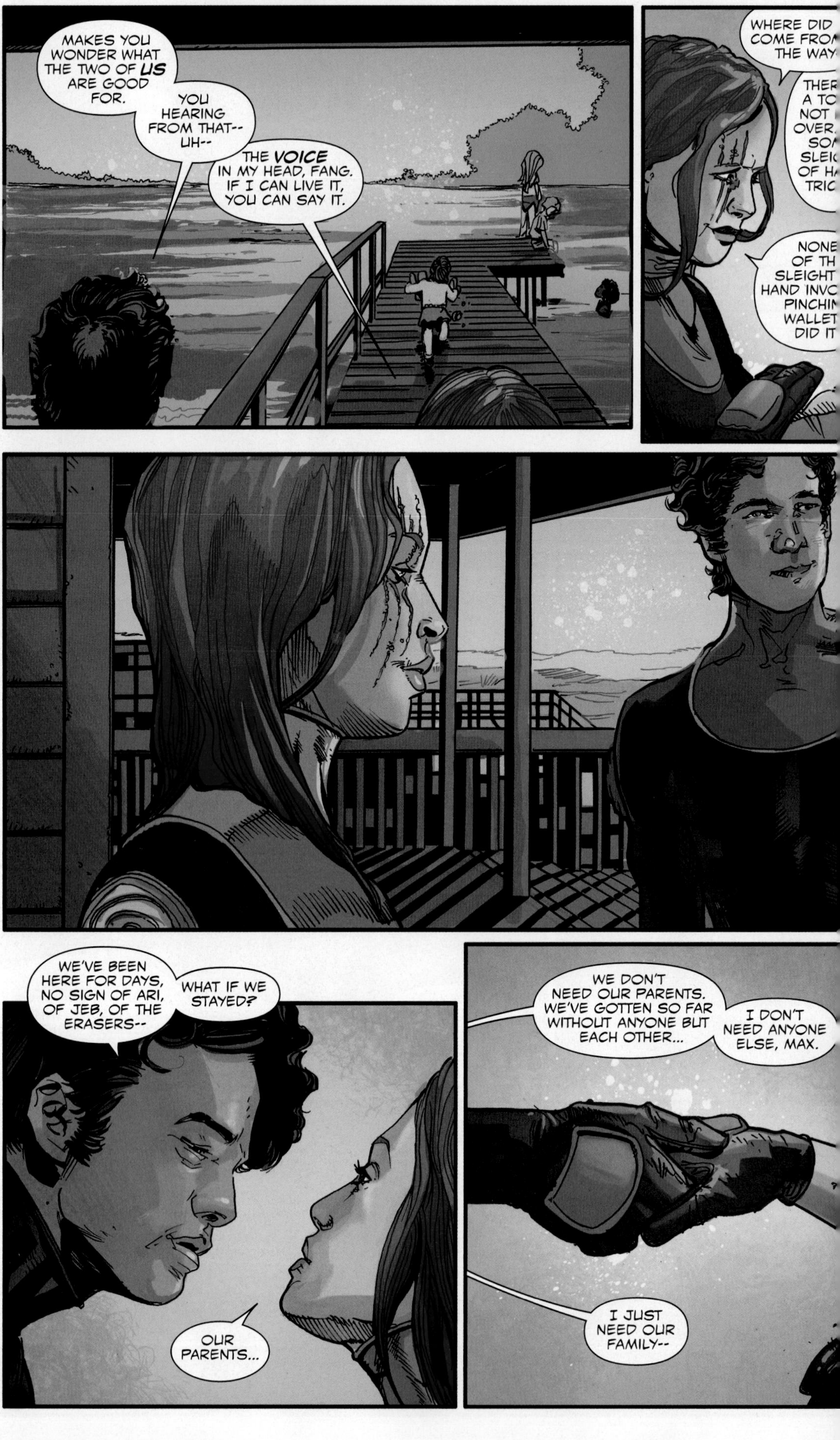
MAKES YOU WONDER WHAT THE TWO OF **US** ARE GOOD FOR.
YOU HEARING FROM THAT-- UH--
THE **VOICE** IN MY HEAD, FANG. IF I CAN LIVE IT, YOU CAN SAY IT.
WHERE DID COME FROM THE WAY
WE'VE BEEN HERE FOR DAYS, NO SIGN OF ARI, OF JEB, OF THE ERASERS--
WHAT IF WE STAYED?
OUR PARENTS...
WE DON'T NEED OUR PARENTS. WE'VE GOTTEN SO FAR WITHOUT ANYONE BUT EACH OTHER...
I DON'T NEED ANYONE ELSE, MAX.
I JUST NEED OUR FAMILY--

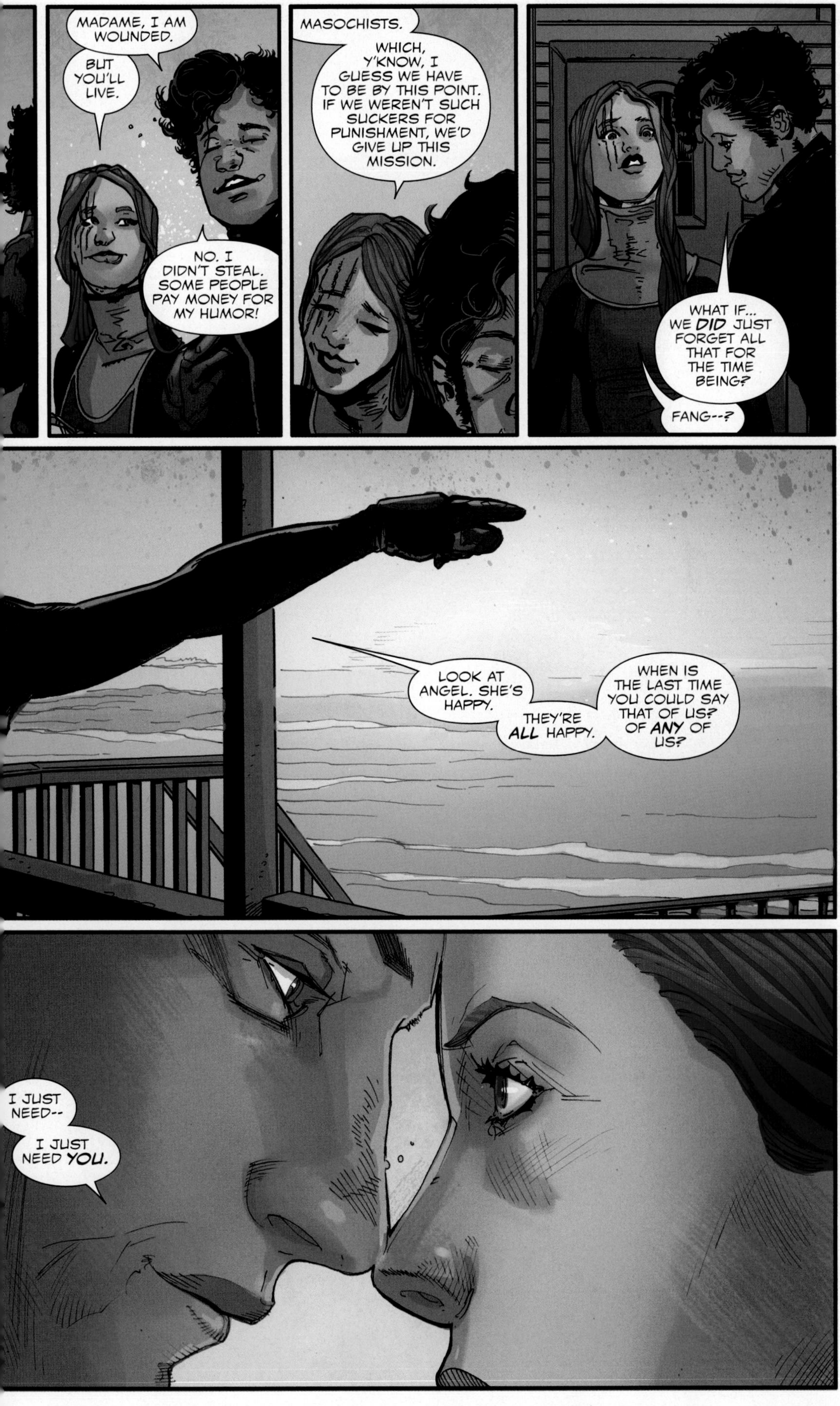
MADAME, I AM WOUNDED.
BUT YOU'LL LIVE.
NO. I DIDN'T STEAL. SOME PEOPLE PAY MONEY FOR MY HUMOR!
MASOCHISTS.
WHICH, Y'KNOW, I GUESS WE HAVE TO BE BY THIS POINT. IF WE WEREN'T SUCH SUCKERS FOR PUNISHMENT, WE'D GIVE UP THIS MISSION.
WHAT IF... WE DID JUST FORGET ALL THAT FOR THE TIME BEING?
FANG--?
LOOK AT ANGEL. SHE'S HAPPY.
THEY'RE ALL HAPPY.
WHEN IS THE LAST TIME YOU COULD SAY THAT OF US? OF ANY OF US?
I JUST NEED--
I JUST NEED YOU.

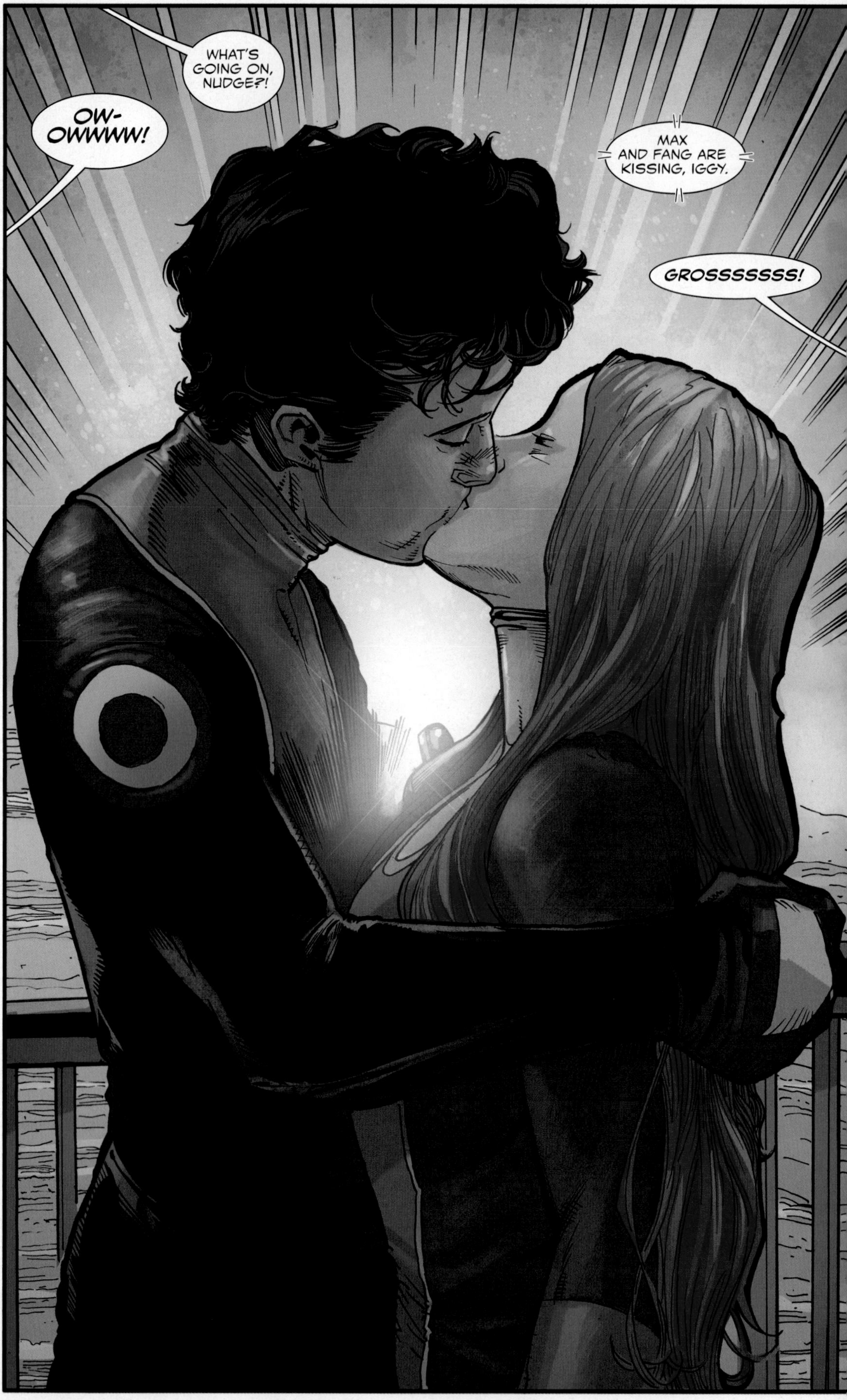
WHAT'S GOING ON, NUDGE?!
OW-OWWWW!
MAX AND FANG ARE KISSING, IGGY.
GROSSSSSSS!

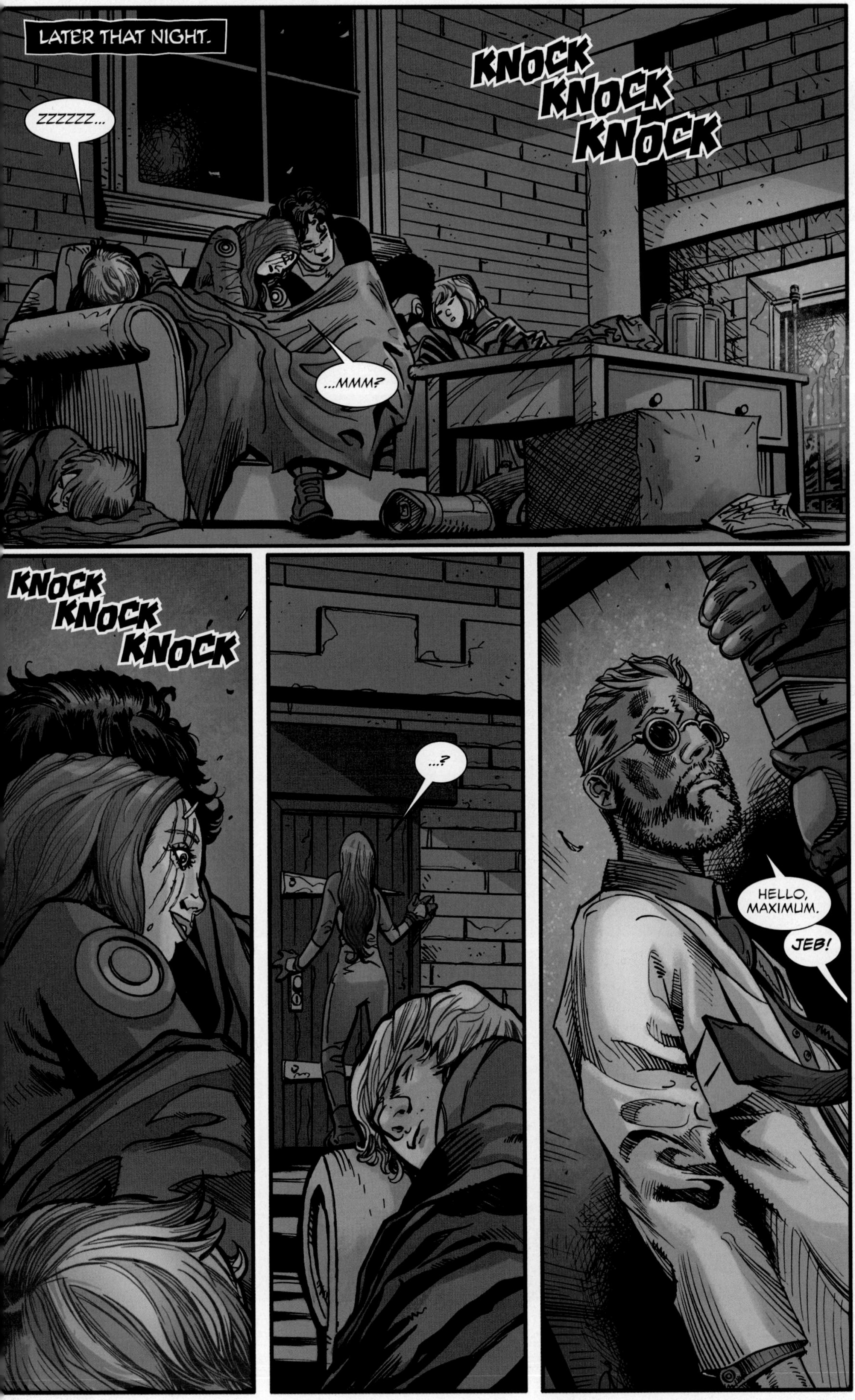
LATER THAT NIGHT.
ZZZZZZ...
KNOCK KNOCK KNOCK
...MMM?
KNOCK KNOCK KNOCK
...?
HELLO, MAXIMUM.
JEB!

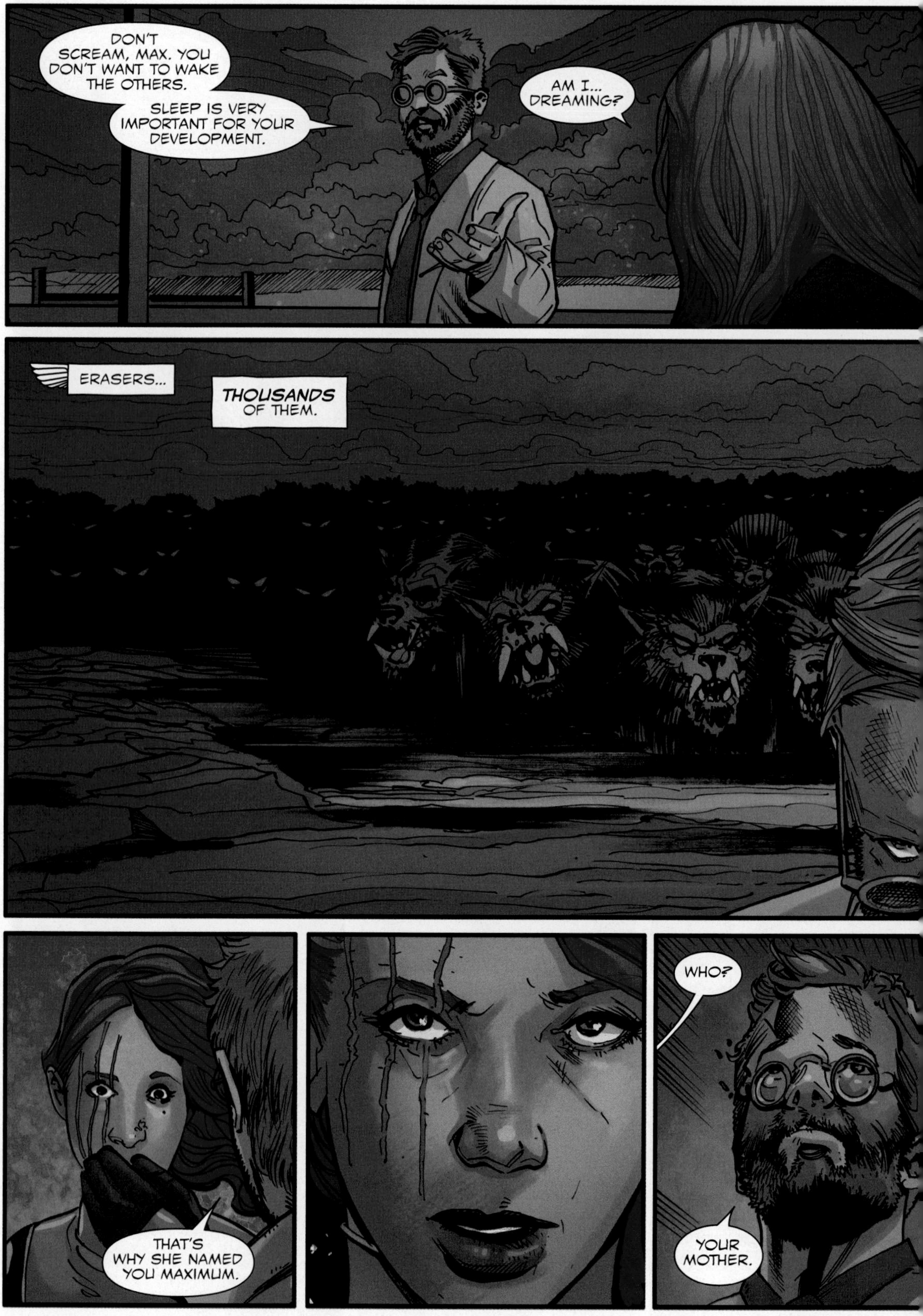

DON'T SCREAM, MAX. YOU DON'T WANT TO WAKE THE OTHERS.
SLEEP IS VERY IMPORTANT FOR YOUR DEVELOPMENT.
AM I... DREAMING?
ERASERS...
THOUSANDS OF THEM.
THAT'S WHY SHE NAMED YOU MAXIMUM.
WHO?
YOUR MOTHER.

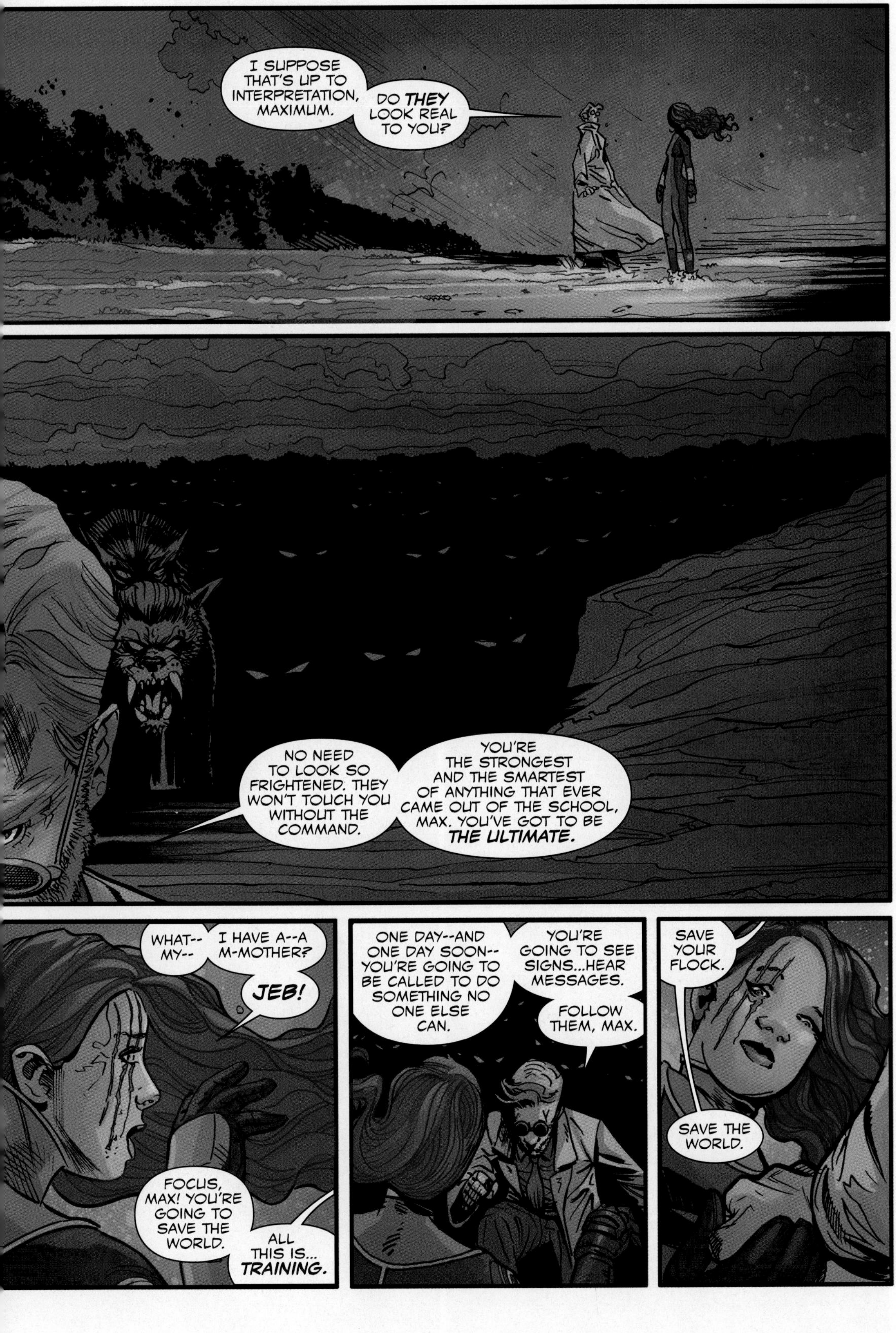
I SUPPOSE THAT'S UP TO INTERPRETATION, MAXIMUM.
DO THEY LOOK REAL TO YOU?
NO NEED TO LOOK SO FRIGHTENED. THEY WON'T TOUCH YOU WITHOUT THE COMMAND.
YOU'RE THE STRONGEST AND THE SMARTEST OF ANYTHING THAT EVER CAME OUT OF THE SCHOOL, MAX. YOU'VE GOT TO BE *THE ULTIMATE.*
WHAT-- MY--
I HAVE A--A M-MOTHER?
JEB!
FOCUS, MAX! YOU'RE GOING TO SAVE THE WORLD.
ALL THIS IS... *TRAINING.*
ONE DAY--AND ONE DAY SOON--YOU'RE GOING TO BE CALLED TO DO SOMETHING NO ONE ELSE CAN.
YOU'RE GOING TO SEE SIGNS...HEAR MESSAGES.
FOLLOW THEM, MAX.
SAVE YOUR FLOCK.
SAVE THE WORLD.

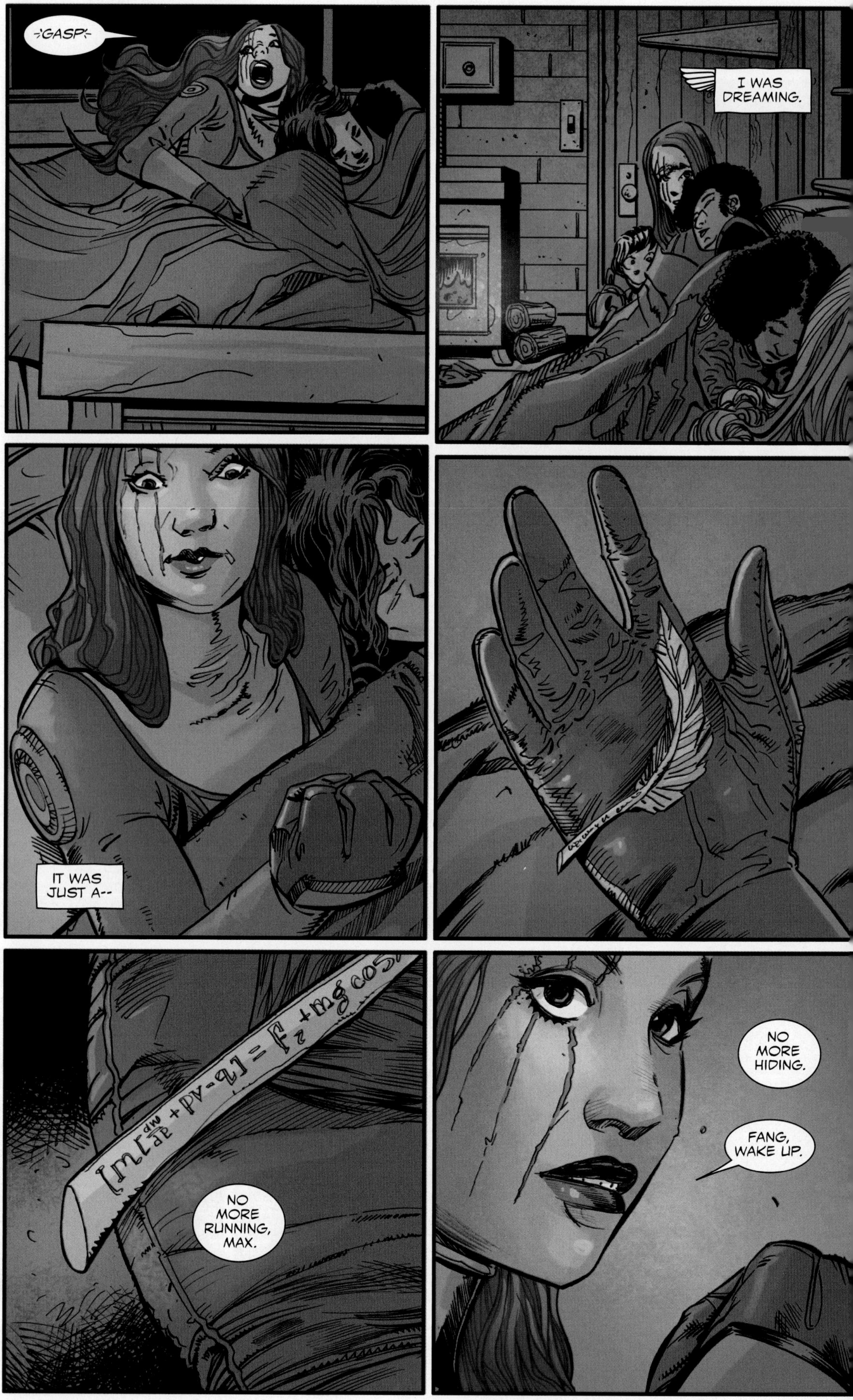
GASP
I WAS DREAMING.
IT WAS JUST A--
NO MORE RUNNING, MAX.
NO MORE HIDING.
FANG, WAKE UP.

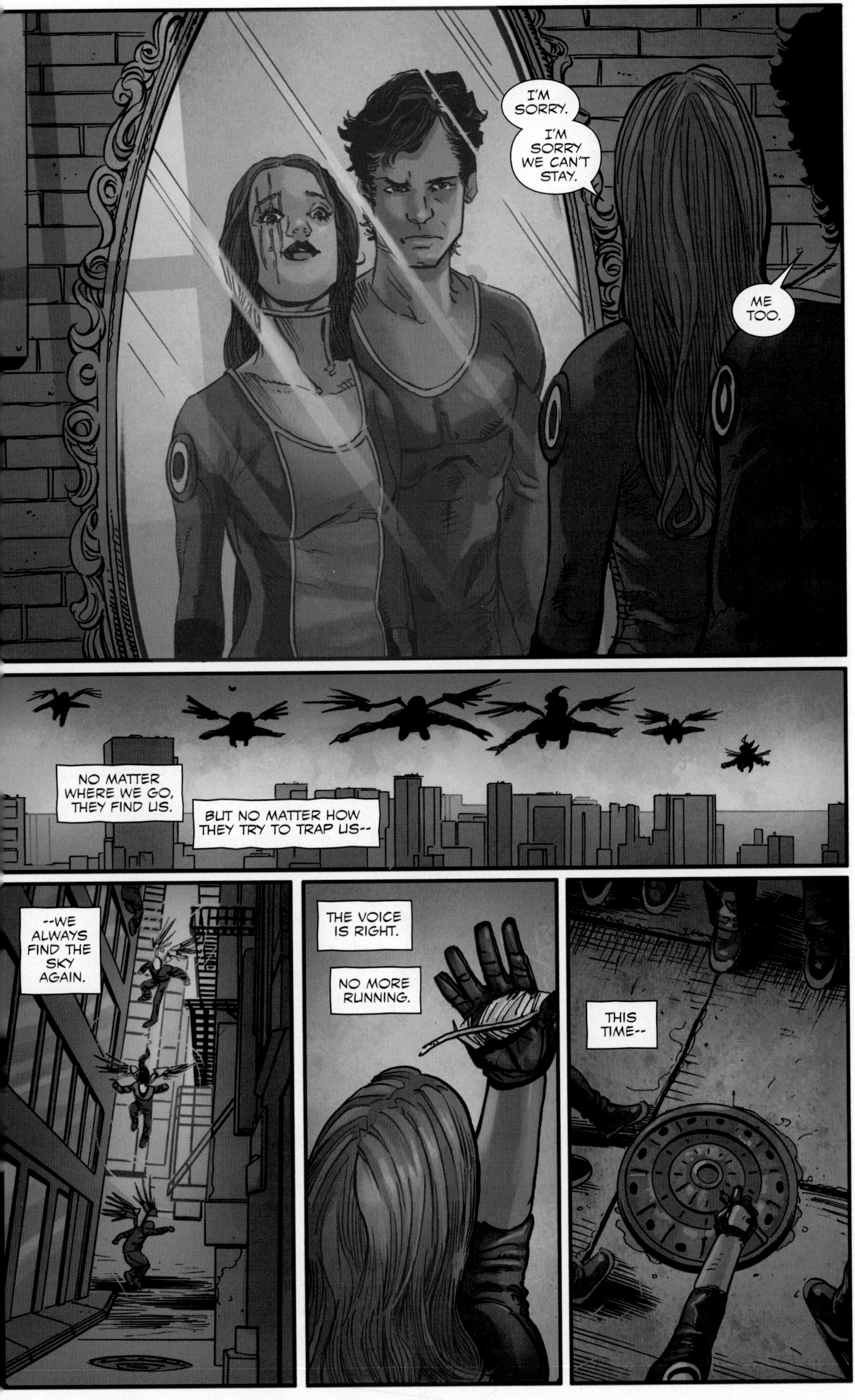
I'M SORRY.
I'M SORRY WE CAN'T STAY.
ME TOO.
NO MATTER WHERE WE GO, THEY FIND US.
BUT NO MATTER HOW THEY TRY TO TRAP US--
--WE ALWAYS FIND THE SKY AGAIN.
THE VOICE IS RIGHT.
NO MORE RUNNING.
THIS TIME--

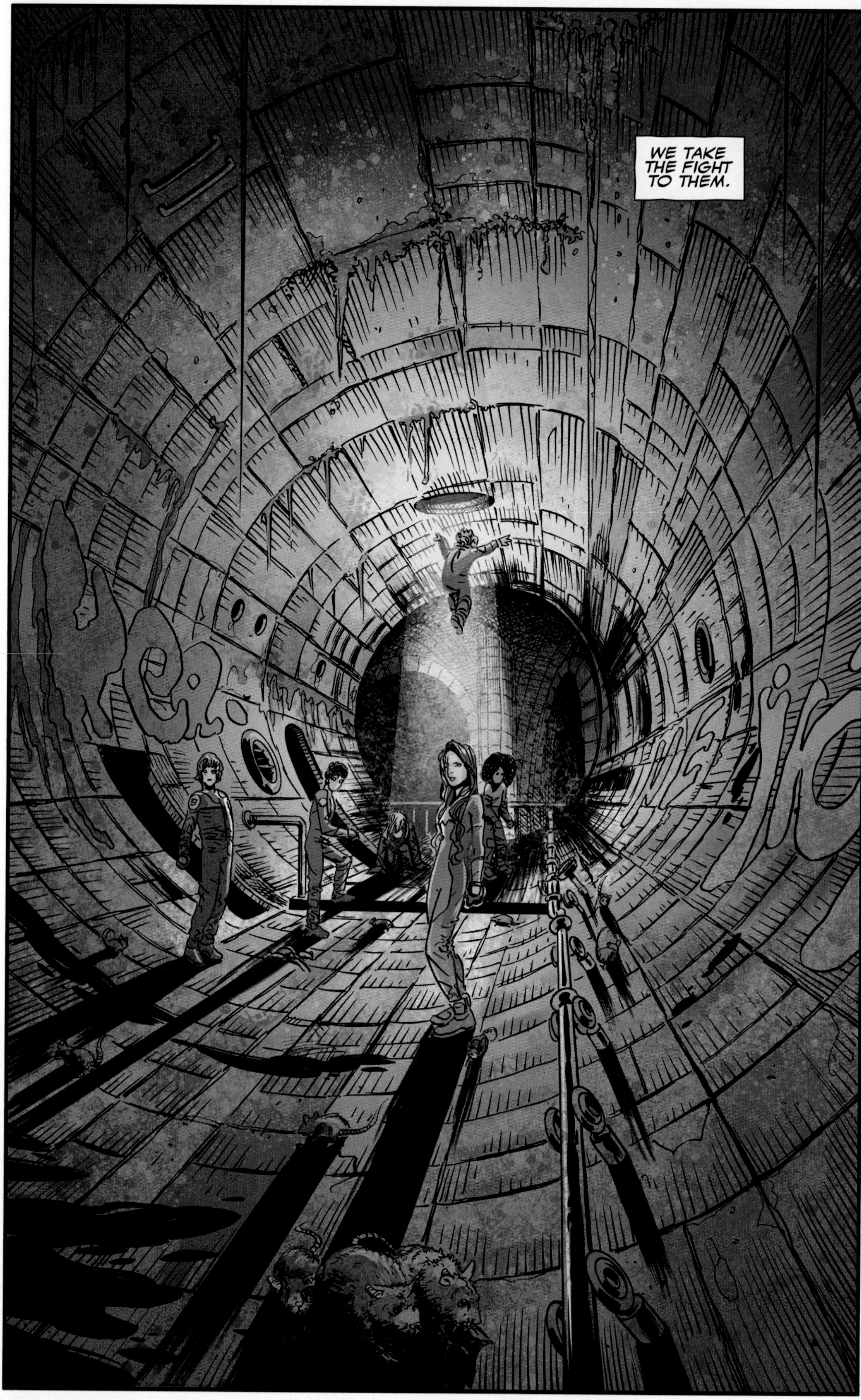
WE TAKE THE FIGHT TO THEM.

CHAPTER 5

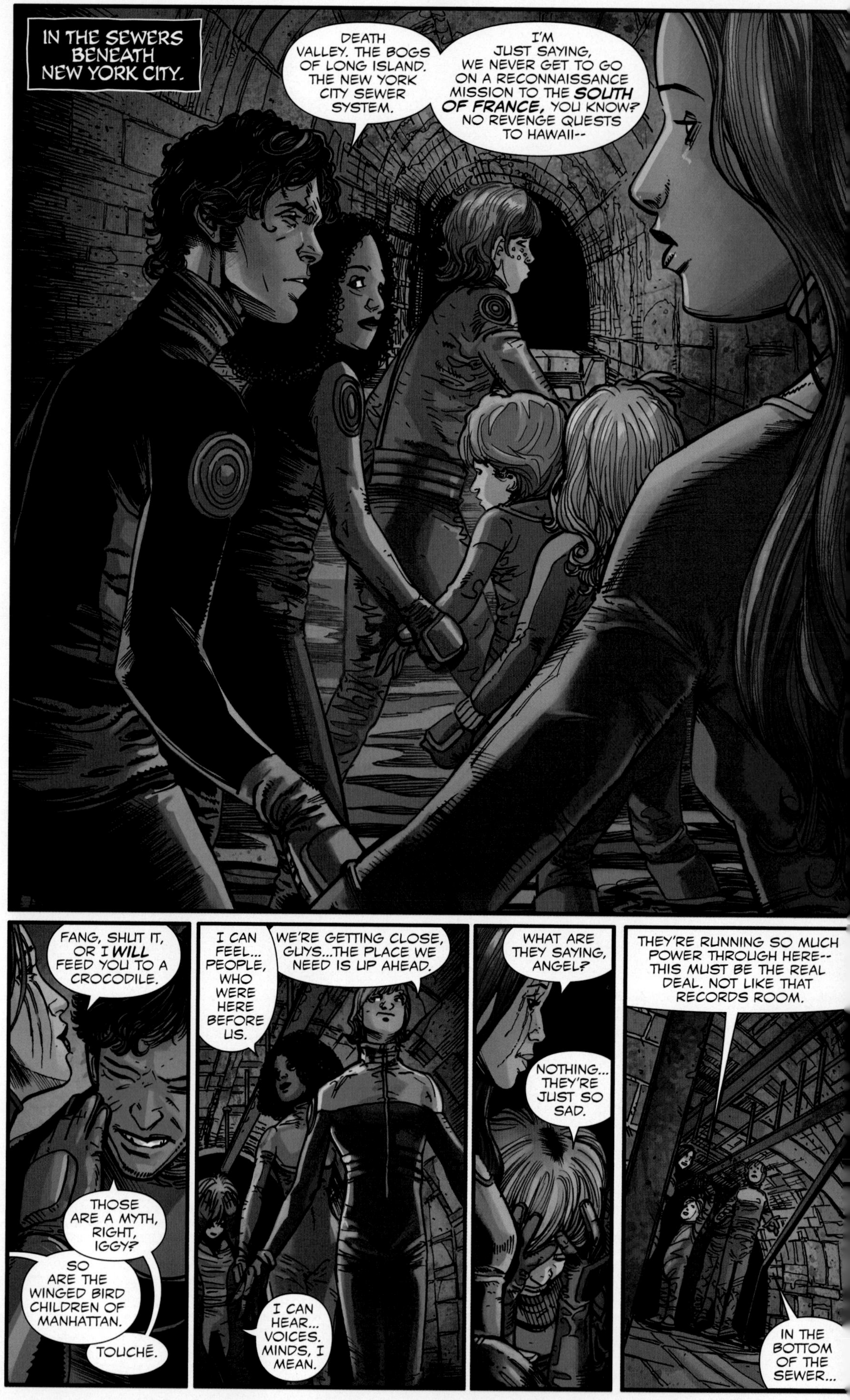
IN THE SEWERS BENEATH NEW YORK CITY.
DEATH VALLEY. THE BOGS OF LONG ISLAND. THE NEW YORK CITY SEWER SYSTEM.
I'M JUST SAYING, WE NEVER GET TO GO ON A RECONNAISSANCE MISSION TO THE SOUTH OF FRANCE, YOU KNOW? NO REVENGE QUESTS TO HAWAII--
FANG, SHUT IT, OR I WILL FEED YOU TO A CROCODILE.
THOSE ARE A MYTH, RIGHT, IGGY?
SO ARE THE WINGED BIRD CHILDREN OF MANHATTAN.
TOUCHÉ.
I CAN FEEL... PEOPLE, WHO WERE HERE BEFORE US.
WE'RE GETTING CLOSE, GUYS...THE PLACE WE NEED IS UP AHEAD.
I CAN HEAR... VOICES. MINDS, I MEAN.
WHAT ARE THEY SAYING, ANGEL?
NOTHING... THEY'RE JUST SO SAD.
THEY'RE RUNNING SO MUCH POWER THROUGH HERE-- THIS MUST BE THE REAL DEAL. NOT LIKE THAT RECORDS ROOM.
IN THE BOTTOM OF THE SEWER...

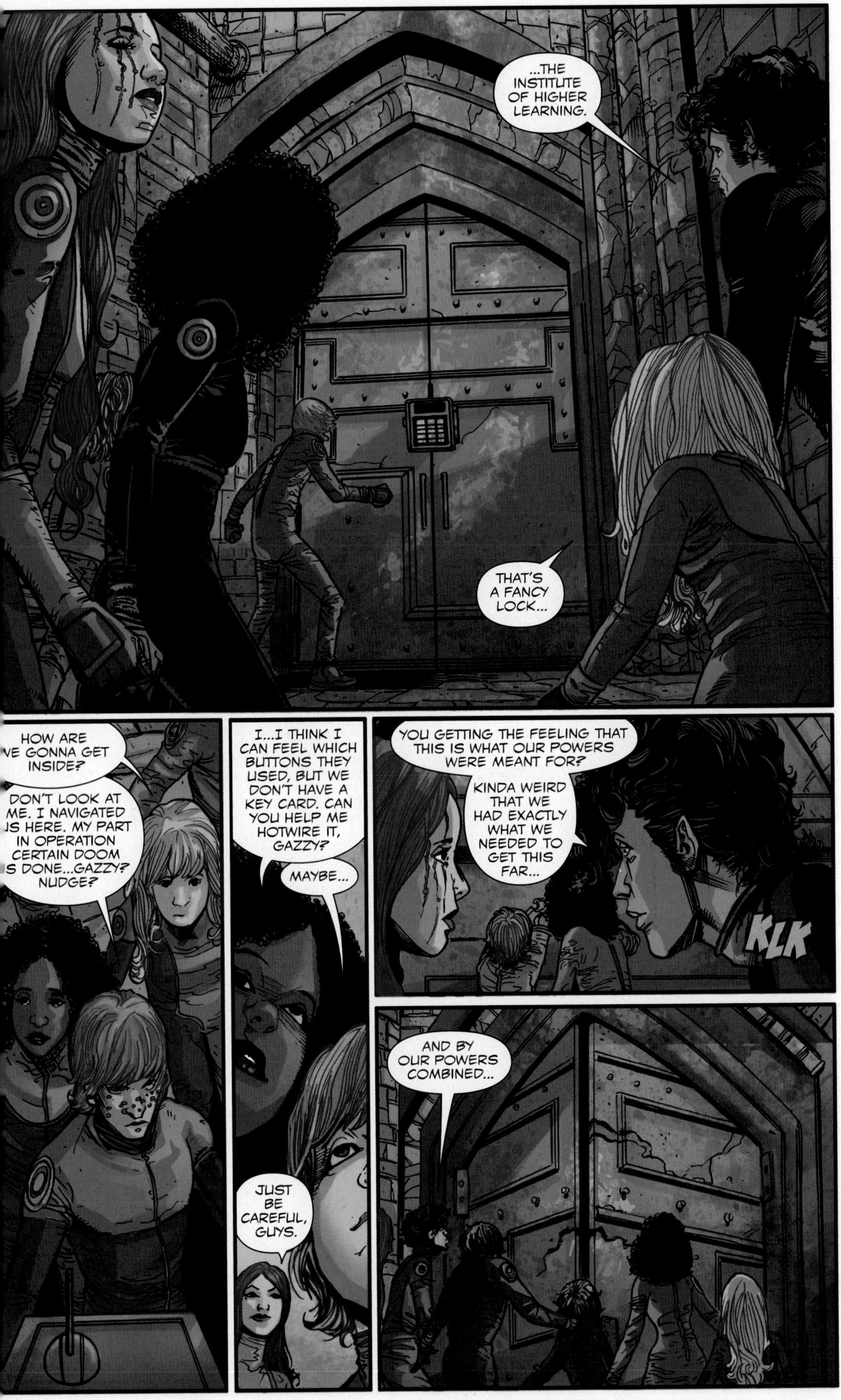
...THE INSTITUTE OF HIGHER LEARNING.
THAT'S A FANCY LOCK...
HOW ARE WE GONNA GET INSIDE?
DON'T LOOK AT ME. I NAVIGATED US HERE. MY PART IN OPERATION CERTAIN DOOM IS DONE...GAZZY? NUDGE?
I...I THINK I CAN FEEL WHICH BUTTONS THEY USED, BUT WE DON'T HAVE A KEY CARD. CAN YOU HELP ME HOTWIRE IT, GAZZY?
MAYBE...
JUST BE CAREFUL, GUYS.
YOU GETTING THE FEELING THAT THIS IS WHAT OUR POWERS WERE MEANT FOR?
KINDA WEIRD THAT WE HAD EXACTLY WHAT WE NEEDED TO GET THIS FAR...
KLK
AND BY OUR POWERS COMBINED...

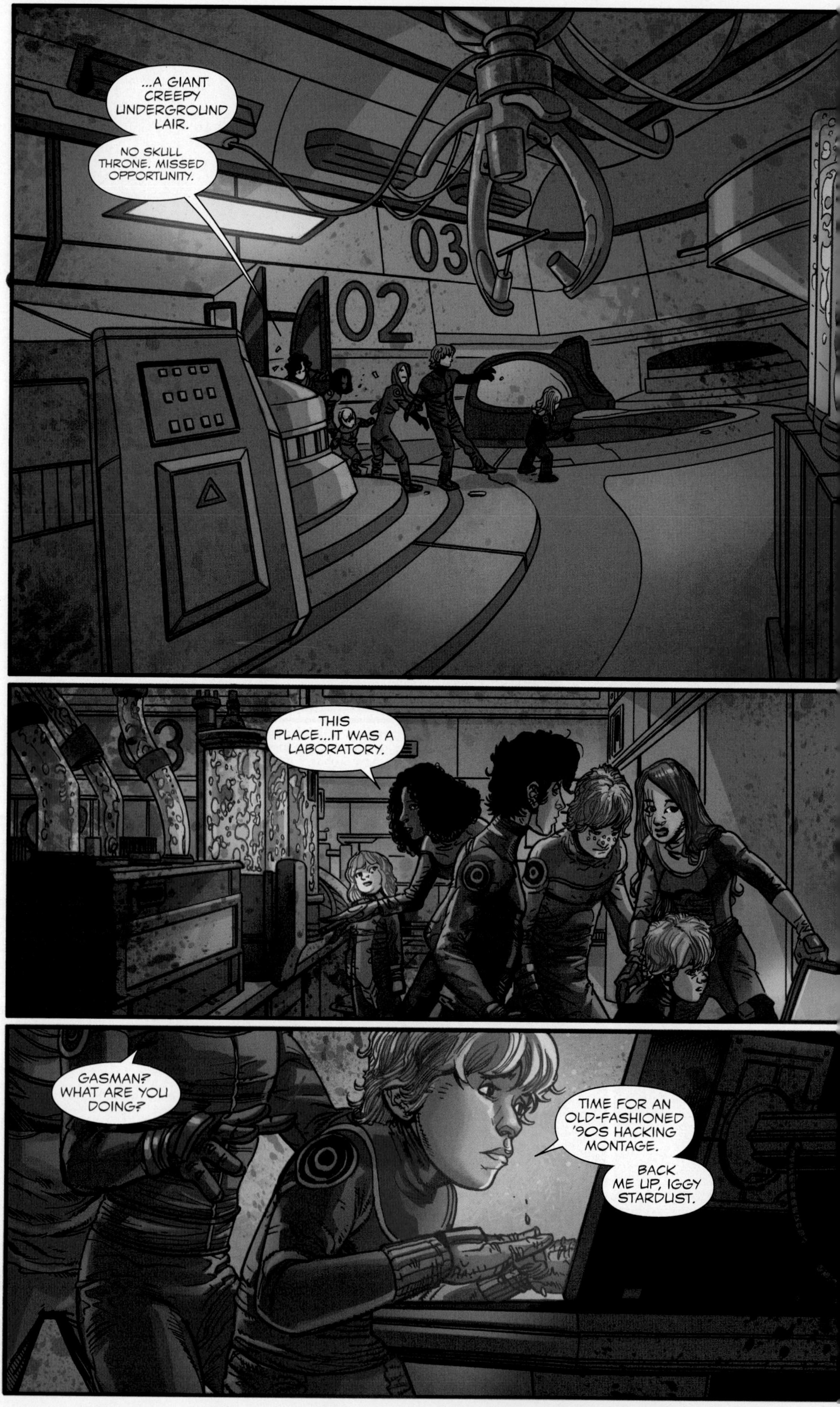
...A GIANT CREEPY UNDERGROUND LAIR.
NO SKULL THRONE. MISSED OPPORTUNITY.
03
02
THIS PLACE...IT WAS A LABORATORY.
GASMAN? WHAT ARE YOU DOING?
TIME FOR AN OLD-FASHIONED '90S HACKING MONTAGE.
BACK ME UP, IGGY STARDUST.

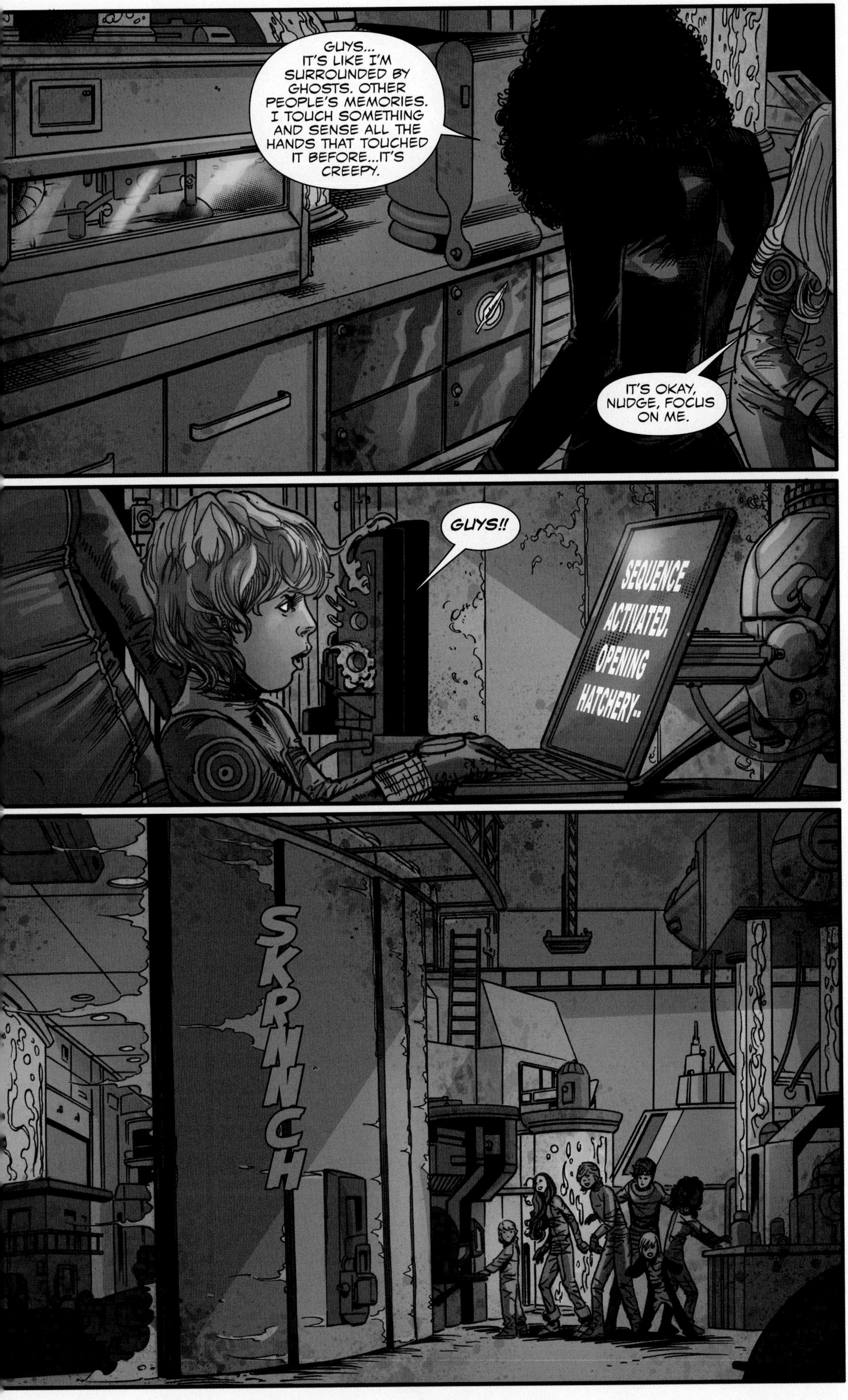
GUYS... IT'S LIKE I'M SURROUNDED BY GHOSTS. OTHER PEOPLE'S MEMORIES. I TOUCH SOMETHING AND SENSE ALL THE HANDS THAT TOUCHED IT BEFORE...IT'S CREEPY.
IT'S OKAY, NUDGE, FOCUS ON ME.
GUYS!!
SEQUENCE ACTIVATED. OPENING HATCHERY..
SKRNNCH

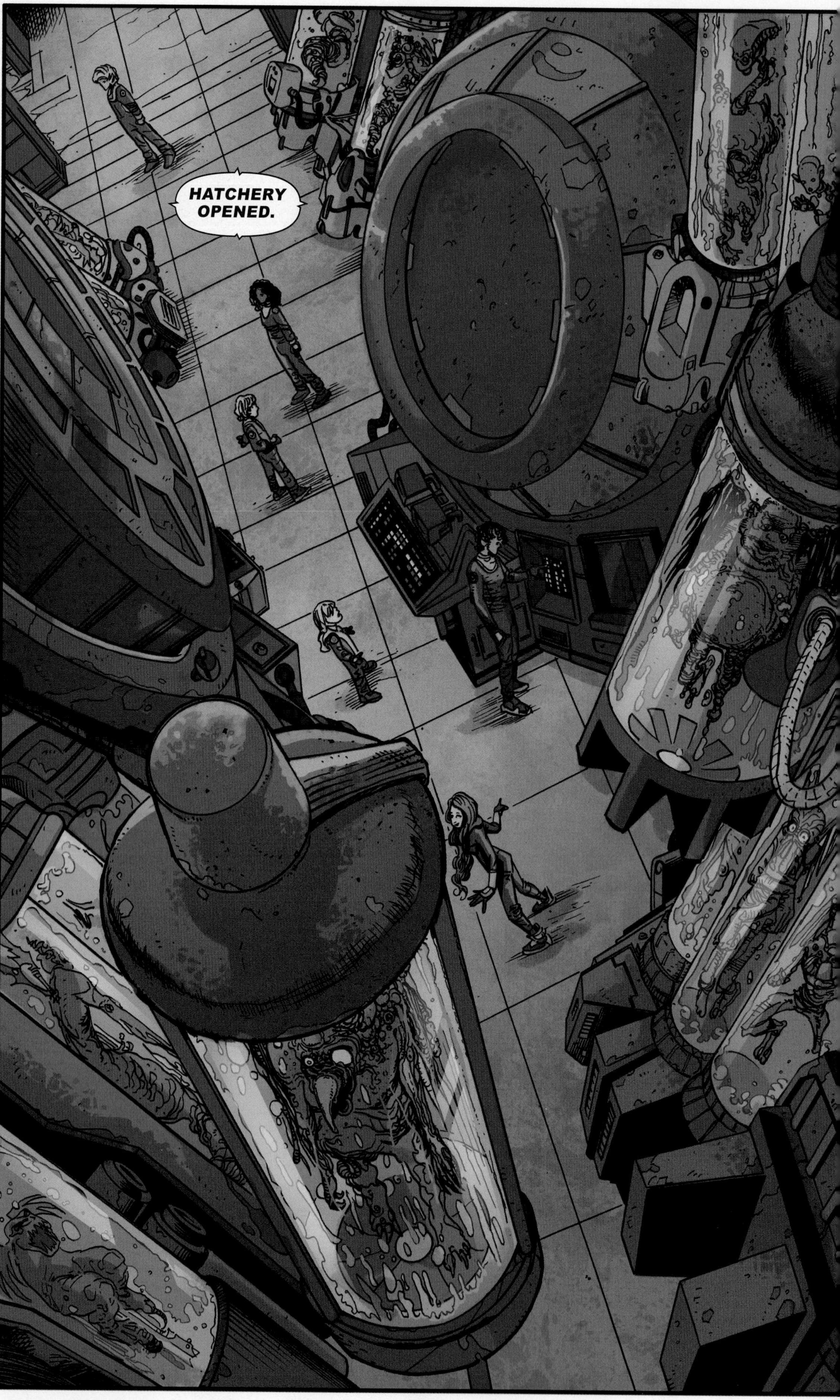
HATCHERY OPENED.

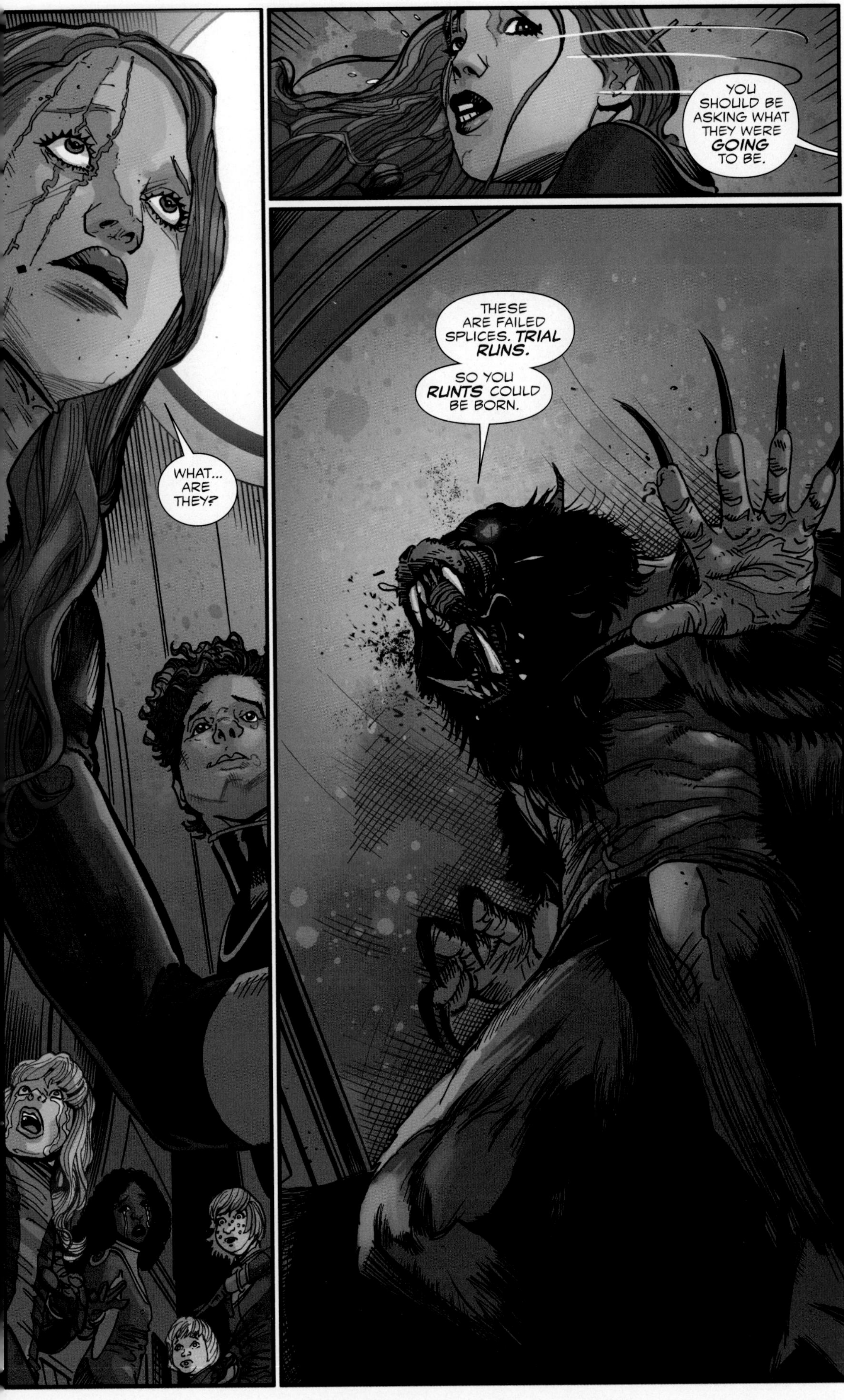
WHAT... ARE THEY?
YOU SHOULD BE ASKING WHAT THEY WERE GOING TO BE.
THESE ARE FAILED SPLICES. TRIAL RUNS.
SO YOU RUNTS COULD BE BORN.

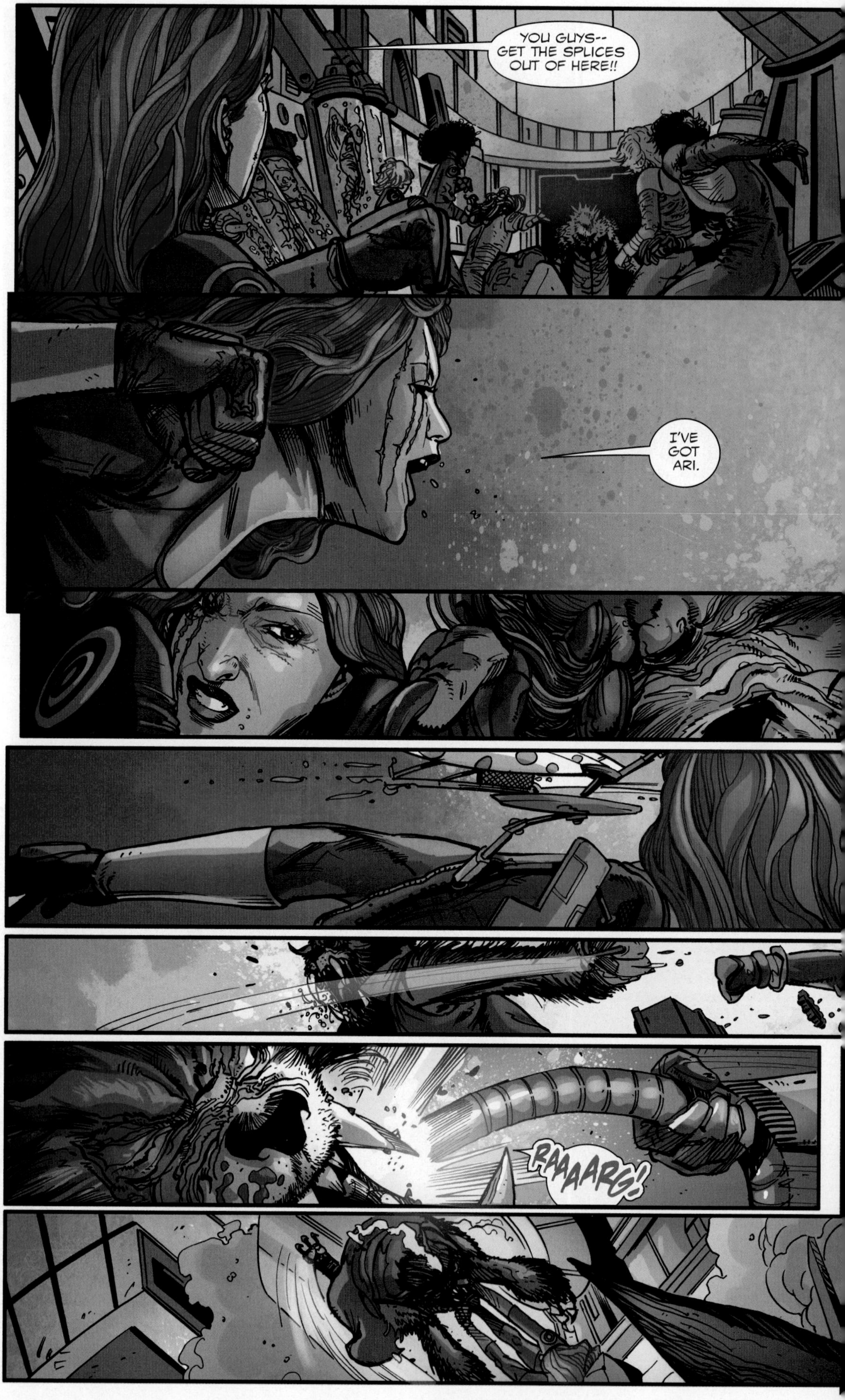
YOU GUYS--
GET THE SPLICES
OUT OF HERE!!
I'VE GOT ARI.
RAAAARG!

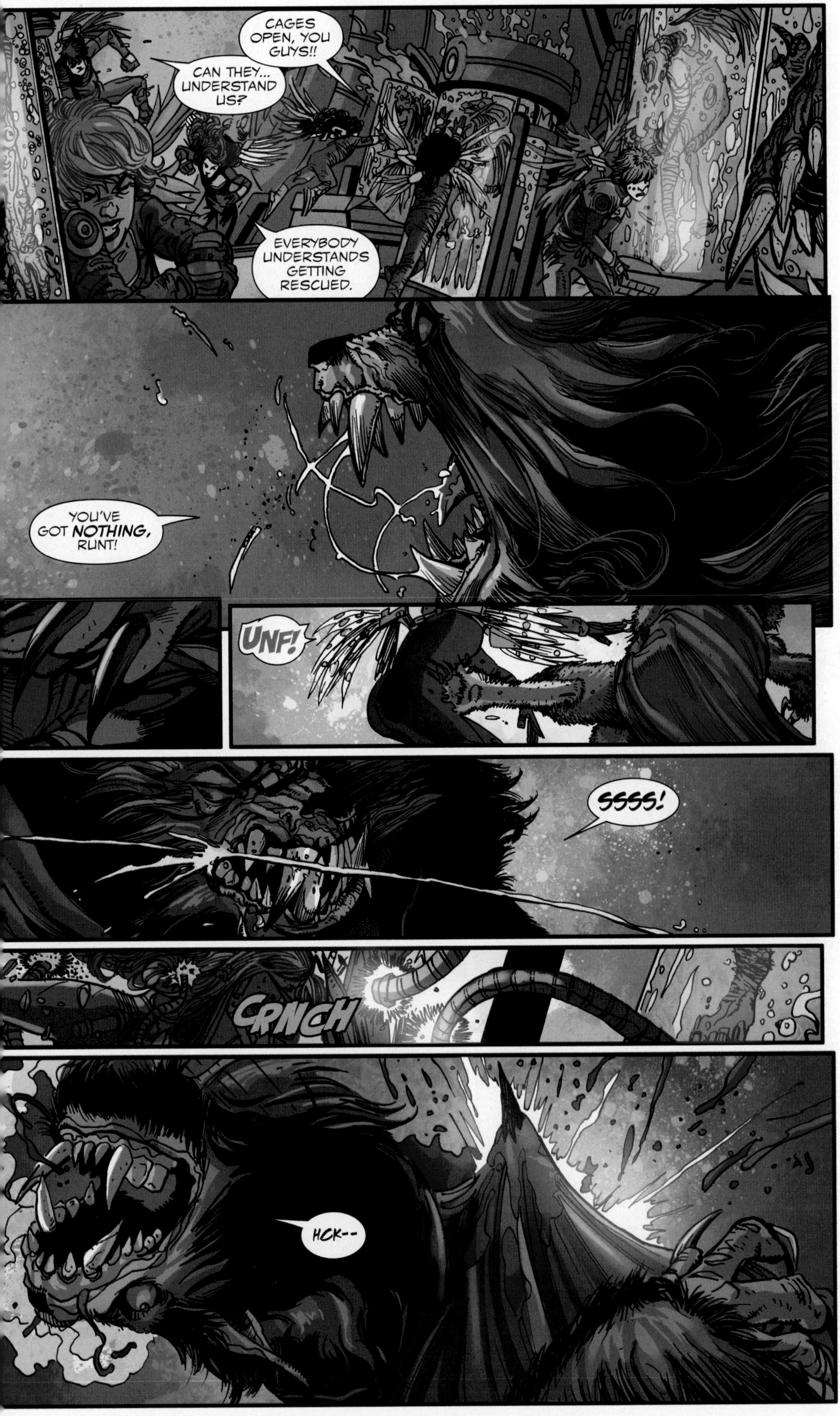
CAGES OPEN, YOU GUYS!!
CAN THEY... UNDERSTAND US?
EVERYBODY UNDERSTANDS GETTING RESCUED.
YOU'VE GOT NOTHING, RUNT!
UNF!
SSSS!
CRNCH
HCK--

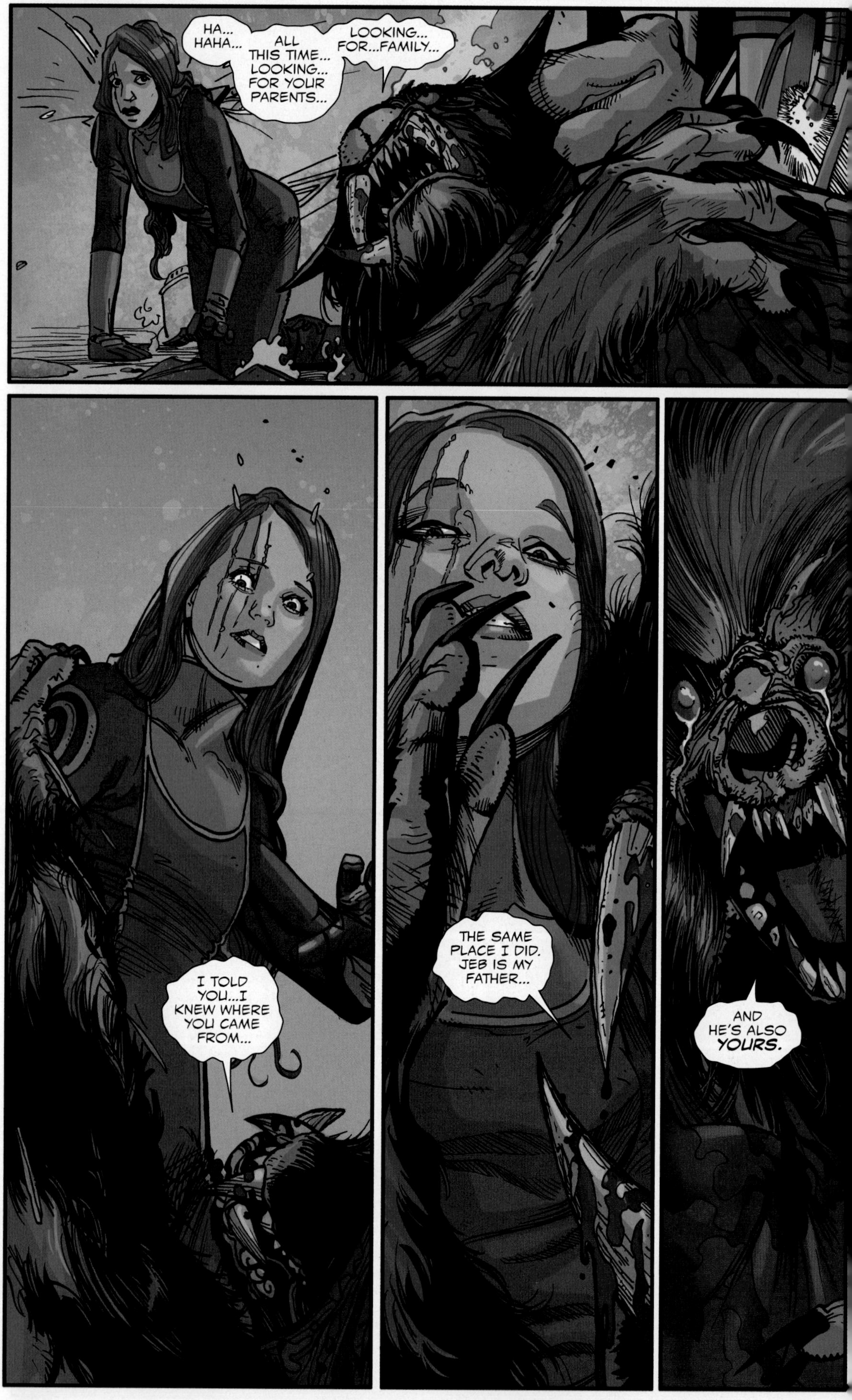
HA... HAHA...
ALL THIS TIME... LOOKING... FOR YOUR PARENTS...
LOOKING... FOR...FAMILY...
I TOLD YOU...I KNEW WHERE YOU CAME FROM...
THE SAME PLACE I DID. JEB IS MY FATHER...
AND HE'S ALSO *YOURS.*

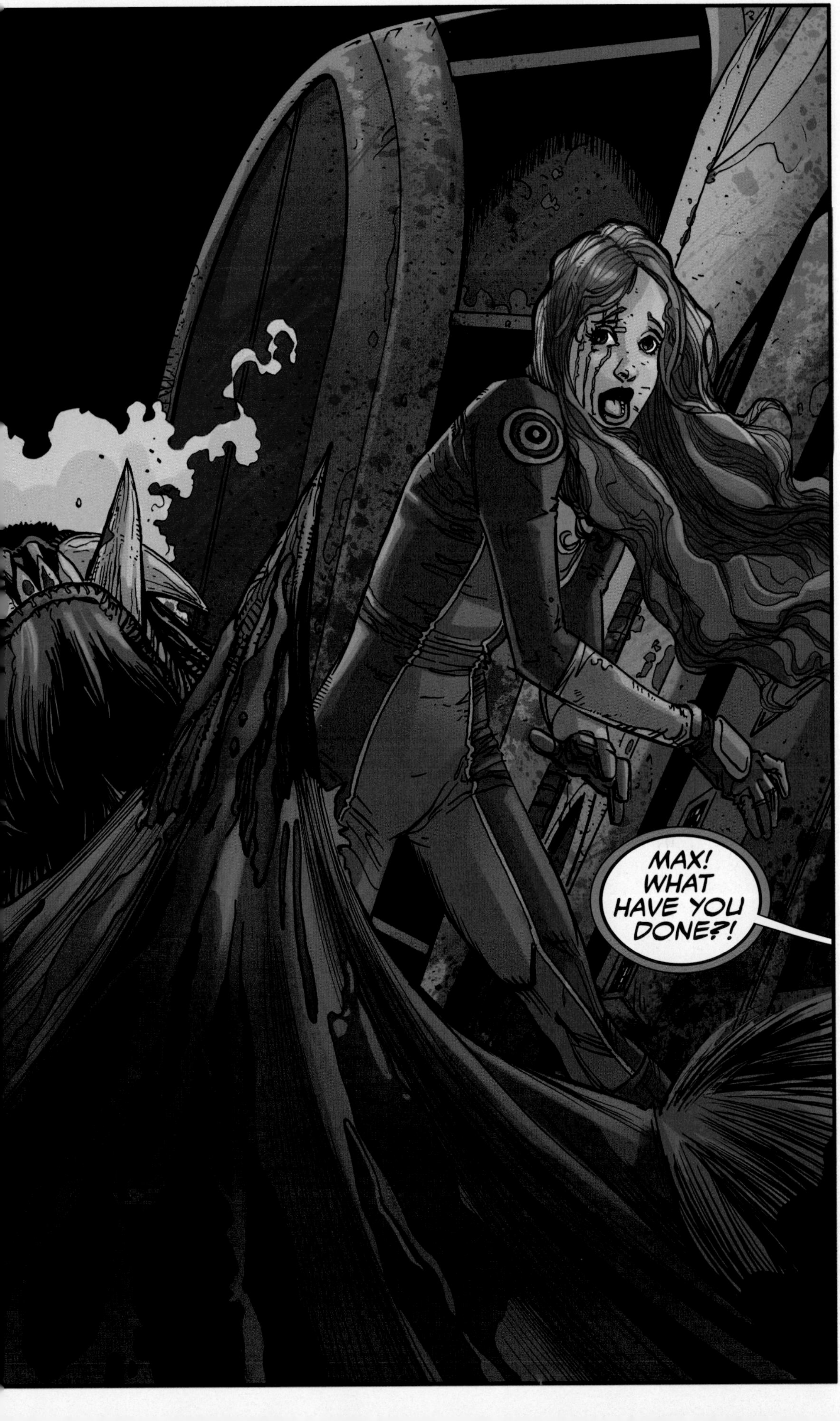
MAX! WHAT HAVE YOU DONE?!

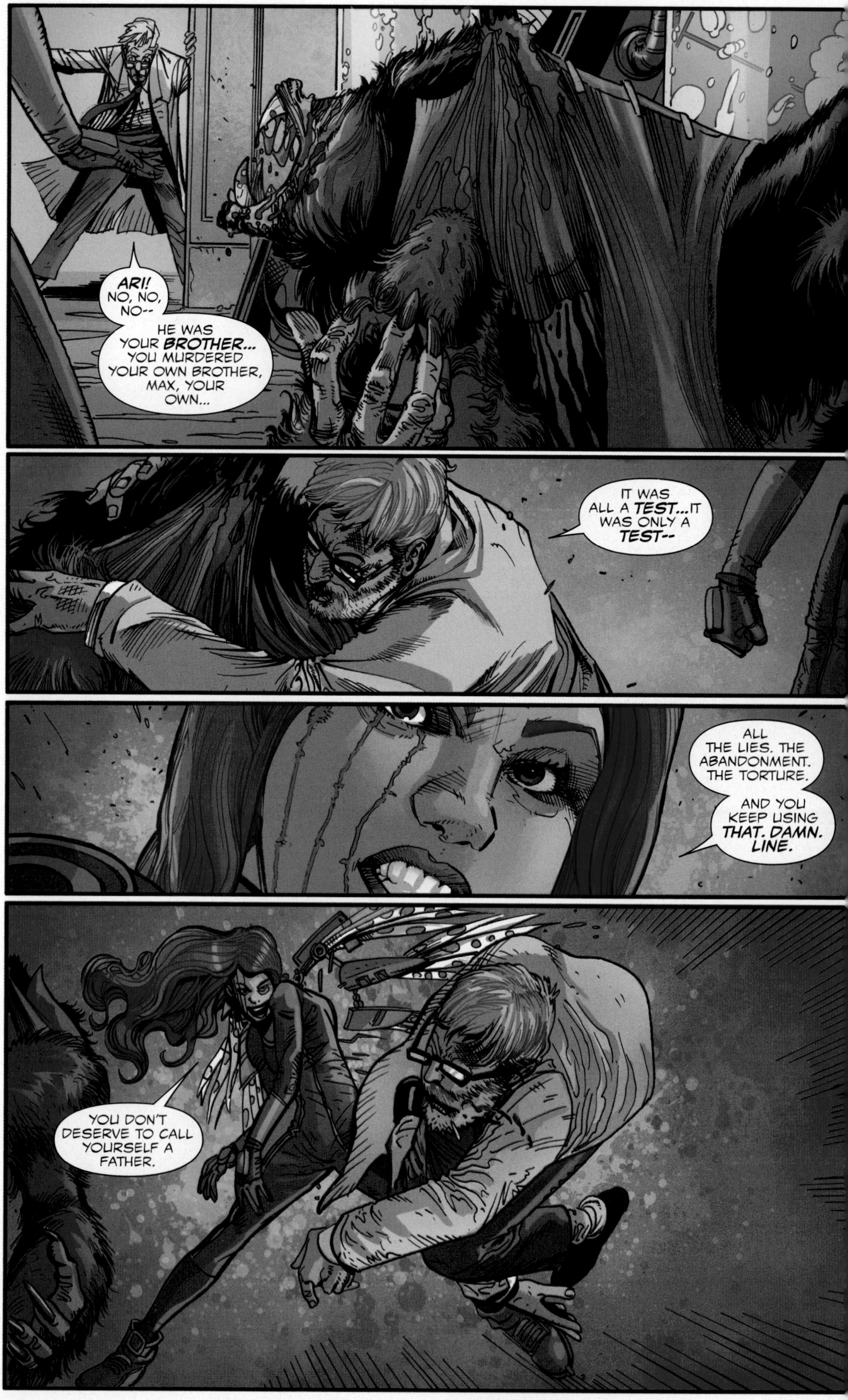
ARI! NO, NO, NO--
HE WAS YOUR BROTHER... YOU MURDERED YOUR OWN BROTHER, MAX, YOUR OWN...
IT WAS ALL A TEST...IT WAS ONLY A TEST--
ALL THE LIES. THE ABANDONMENT. THE TORTURE.
AND YOU KEEP USING THAT. DAMN. LINE.
YOU DON'T DESERVE TO CALL YOURSELF A FATHER.

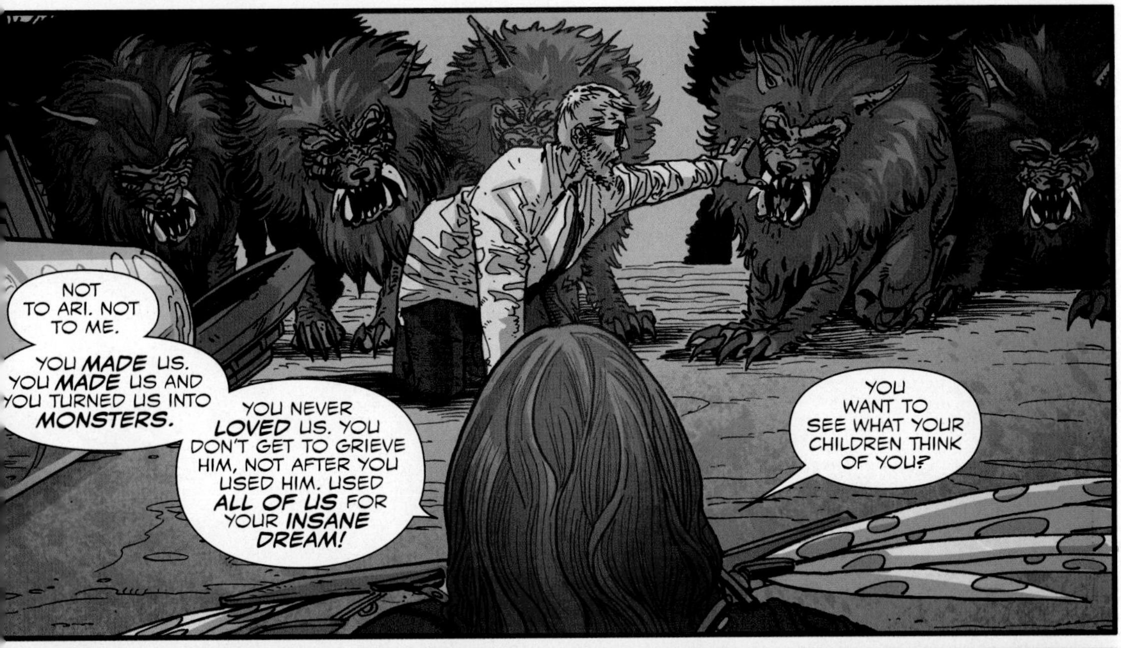
NOT TO ARI. NOT TO ME.
YOU MADE US. YOU MADE US AND YOU TURNED US INTO MONSTERS.
YOU NEVER LOVED US. YOU DON'T GET TO GRIEVE HIM, NOT AFTER YOU USED HIM. USED ALL OF US FOR YOUR INSANE DREAM!
YOU WANT TO SEE WHAT YOUR CHILDREN THINK OF YOU?

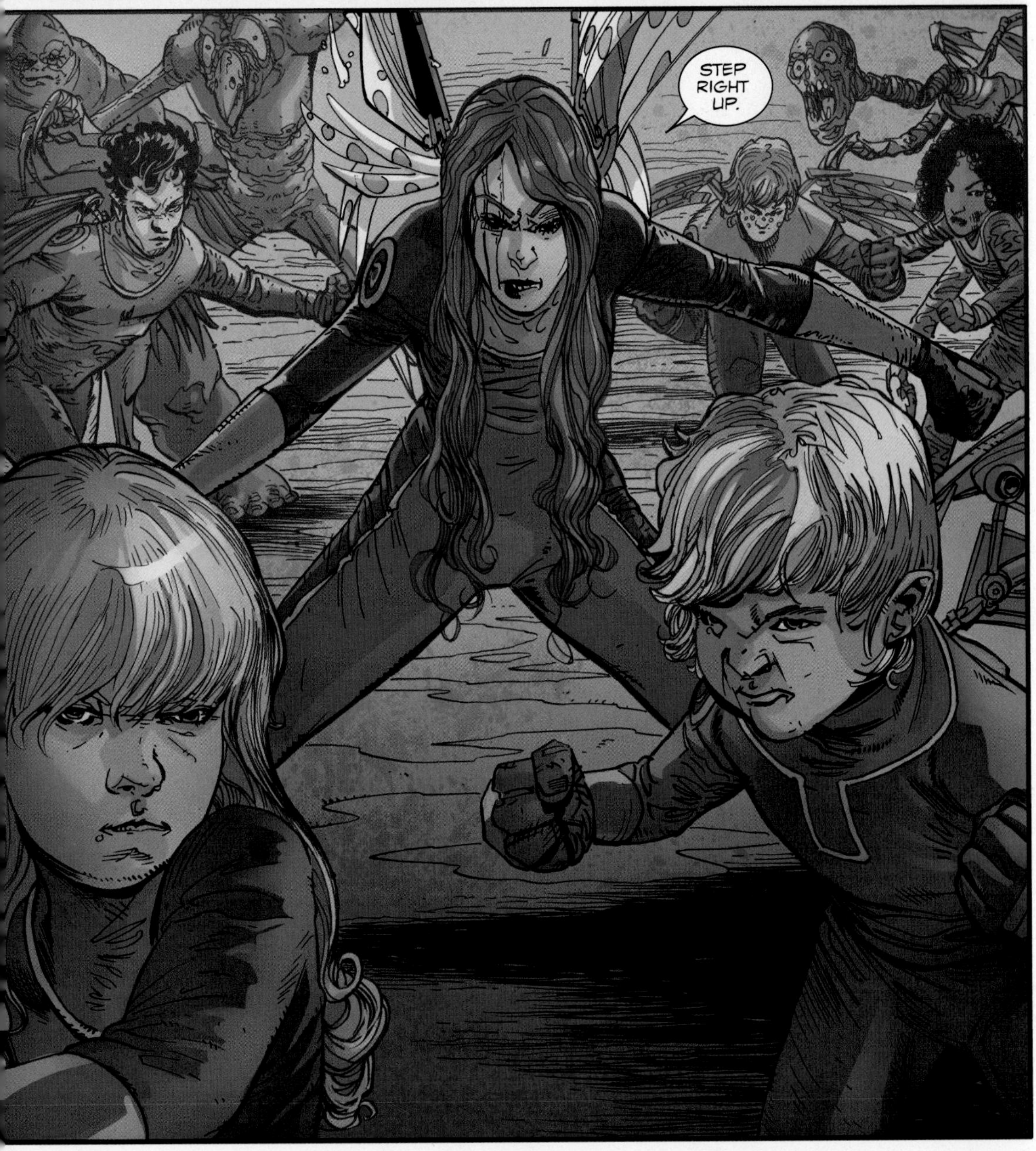
STEP RIGHT UP.

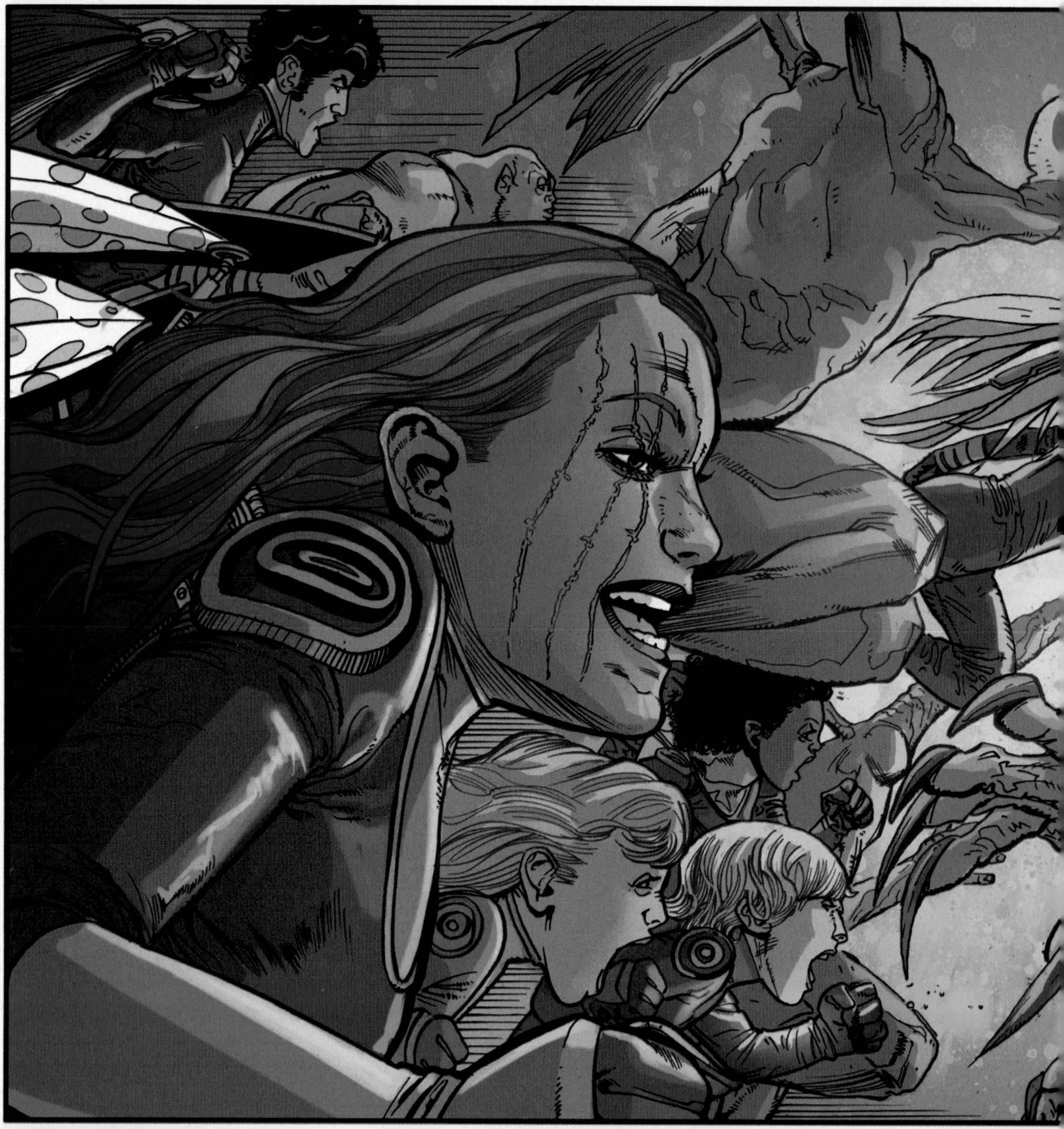
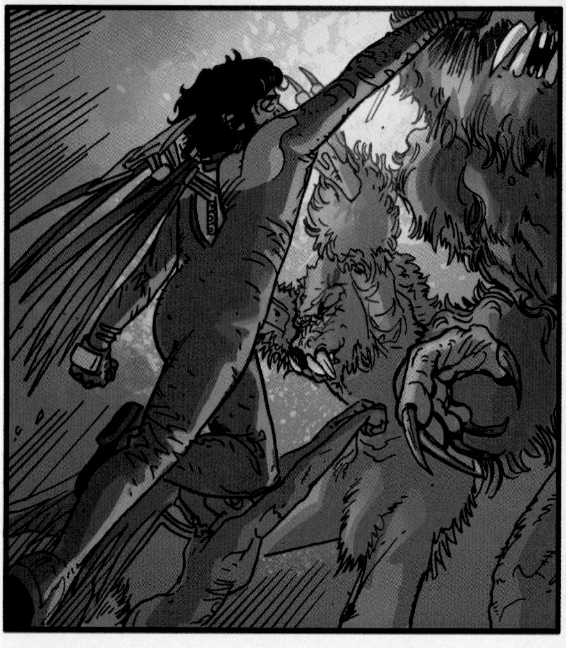
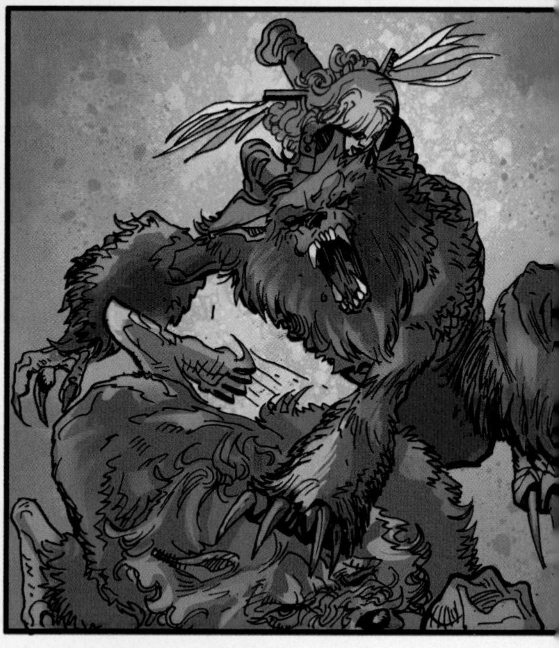

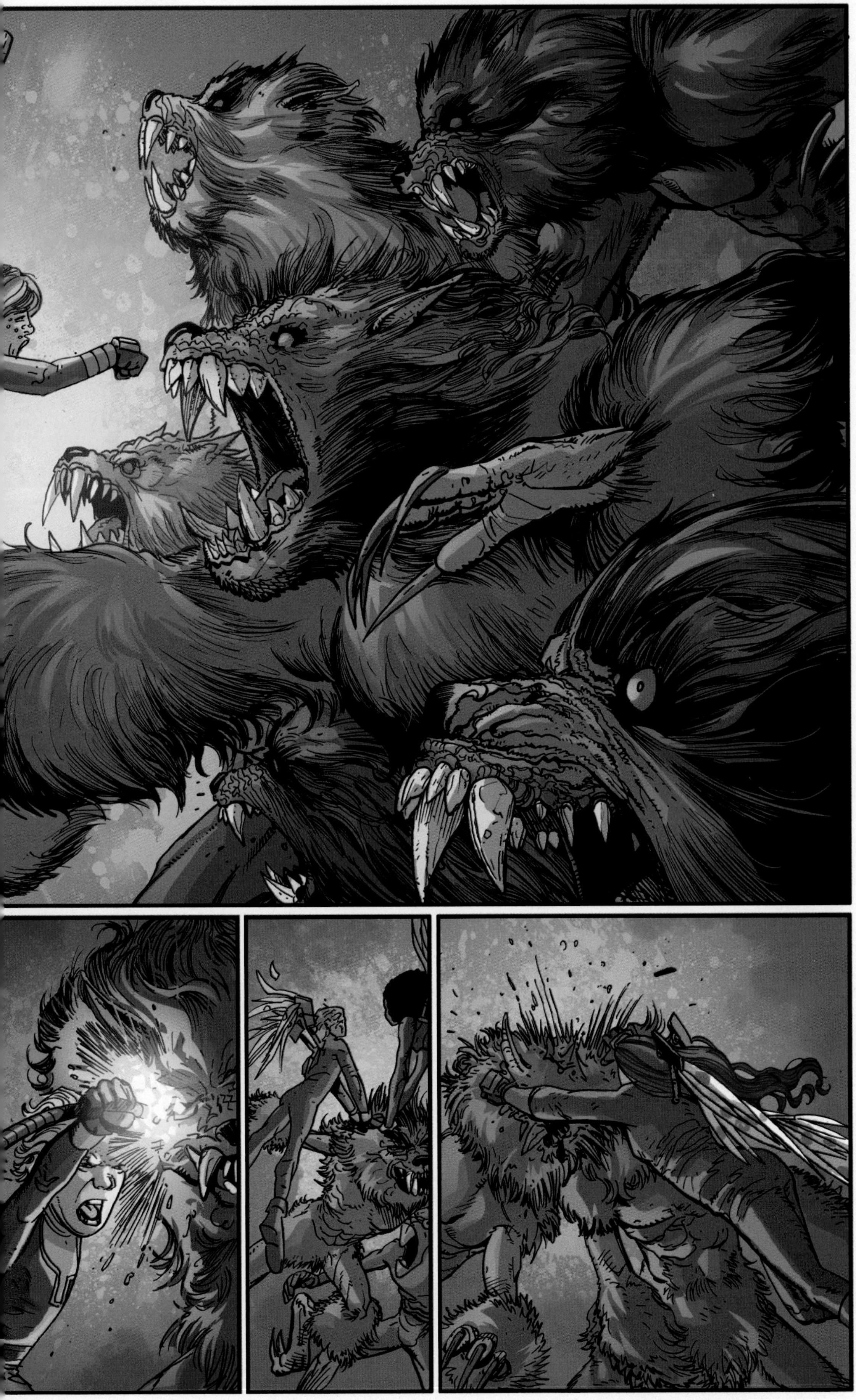

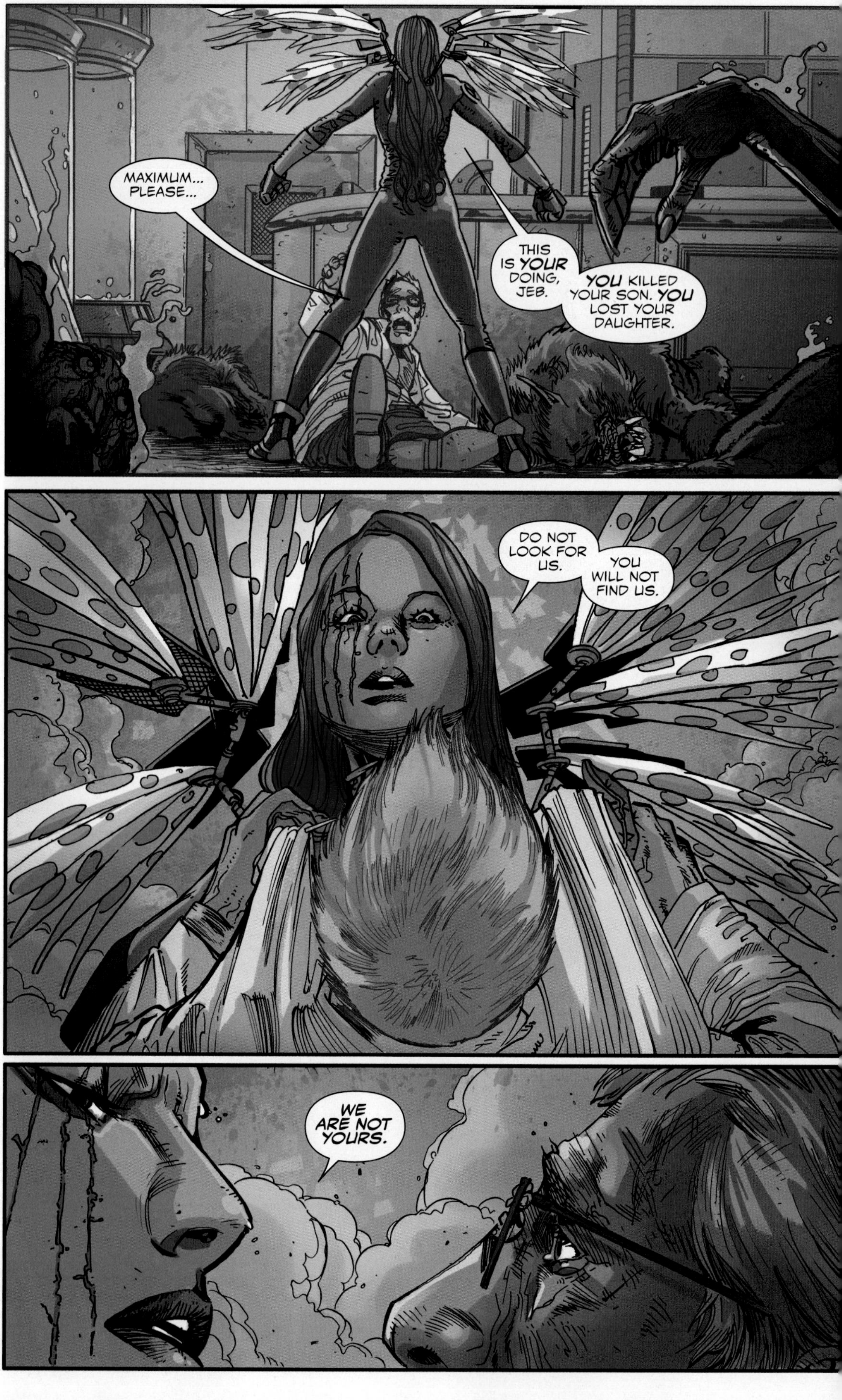
MAXIMUM... PLEASE...
THIS IS YOUR DOING, JEB.
YOU KILLED YOUR SON. YOU LOST YOUR DAUGHTER.
DO NOT LOOK FOR US.
YOU WILL NOT FIND US.
WE ARE NOT YOURS.

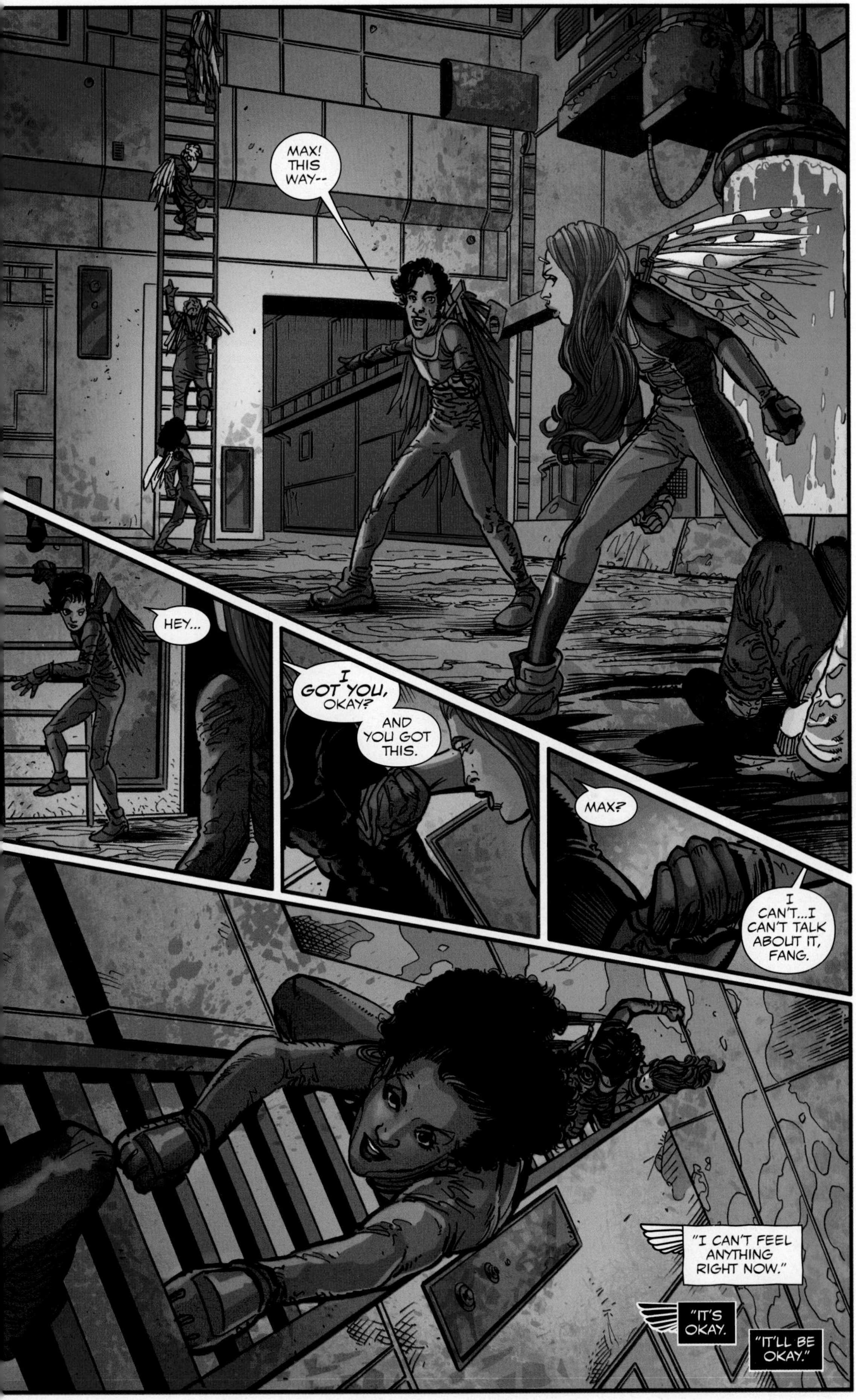
MAX! THIS WAY--
HEY...
I GOT YOU, OKAY?
AND YOU GOT THIS.
MAX?
I CAN'T...I CAN'T TALK ABOUT IT, FANG.
"I CAN'T FEEL ANYTHING RIGHT NOW."
"IT'S OKAY.
"IT'LL BE OKAY."

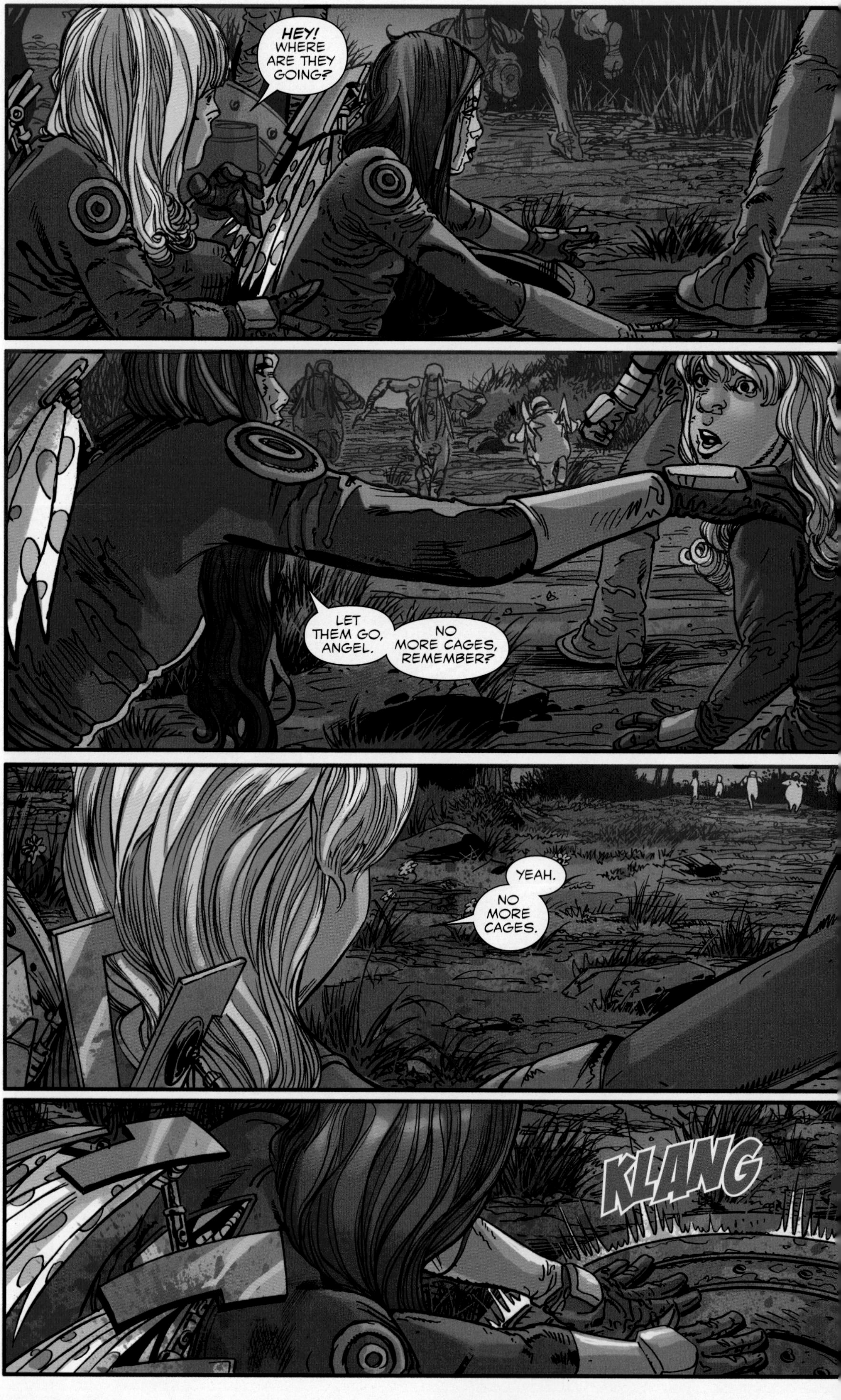
HEY! WHERE ARE THEY GOING?
LET THEM GO, ANGEL.
NO MORE CAGES, REMEMBER?
YEAH.
NO MORE CAGES.
KLANG

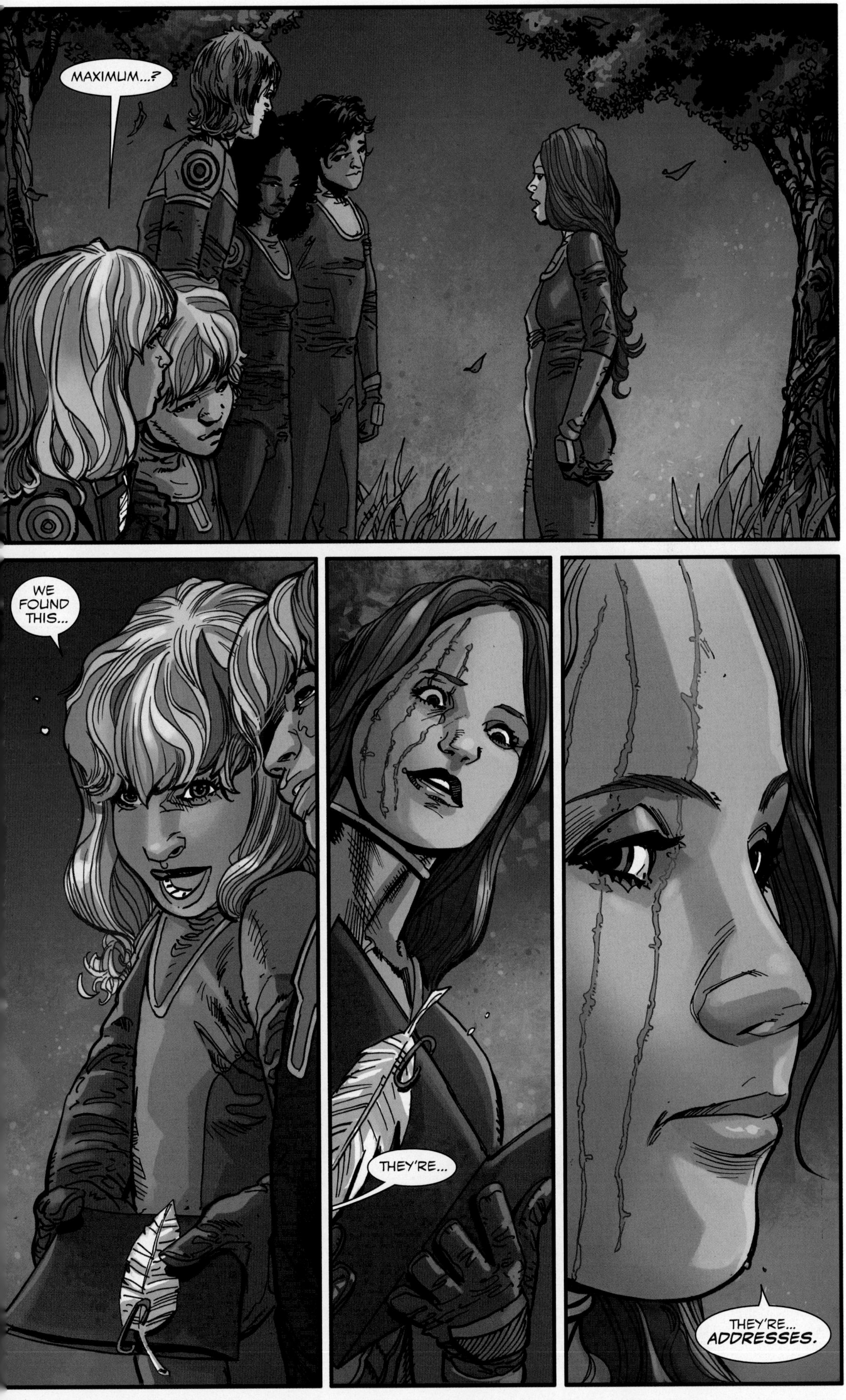
MAXIMUM...?
WE FOUND THIS...
THEY'RE...
THEY'RE... ADDRESSES.

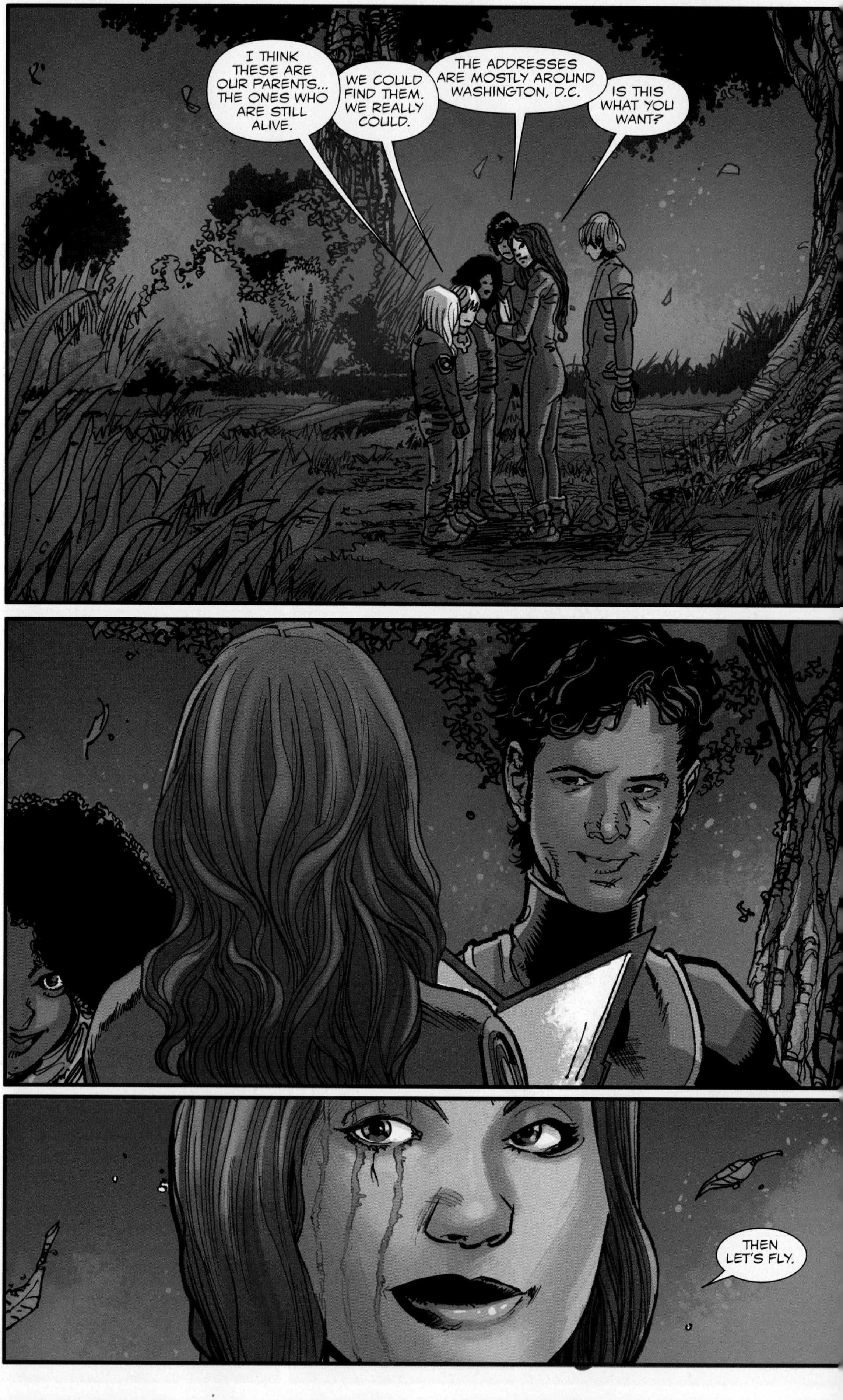
I THINK THESE ARE OUR PARENTS... THE ONES WHO ARE STILL ALIVE.
WE COULD FIND THEM. WE REALLY COULD.
THE ADDRESSES ARE MOSTLY AROUND WASHINGTON, D.C.
IS THIS WHAT YOU WANT?
THEN LET'S FLY.

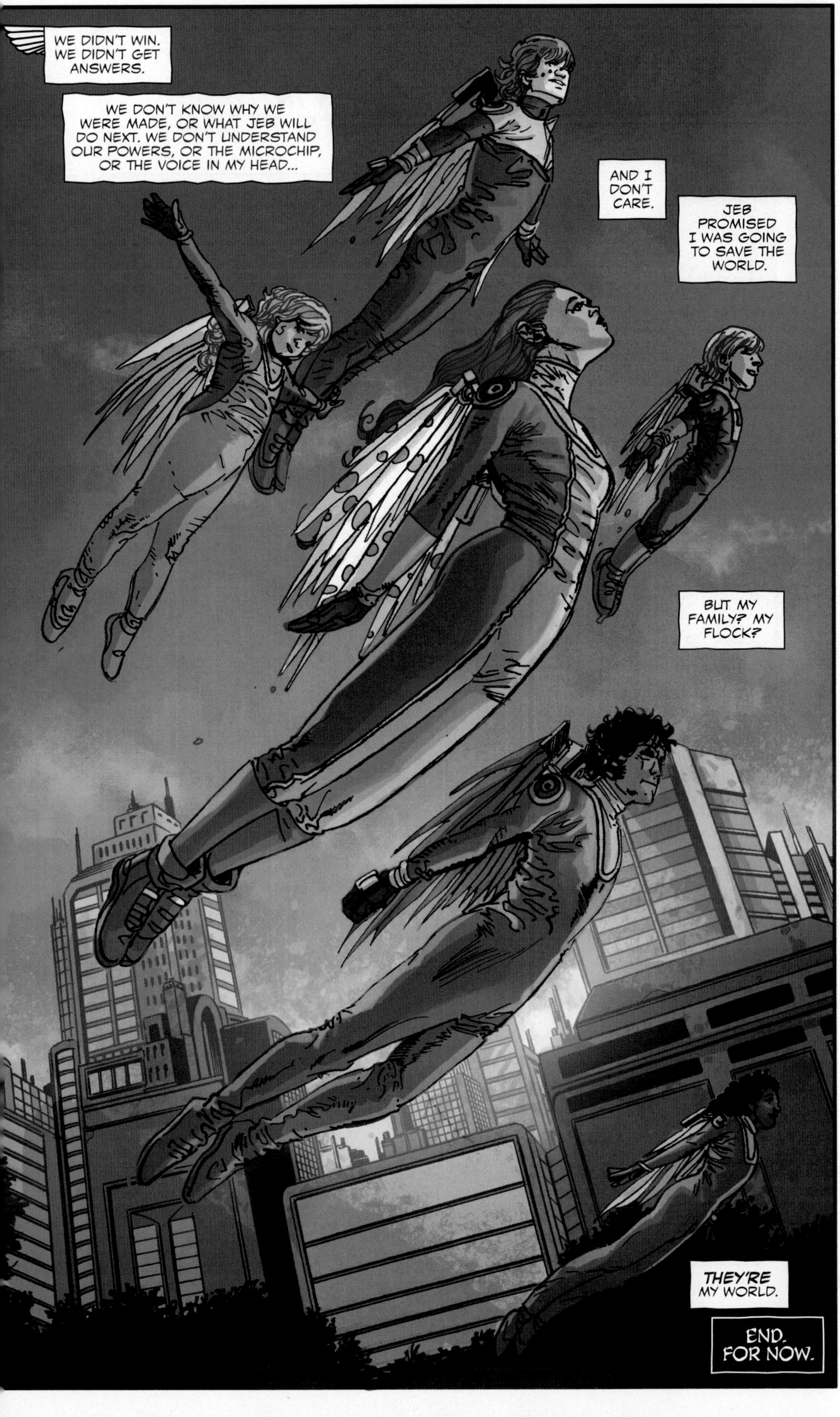

WE DIDN'T WIN. WE DIDN'T GET ANSWERS.
WE DON'T KNOW WHY WE WERE MADE, OR WHAT JEB WILL DO NEXT. WE DON'T UNDERSTAND OUR POWERS, OR THE MICROCHIP, OR THE VOICE IN MY HEAD...
AND I DON'T CARE.
JEB PROMISED I WAS GOING TO SAVE THE WORLD.
BUT MY FAMILY? MY FLOCK?
THEY'RE MY WORLD.
END. FOR NOW.

THE STORY CONTINUES IN...
MAX RIDE: ULTIMATE FLIGHT

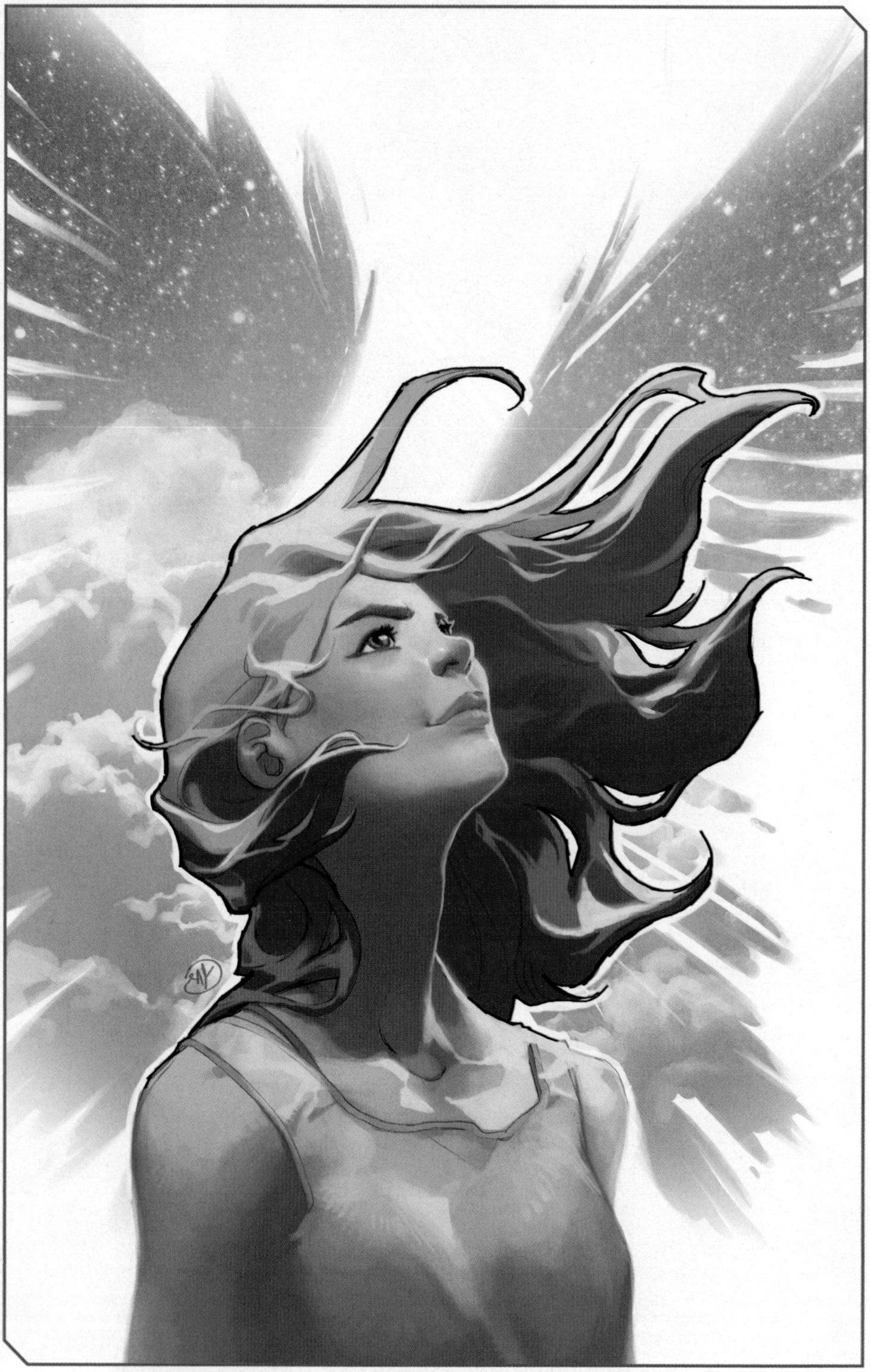

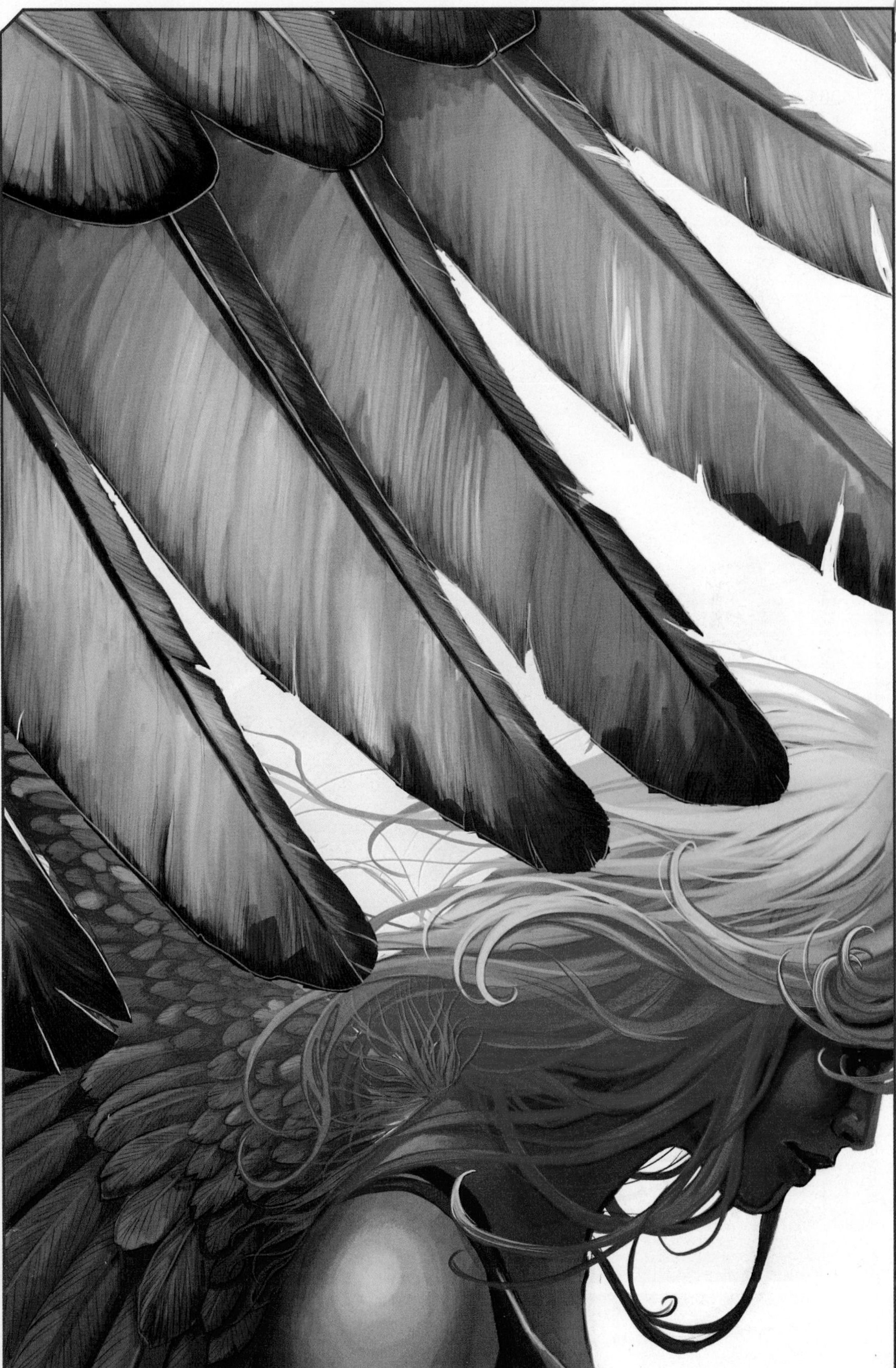

MAX RIDE #1 COVER
by STEPHANIE HANS

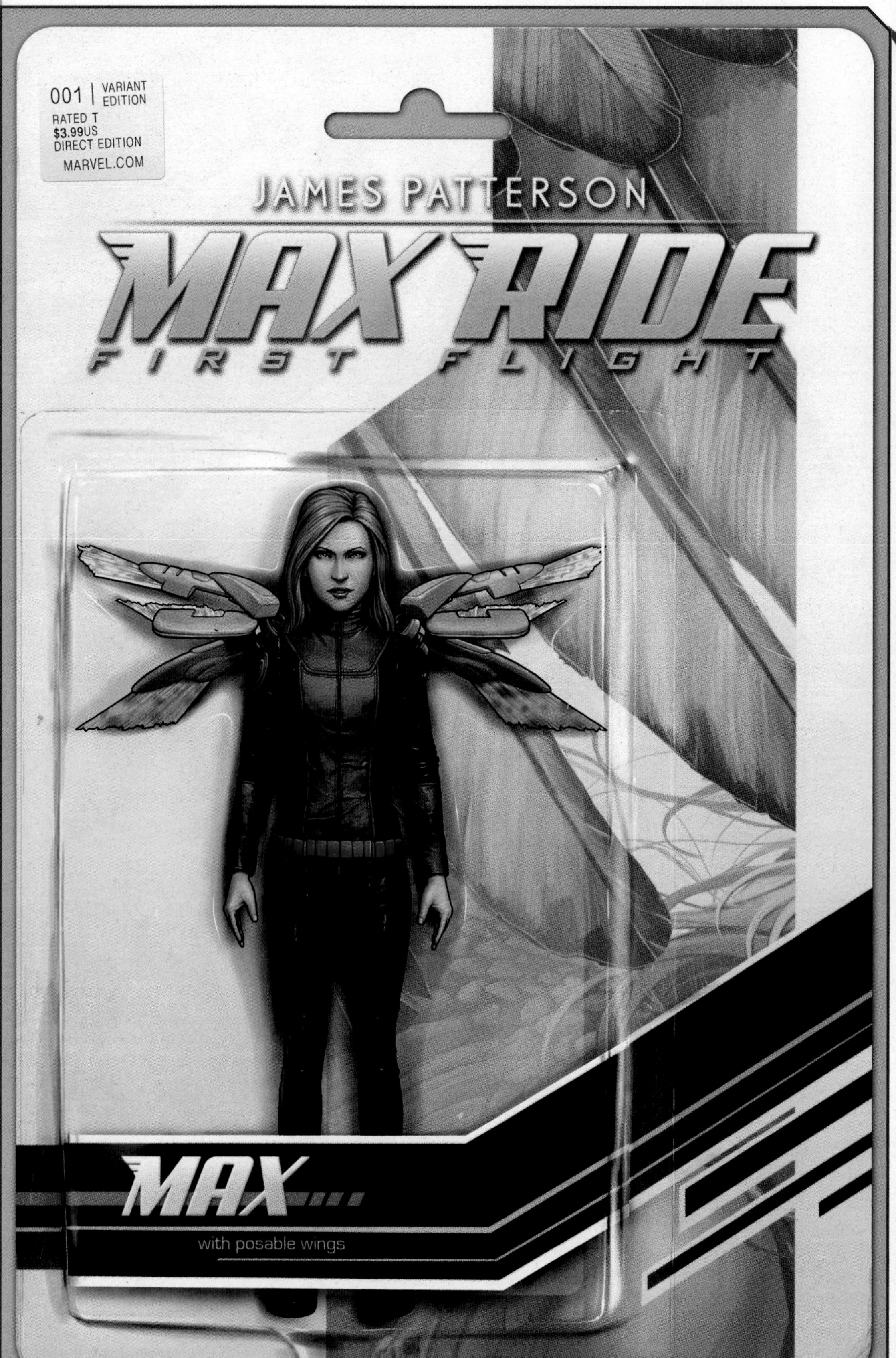
001 | VARIANT EDITION
RATED T
$3.99US
DIRECT EDITION
MARVEL.COM
JAMES PATTERSON
MAX RIDE
FIRST FLIGHT
MAX...
with posable wings

MAX RIDE #1 ACTION FIGURE VARIANT COVER
by JOHN TYLER CHRISTOPHER

MAX RIDE #1 B&W ACTION FIGURE VARIANT COVER
by JOHN TYLER CHRISTOPHER

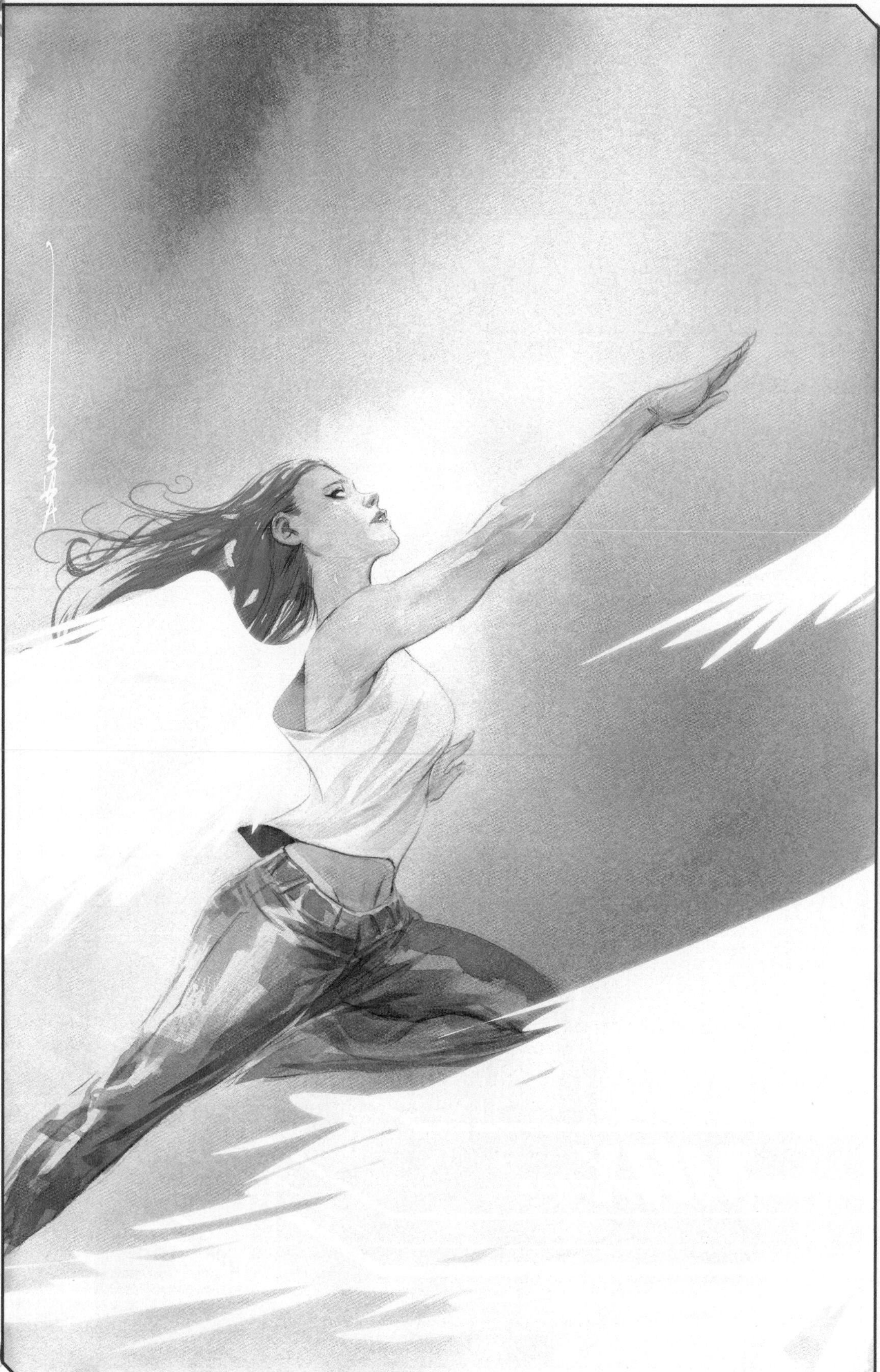

MAX RIDE #1 VARIANT COVER
by DUSTIN NGUYEN

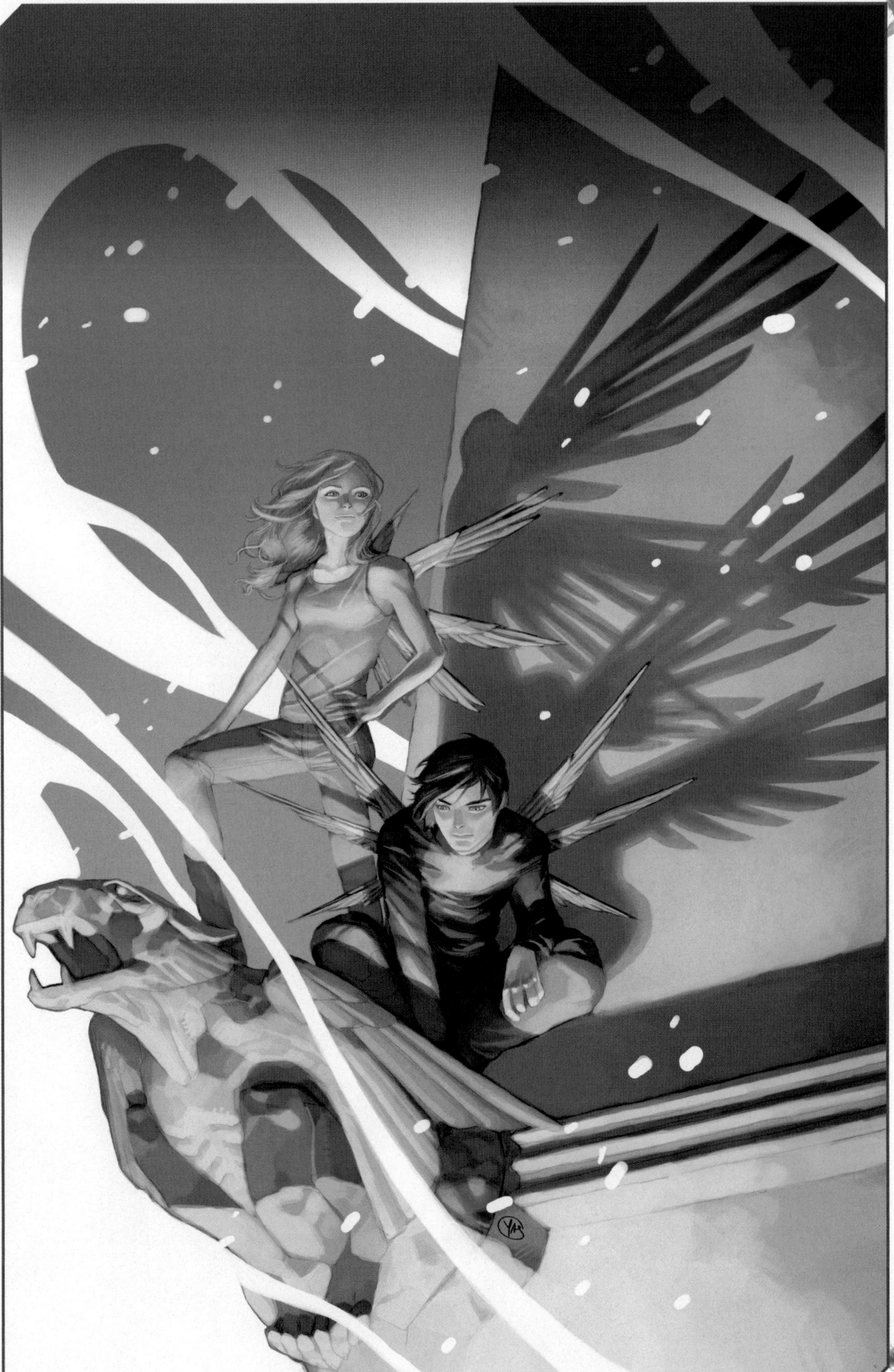

MAX RIDE #2 COVER
by YASMINE PUTRI

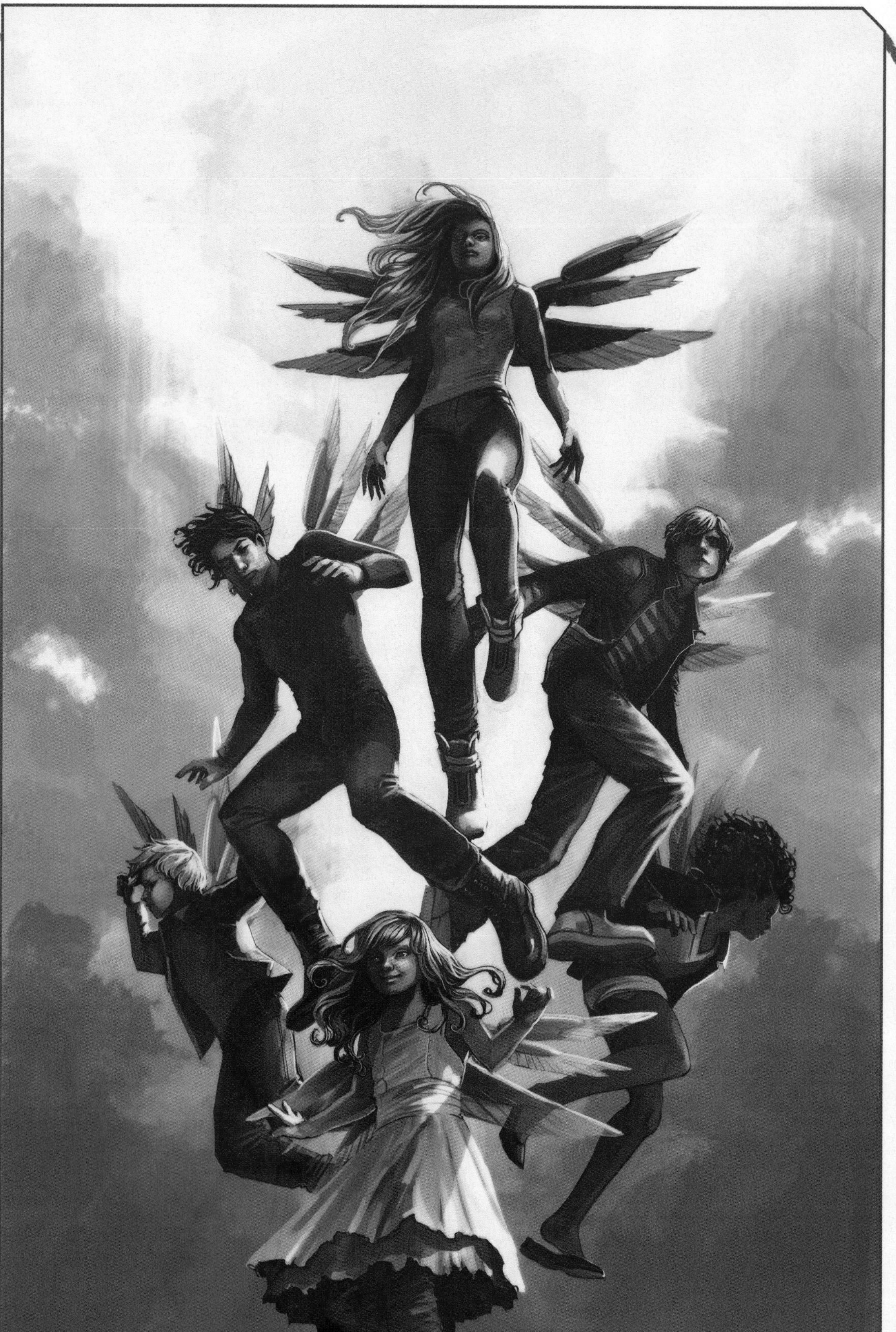

MAX RIDE #3 COVER
by STEPHANIE HANS

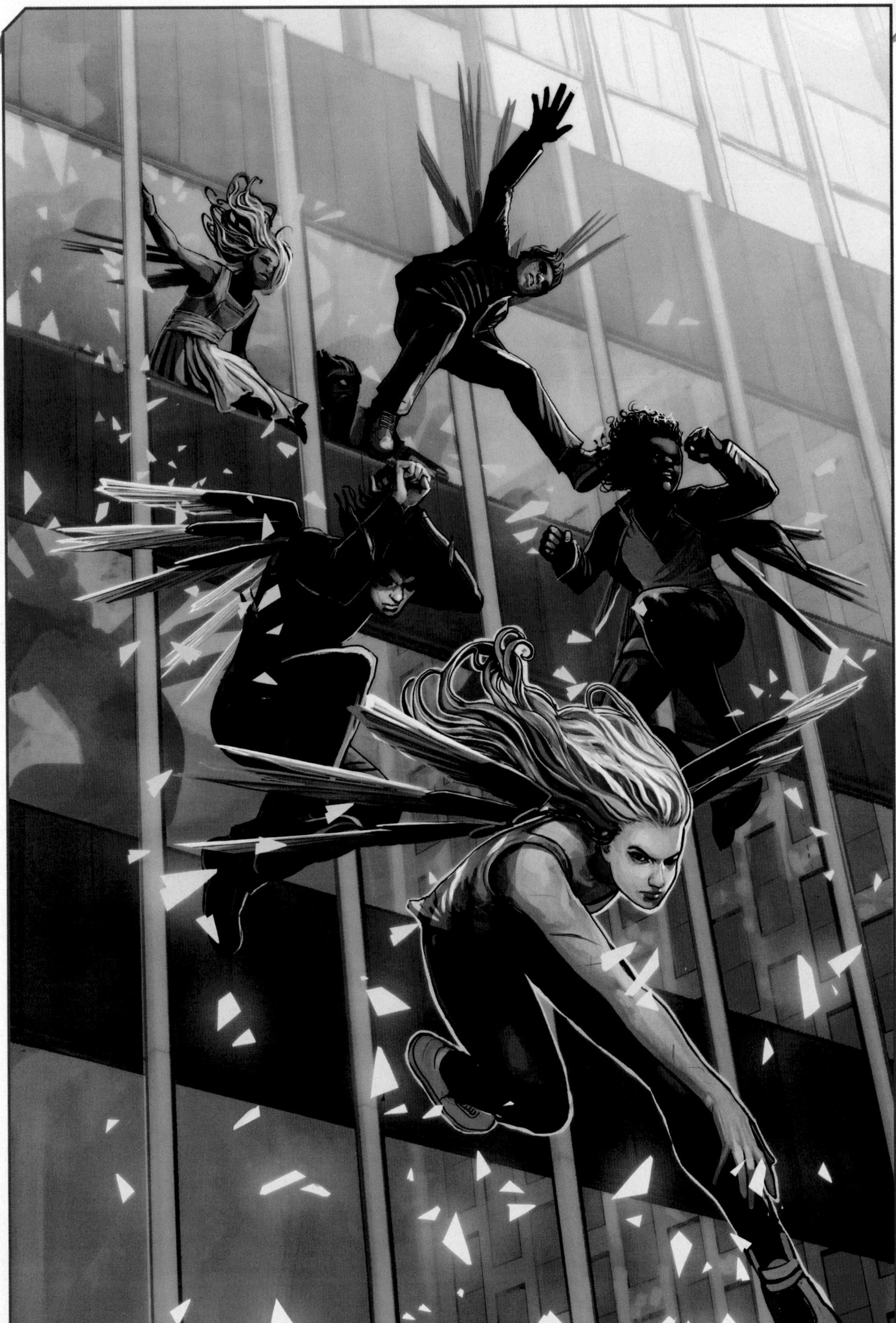

MAX RIDE #4 COVER
by STEPHANIE HANS

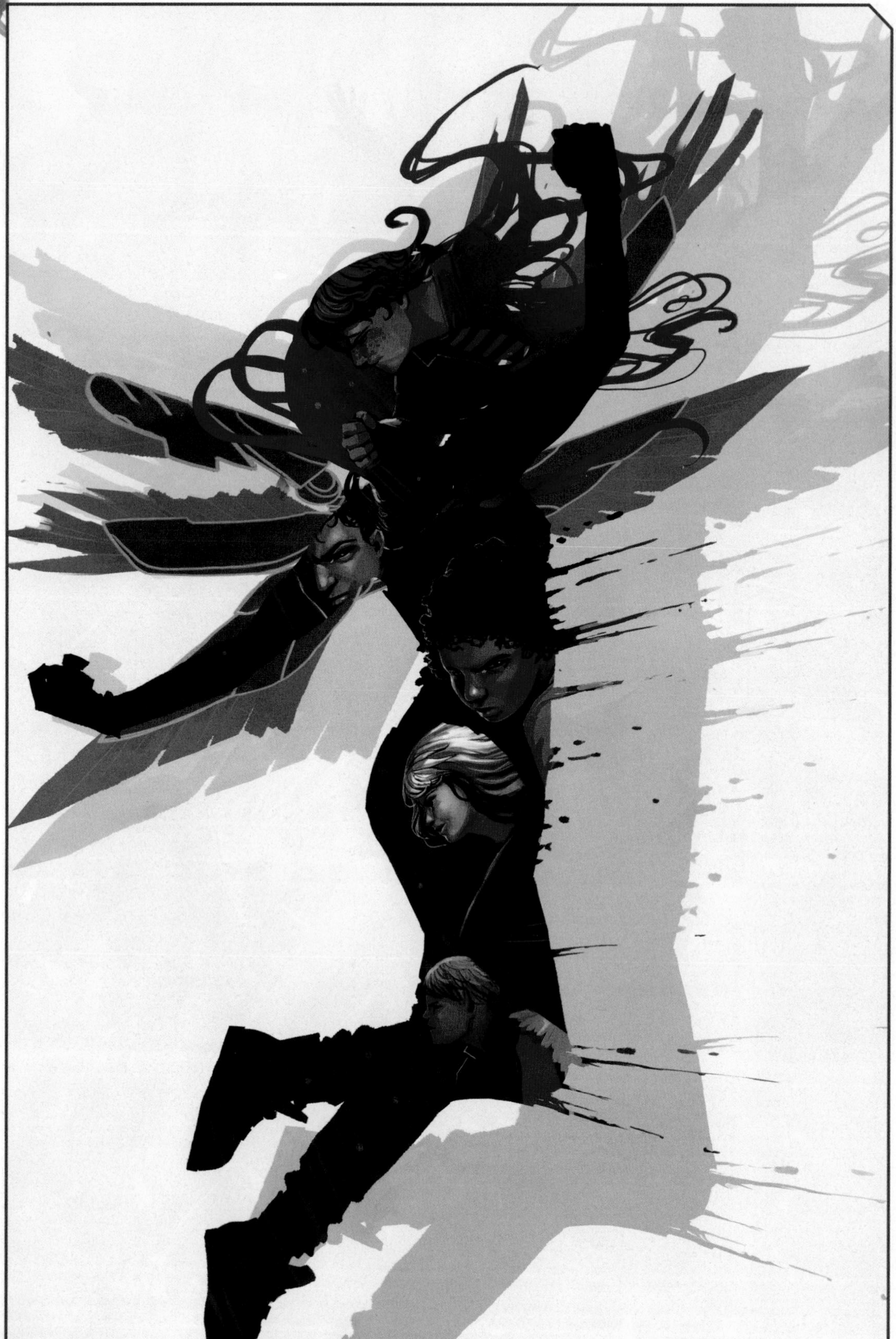
SH

MAX RIDE #5 COVER
by STEPHANIE HANS

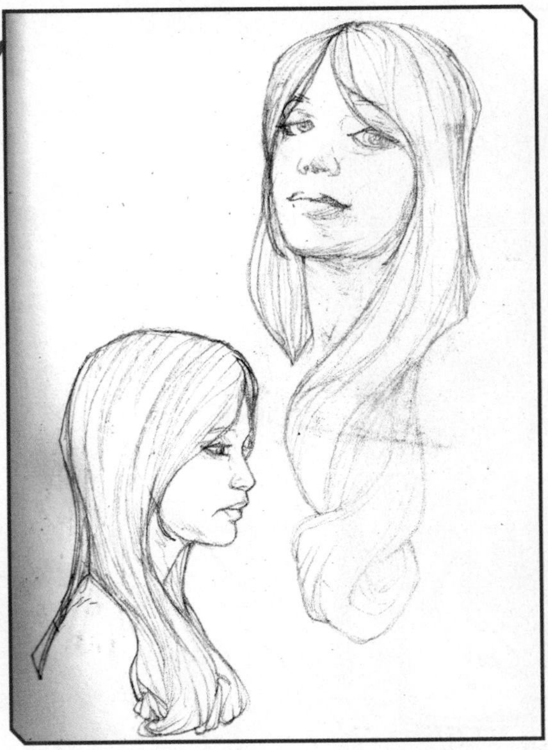

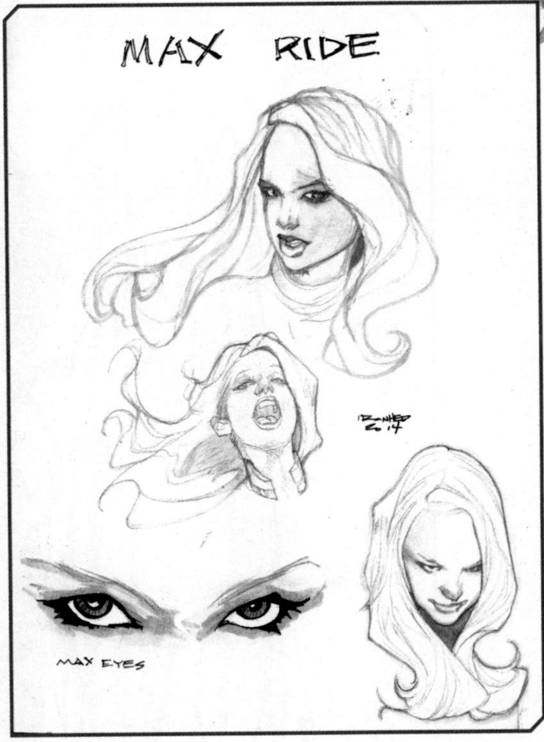
MAX RIDE
MAX EYES

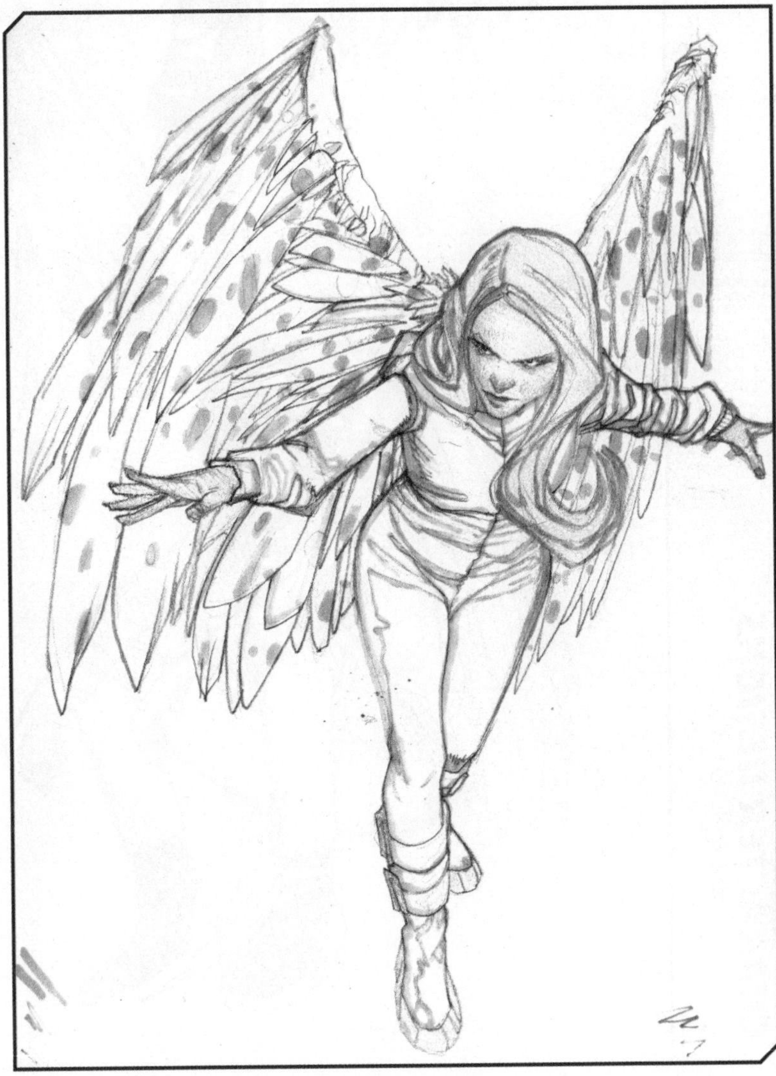

MAX CHARACTER DESIGNS

by ALEX SANCHEZ

CHARACTER DESIGNS
by ALEX SANCHEZ

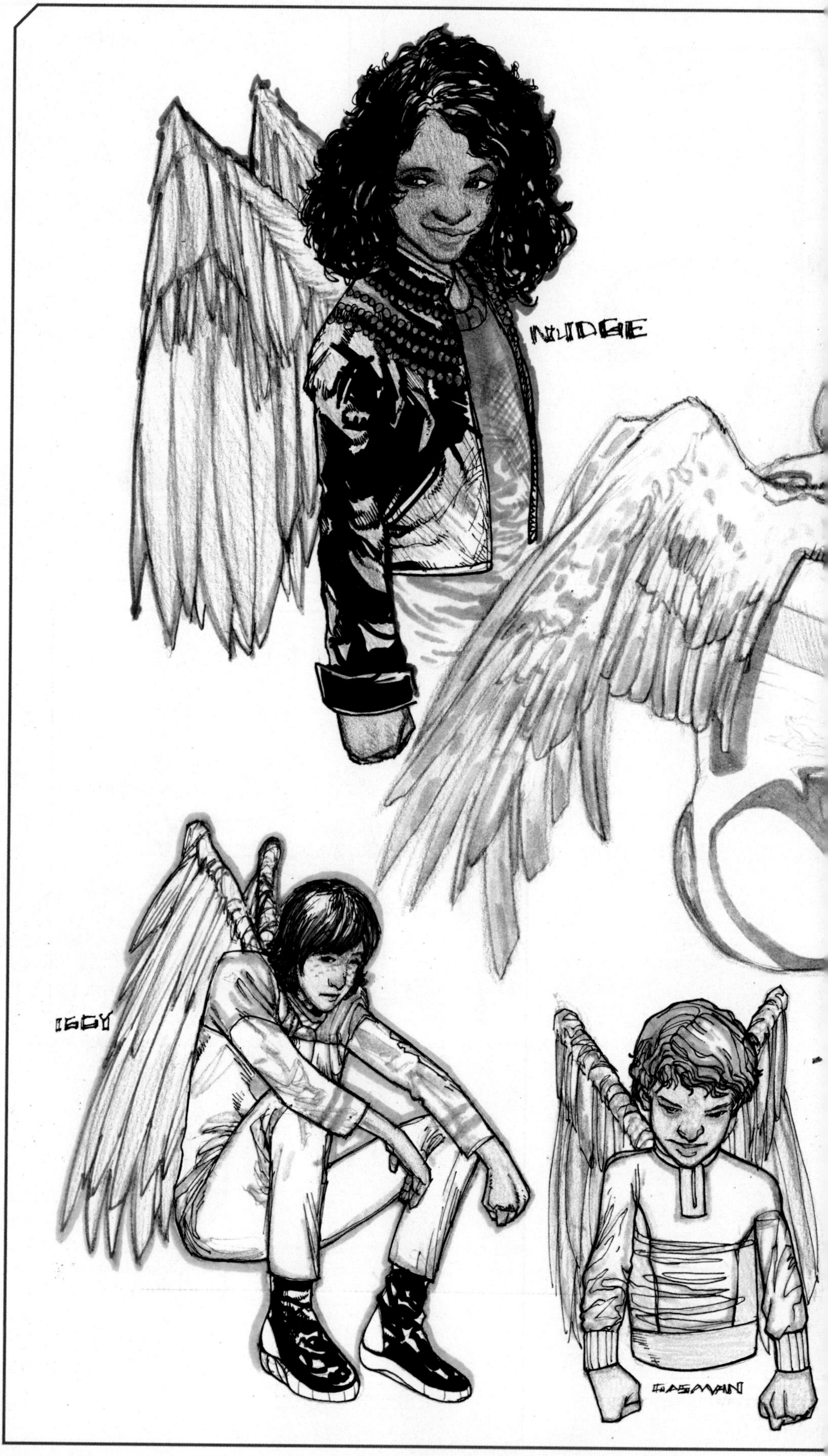
NUDGE
IGGY
GASMAN

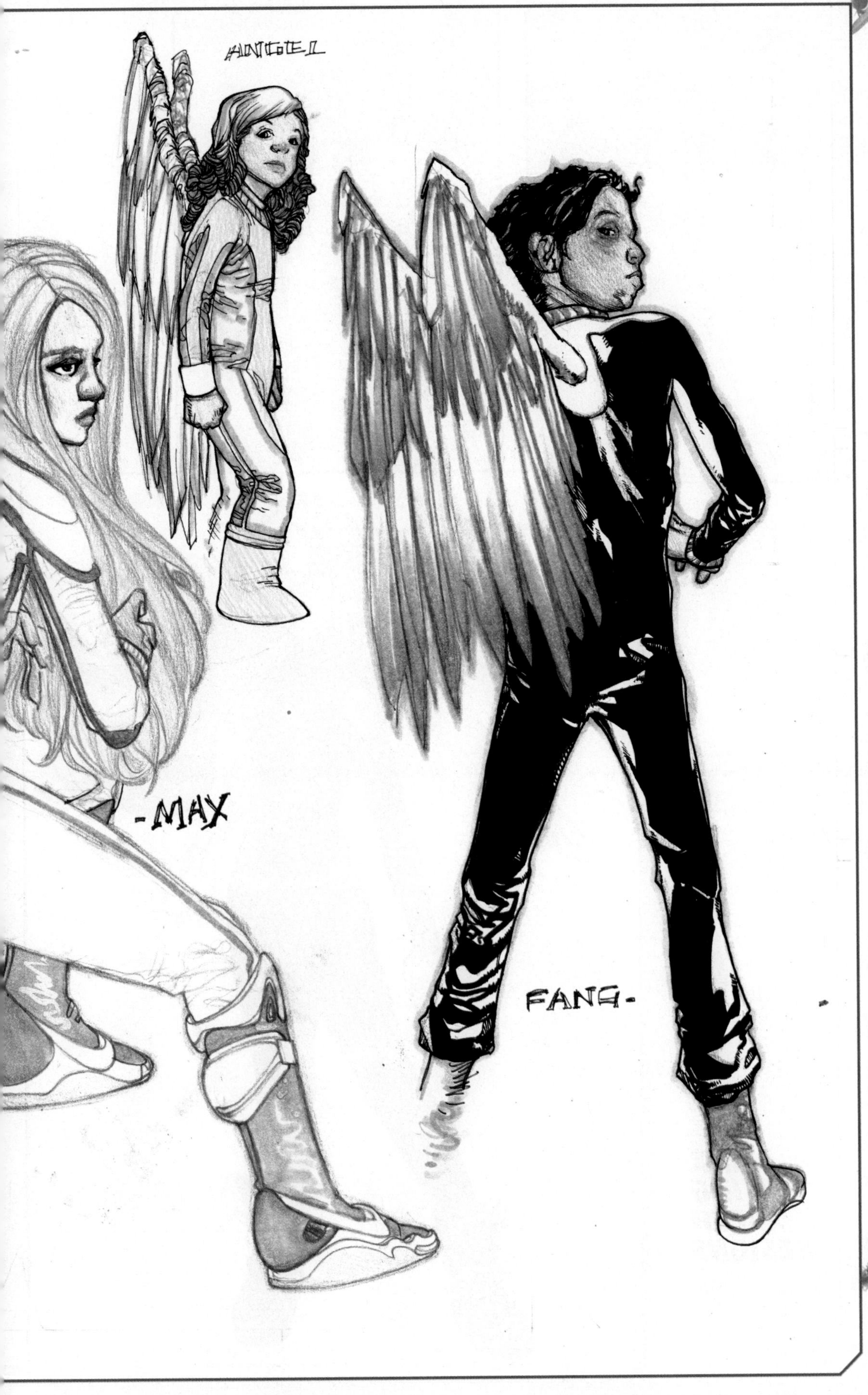
ANGEL
-MAX
FANG-

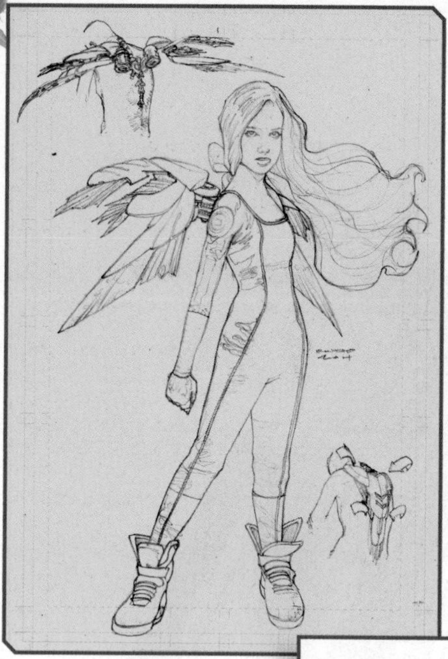

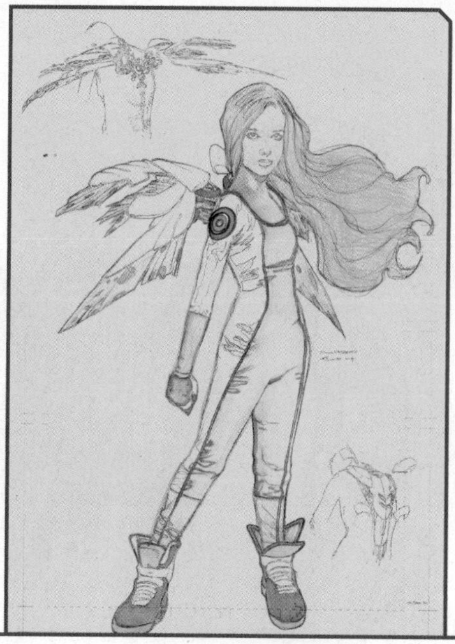

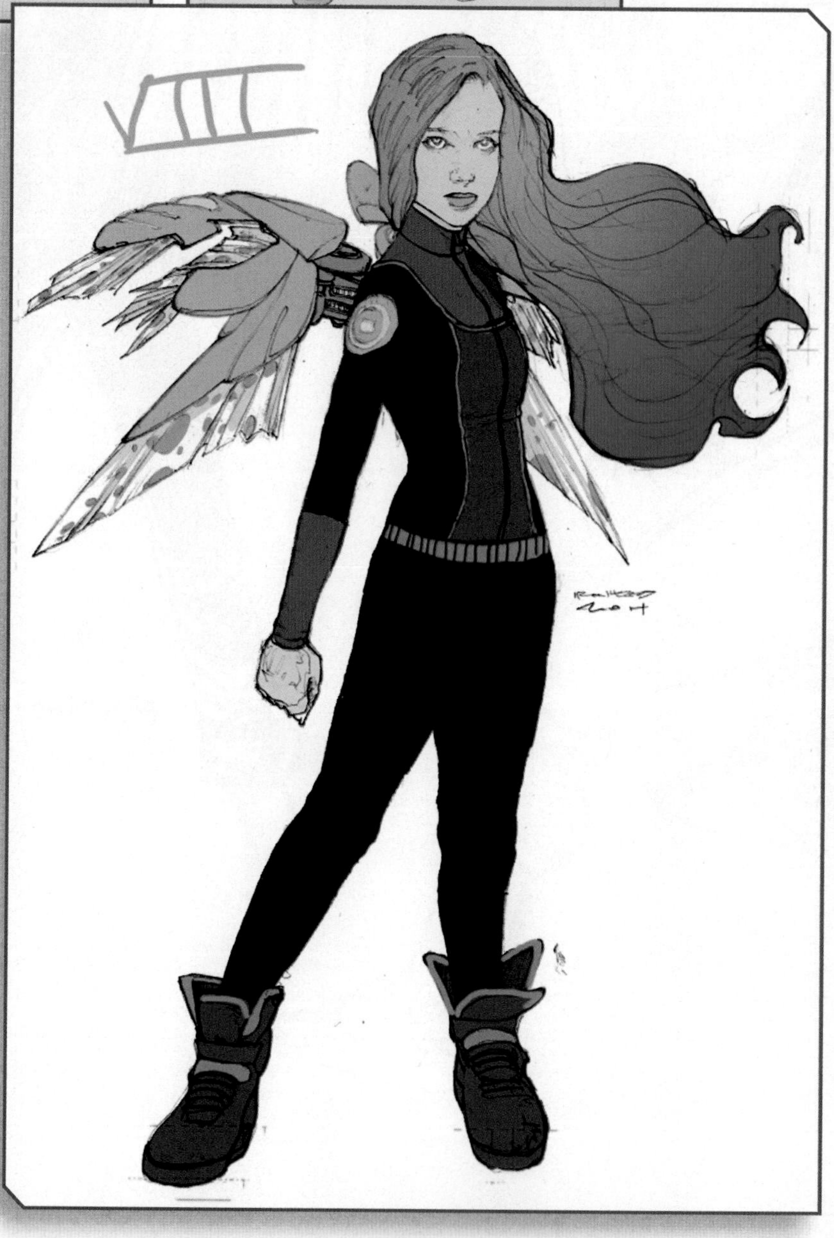
VIII

MAX WING MECH DESIGNS

by ALEX SANCHEZ

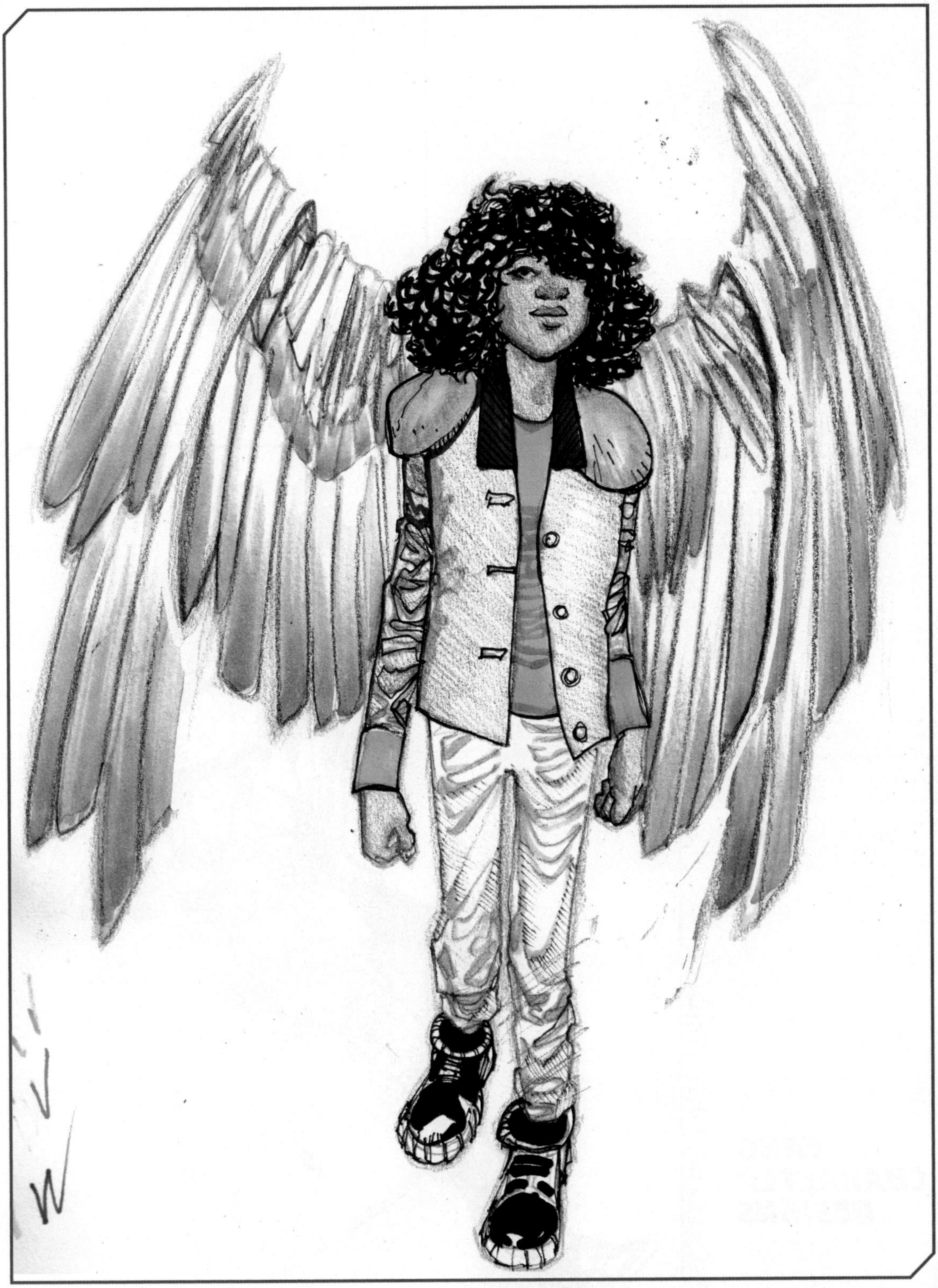

NUDGE CHARACTER DESIGN
by ALEX SANCHEZ

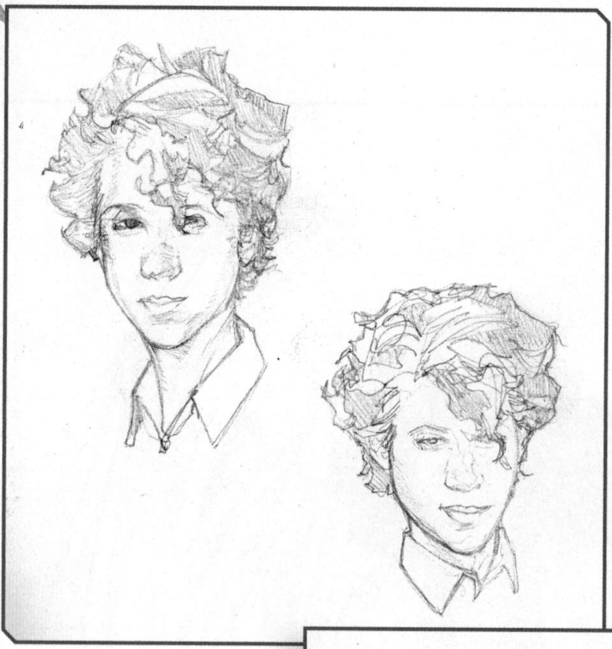

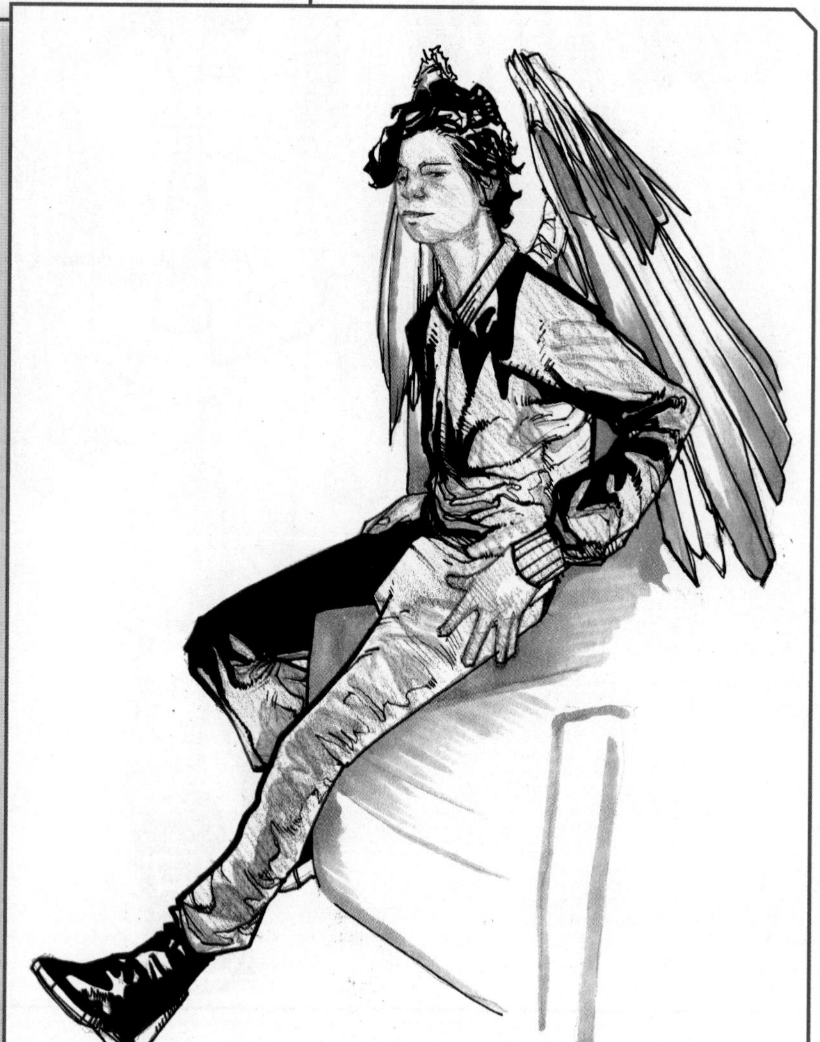

FANG CHARACTER DESIGNS

by ALEX SANCHEZ

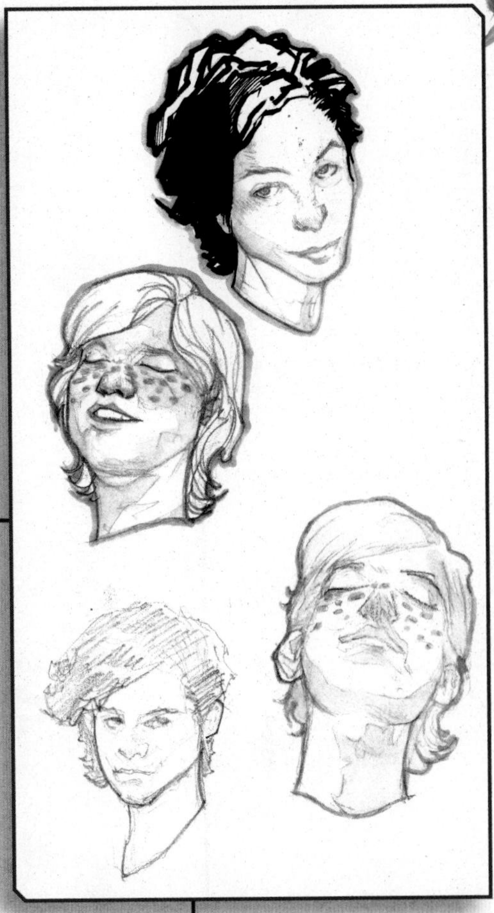

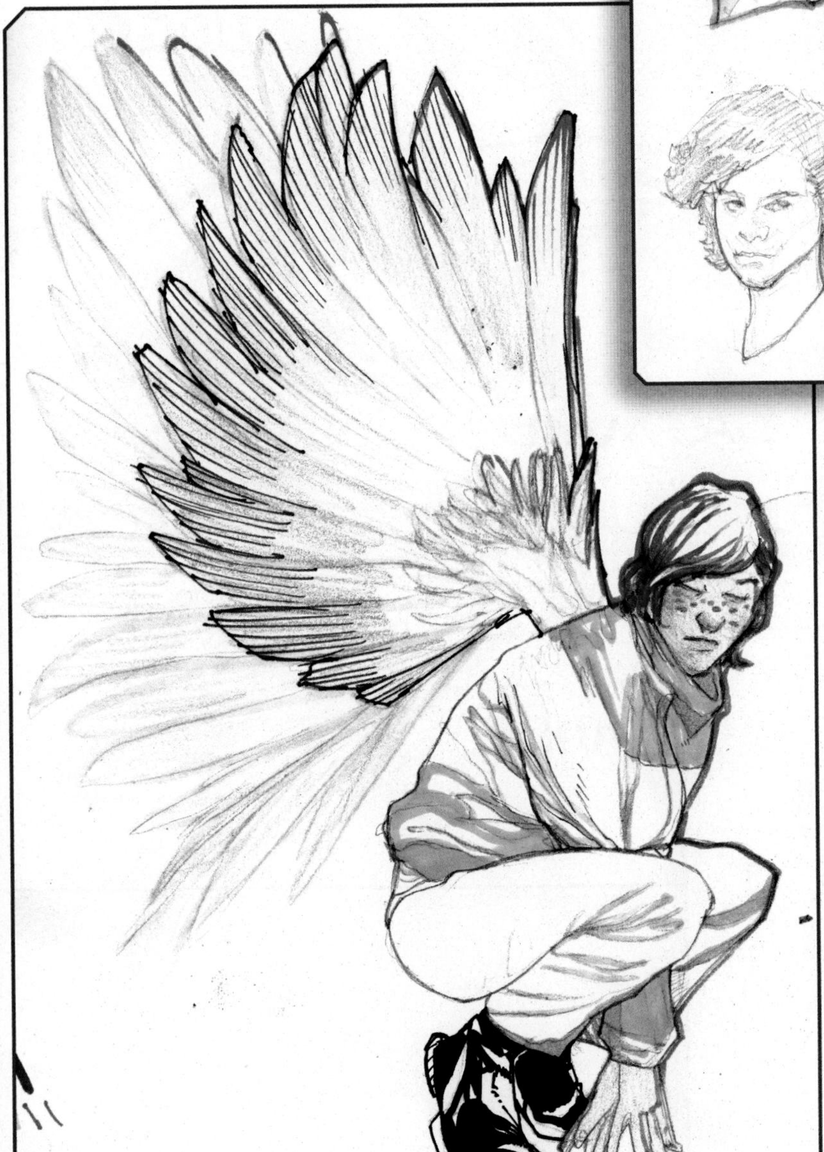

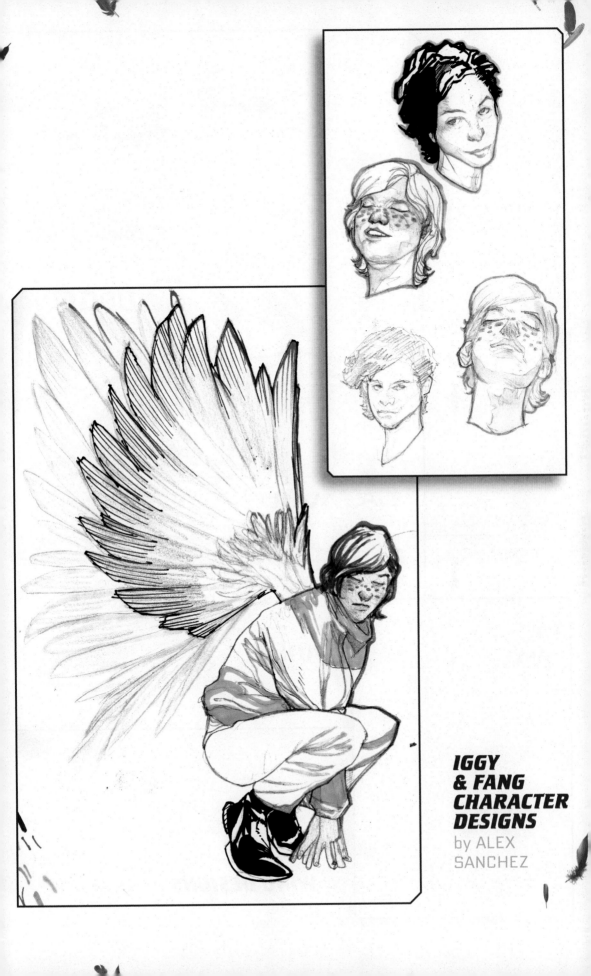

IGGY & FANG CHARACTER DESIGNS
by ALEX SANCHEZ

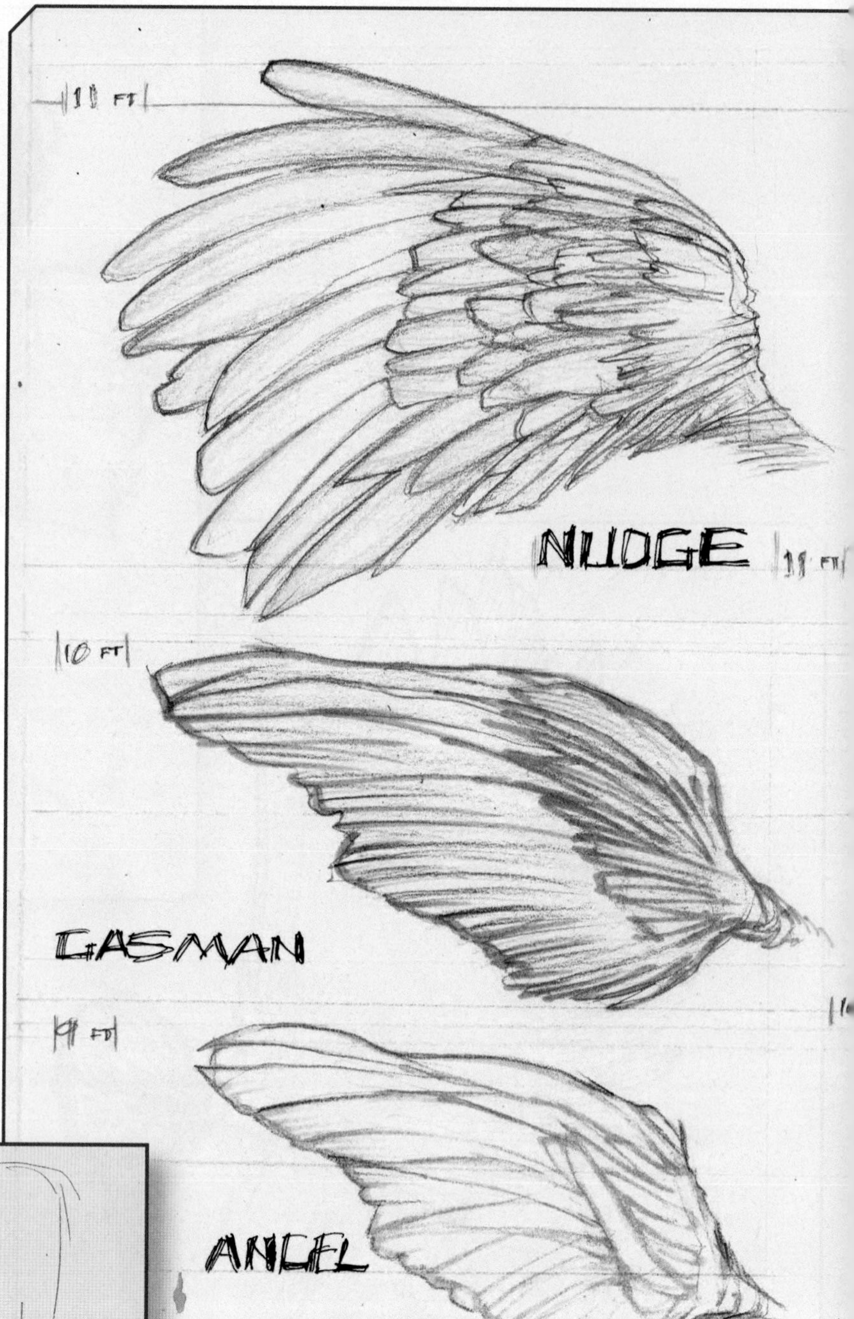
11 FT
NUDGE
11 FT
10 FT
GASMAN
9 FT
ANGEL
9

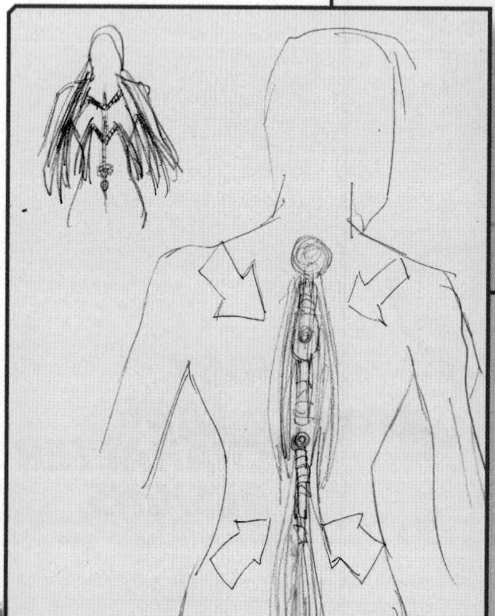

WING DESIGNS
by ALEX SANCHEZ

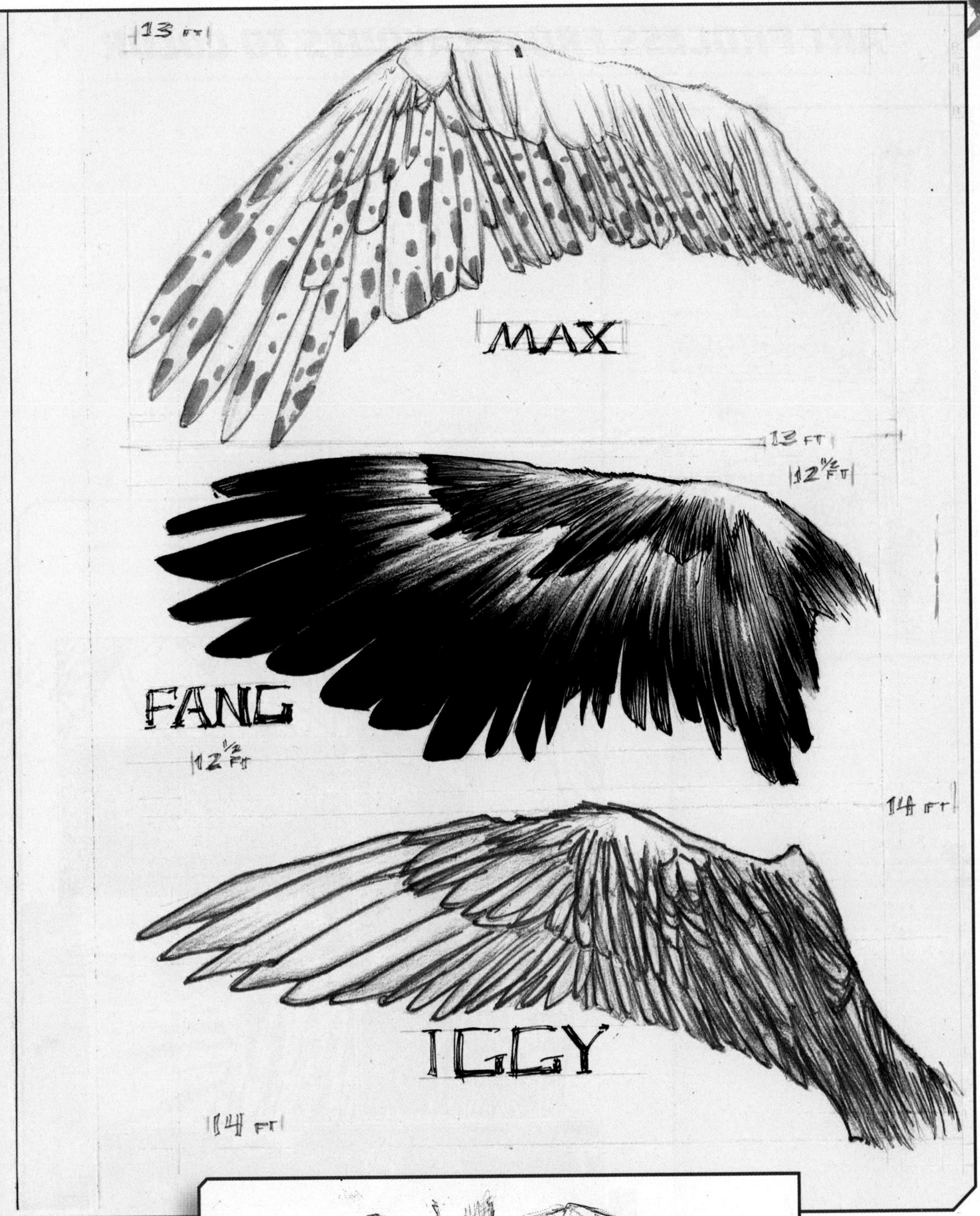
13 FT
MAX
13 FT
12 1/2 FT
FANG
12 1/2 FT
14 FT
IGGY
14 FT

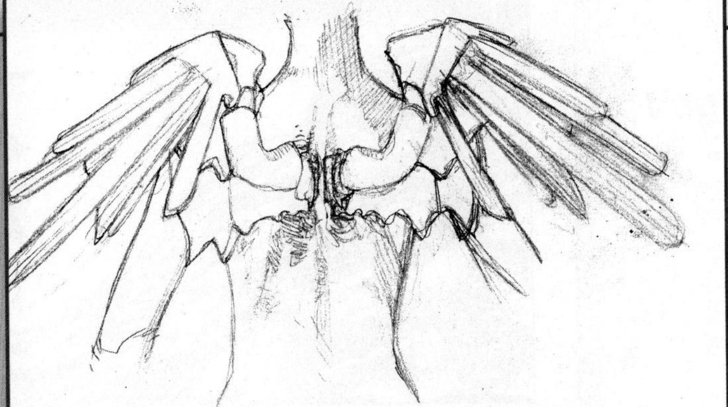

ART PROCESS FROM LAYOUTS TO COLOR

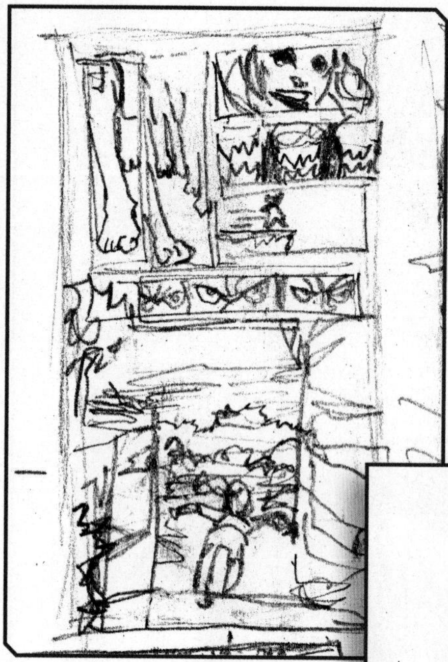

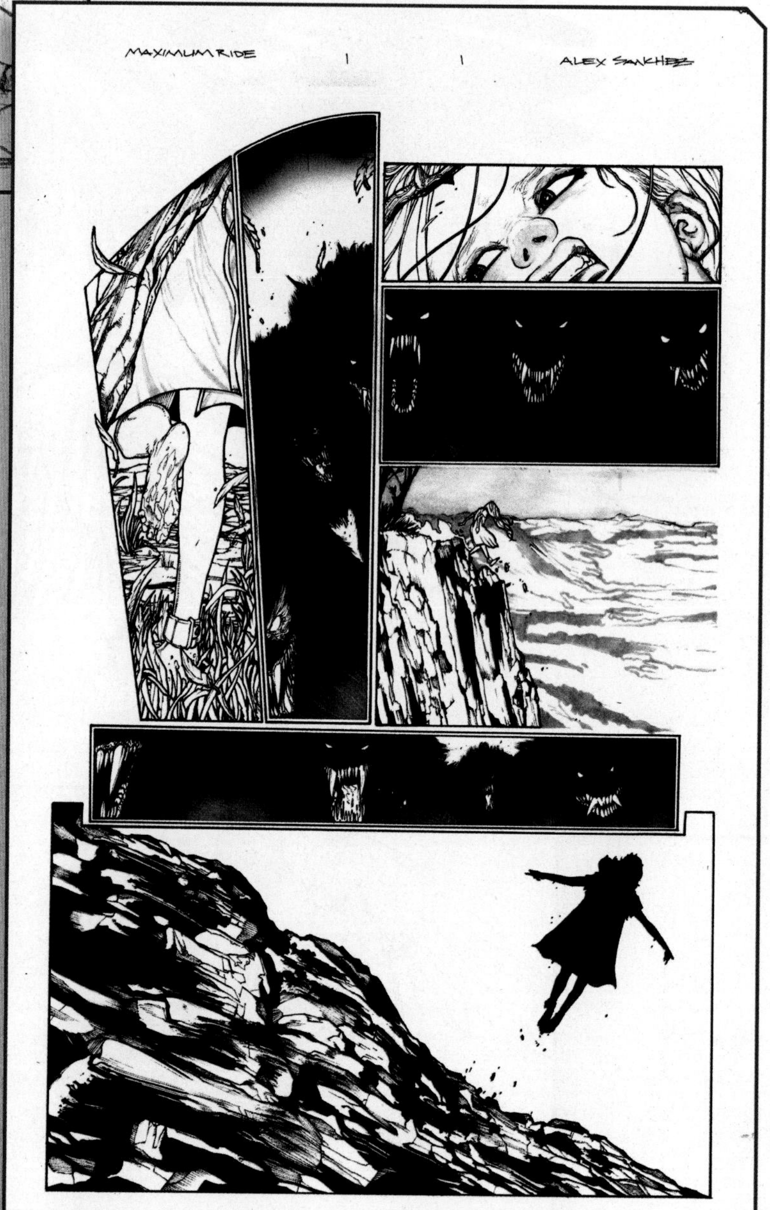
MAXIMUM RIDE
1
1
ALEX SANCHEZ

Issue 1, page 1
by ALEX SANCHEZ
& ESTHER SANZ

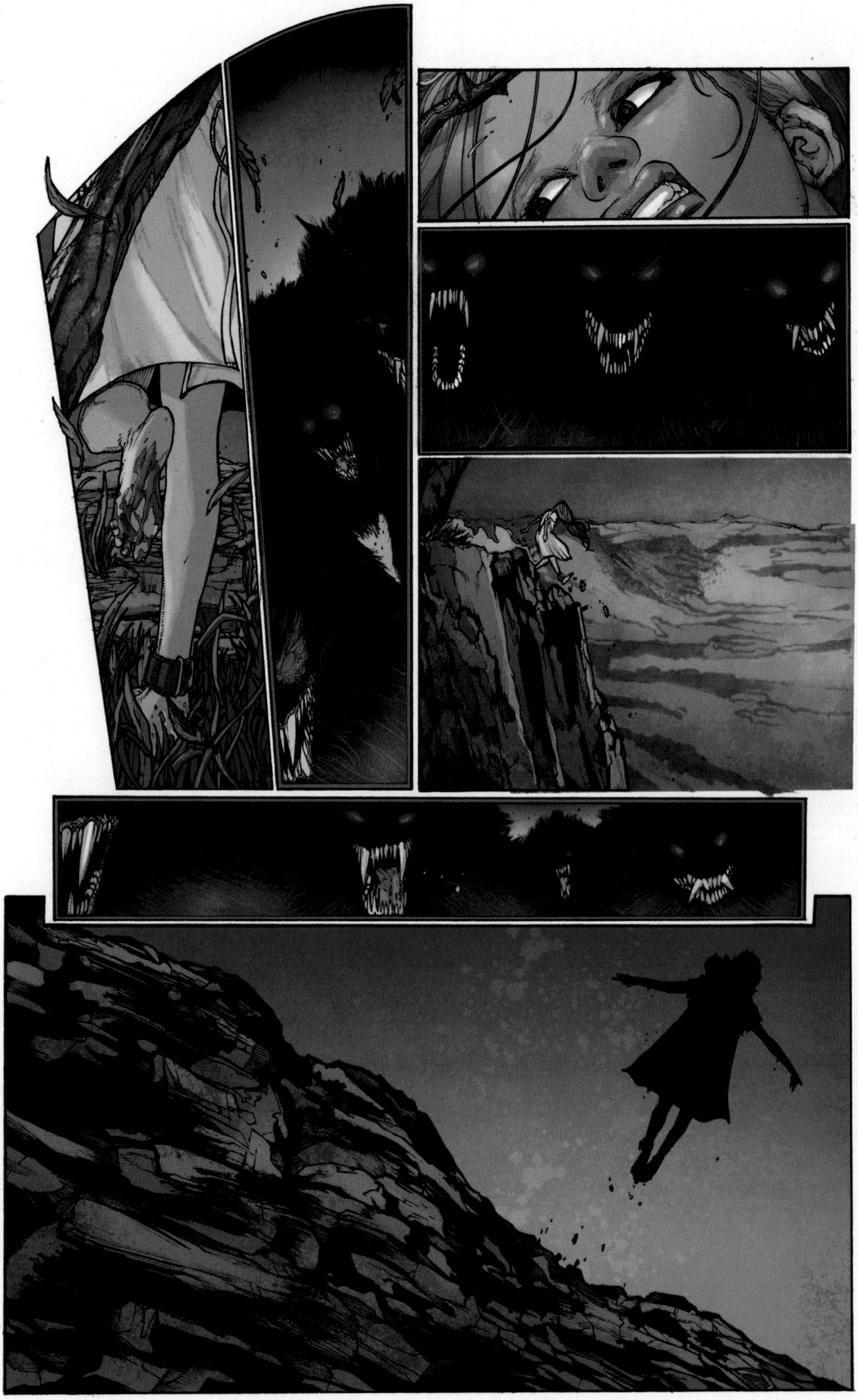

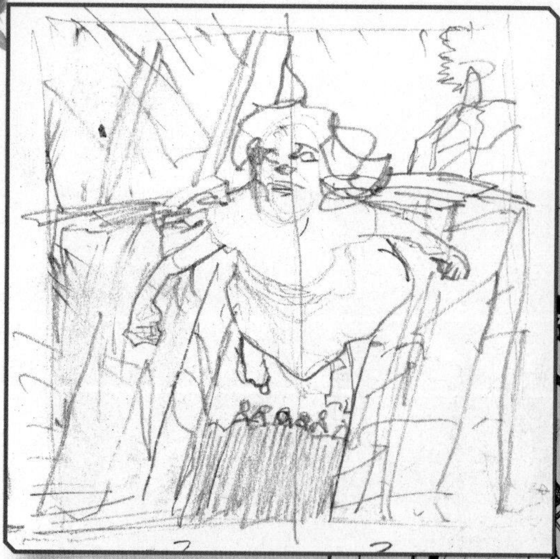

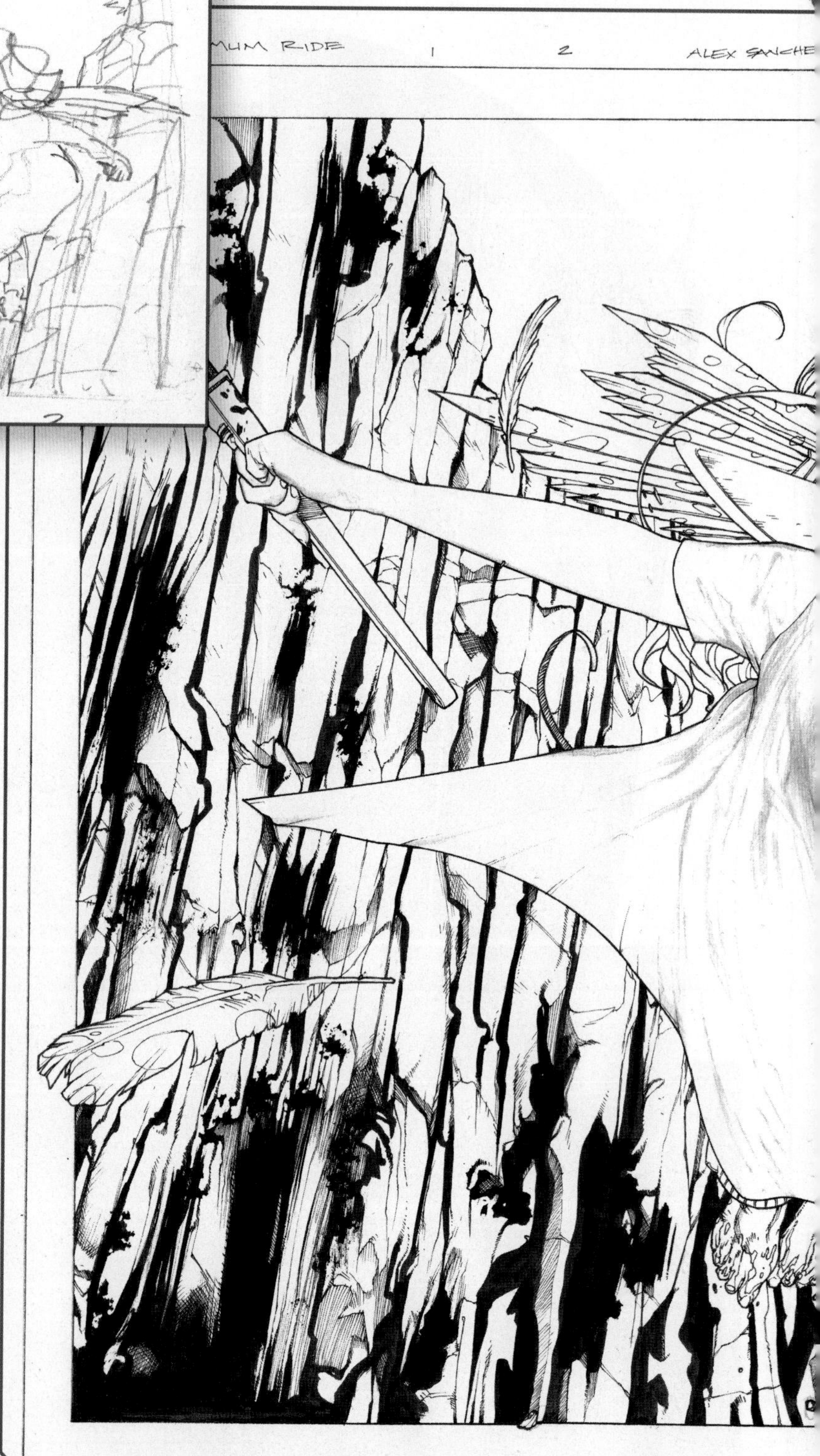
MUM RIDE
1
2
ALEX SANCHE

Issue 1, pages 2-3
by ALEX SANCHEZ & ESTHER SANZ

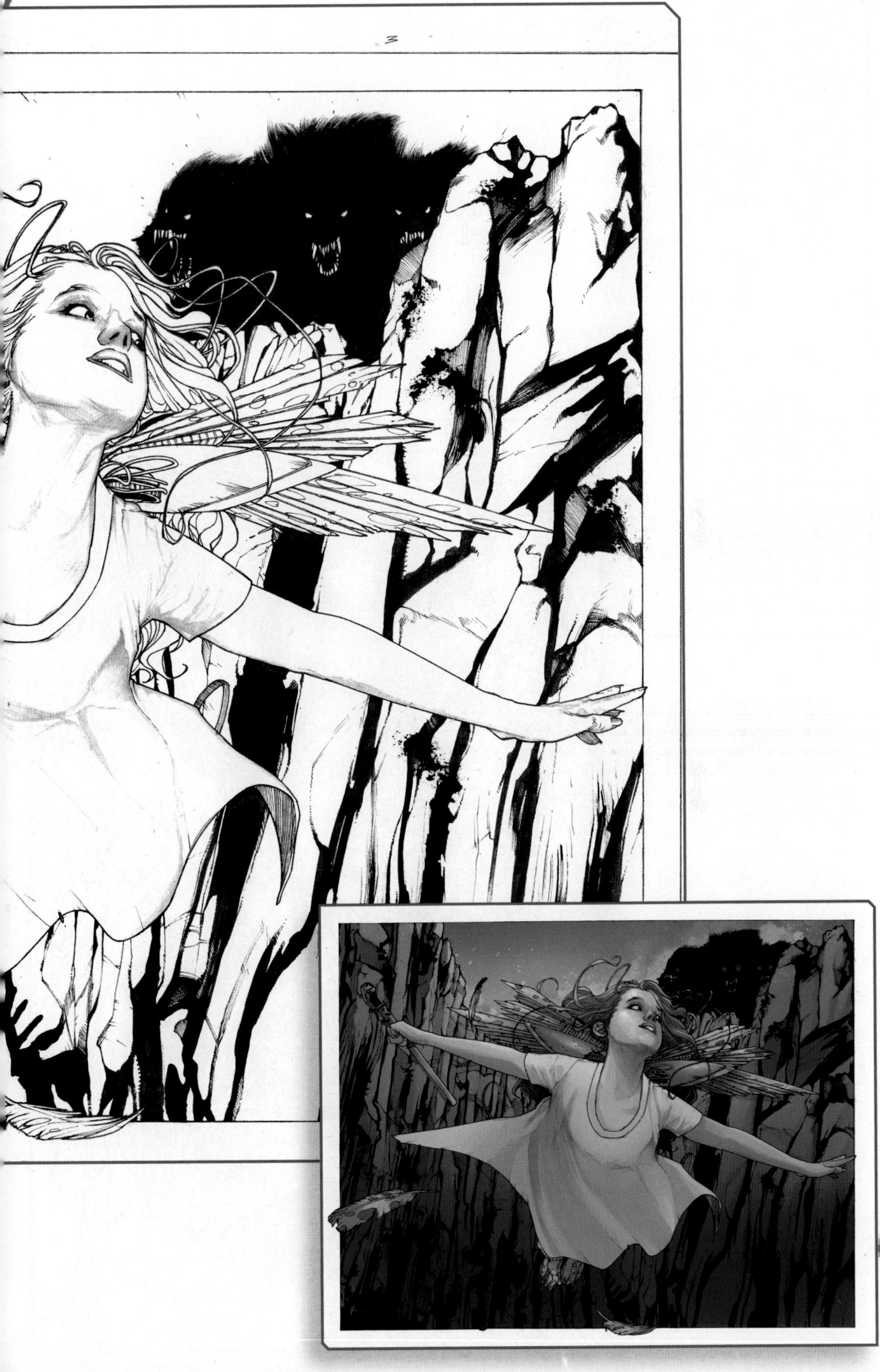

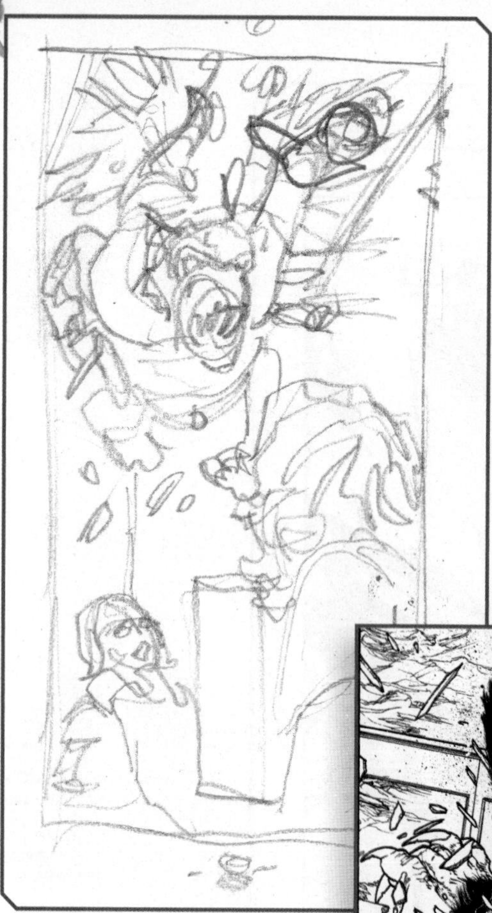

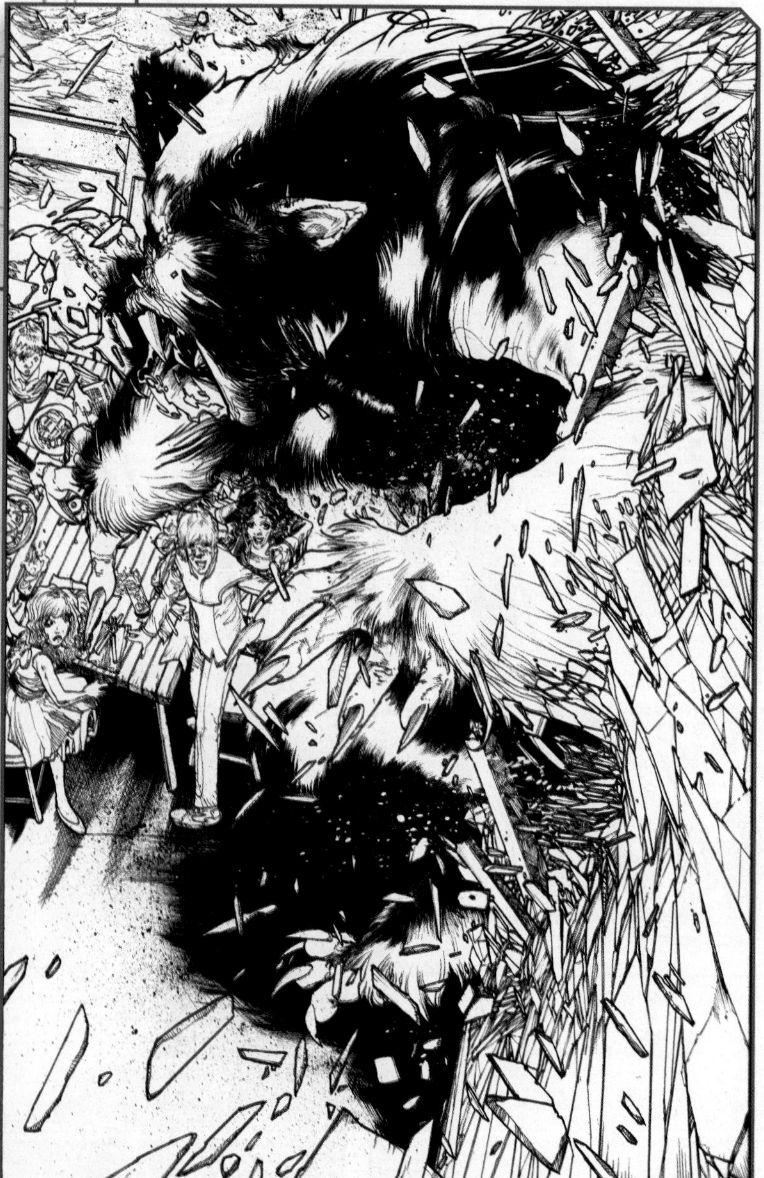

Issue 1, page 8
by ALEX SANCHEZ
& ESTHER SANZ

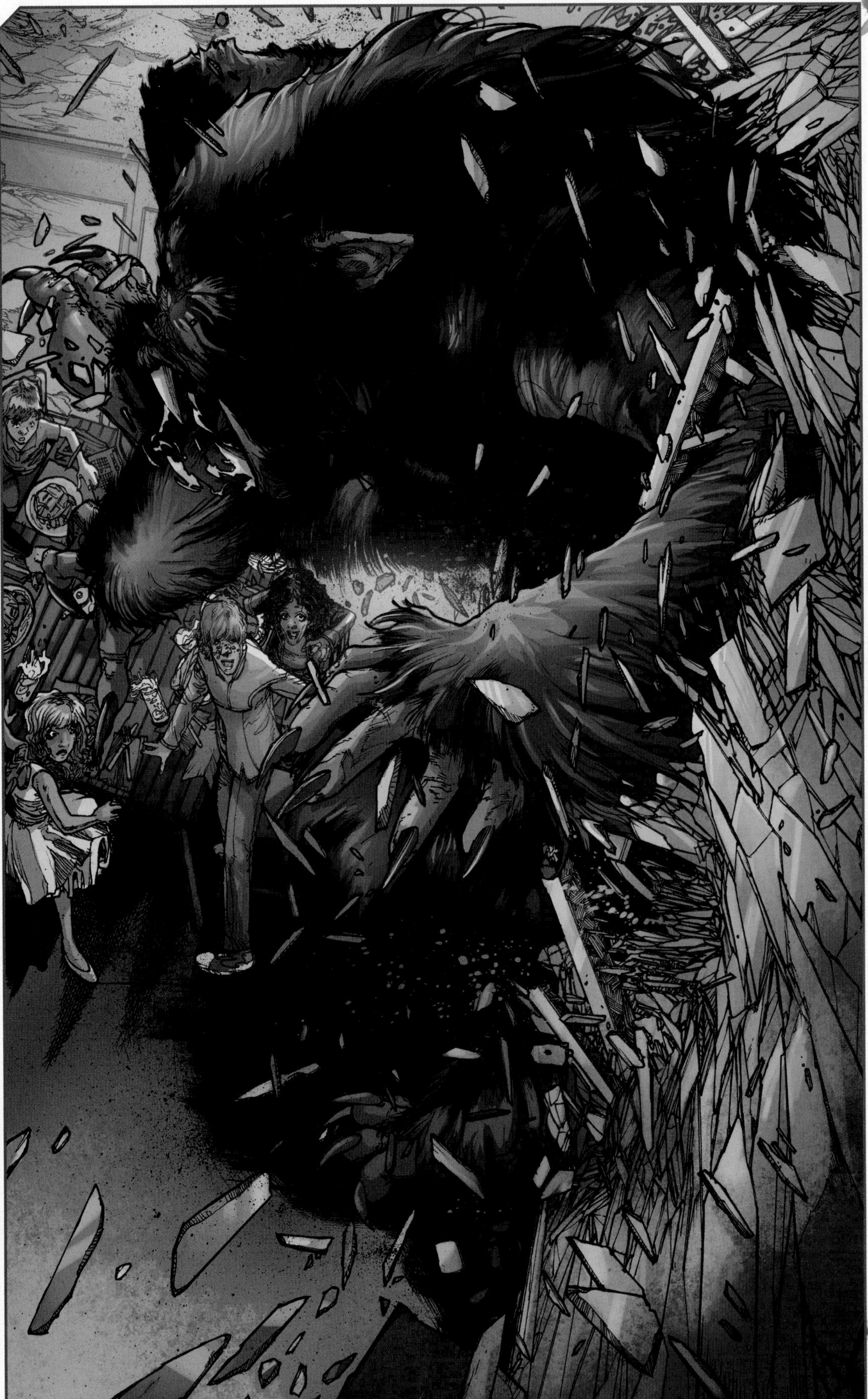

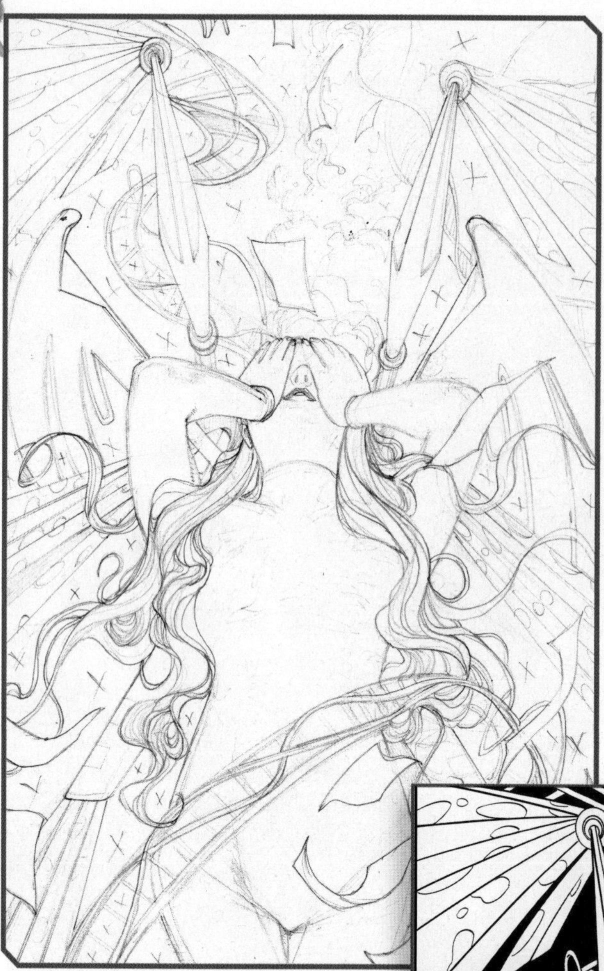

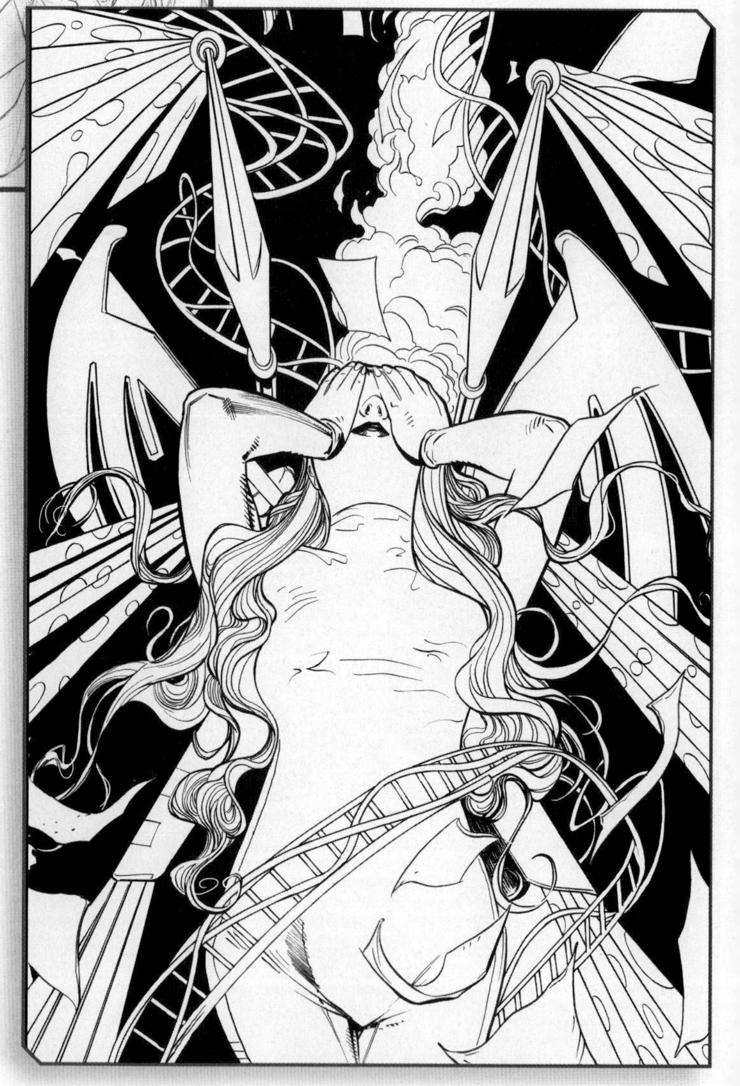

Issue 3, page 19
by ALEX SANCHEZ, MARK PENNINGTON & ESTHER SANZ

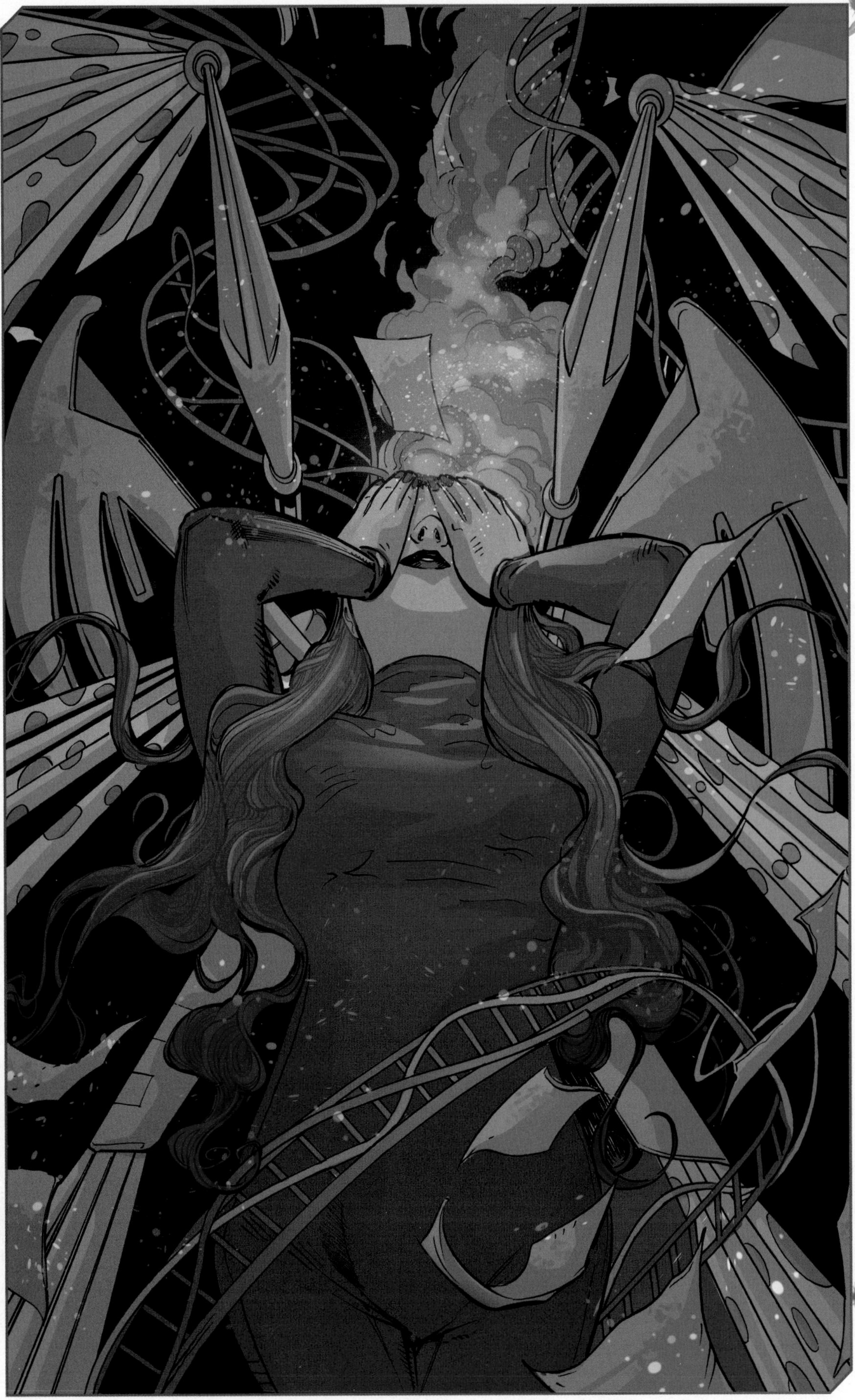

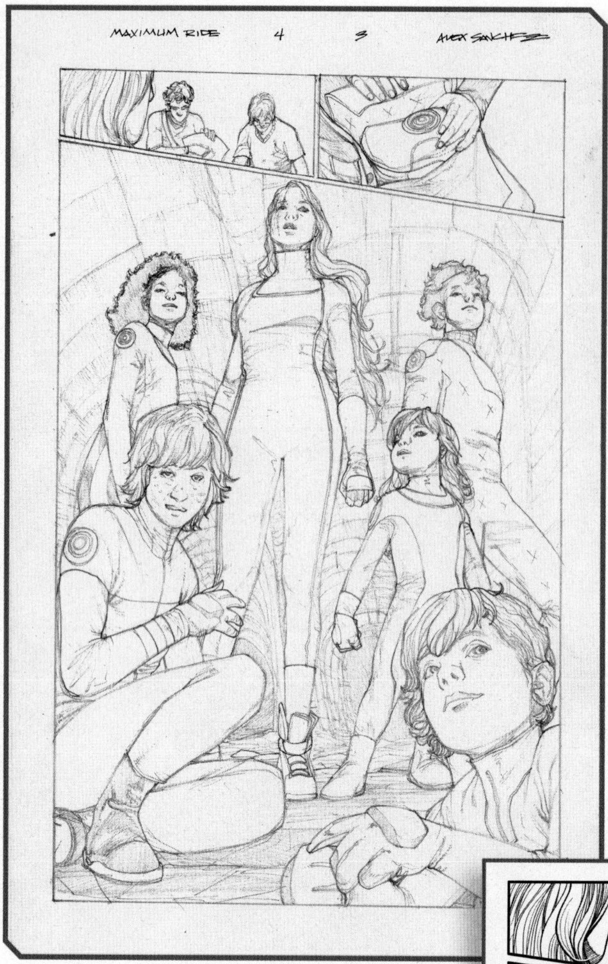
MAXIMUM RIDE 4 3 ALEX SANCHEZ

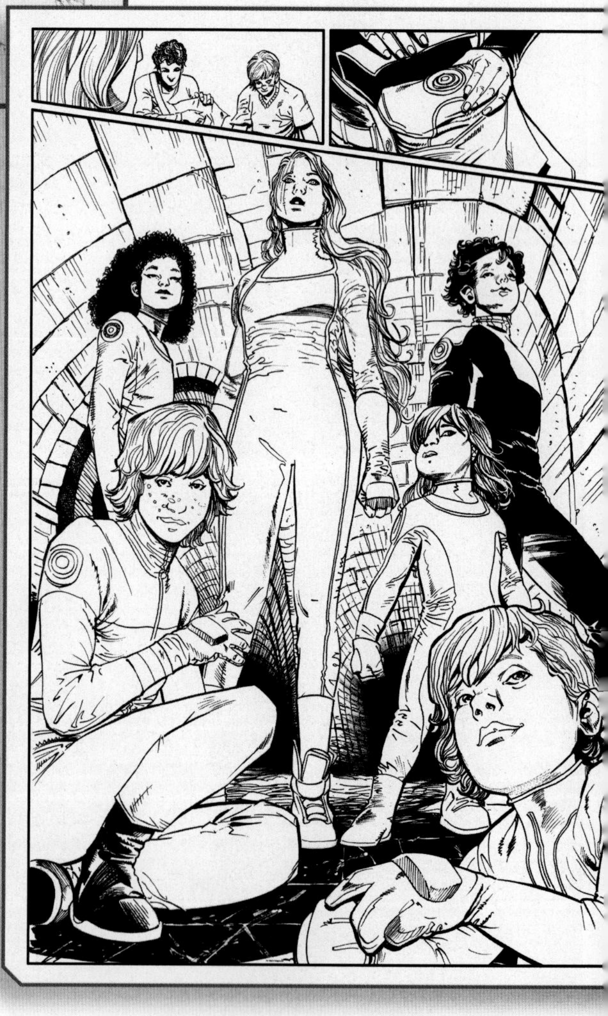

Issue 4, page 3
by ALEX SANCHEZ,
MARK PENNINGTON
& ESTHER SANZ

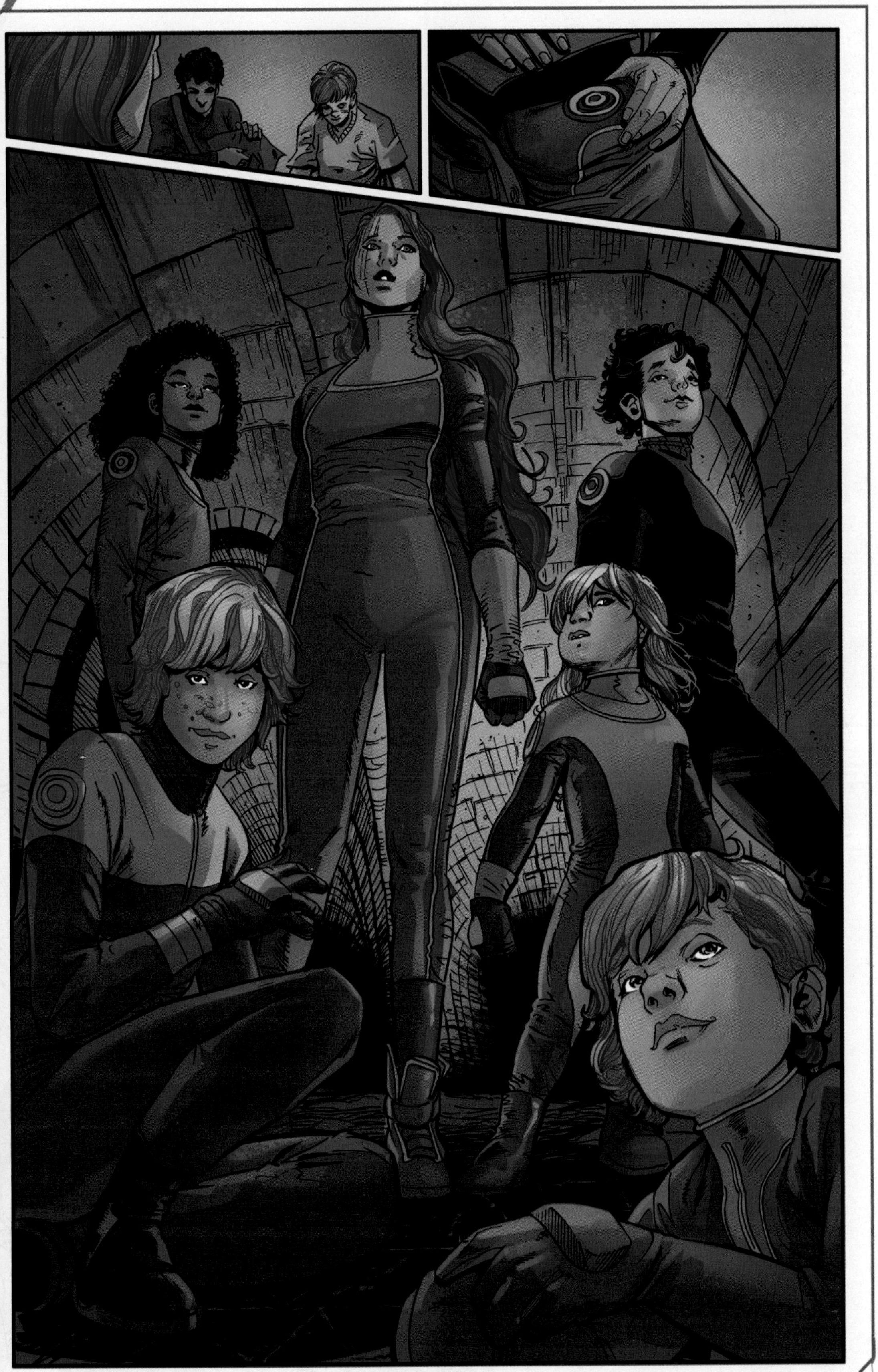

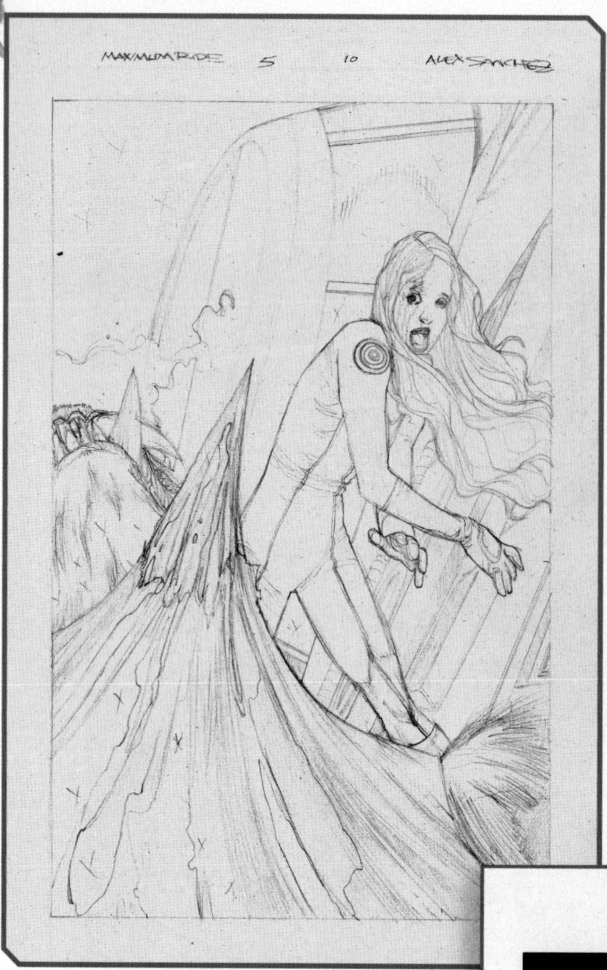
MAXIMUM RIDE
5
10
ALEX SANCHEZ

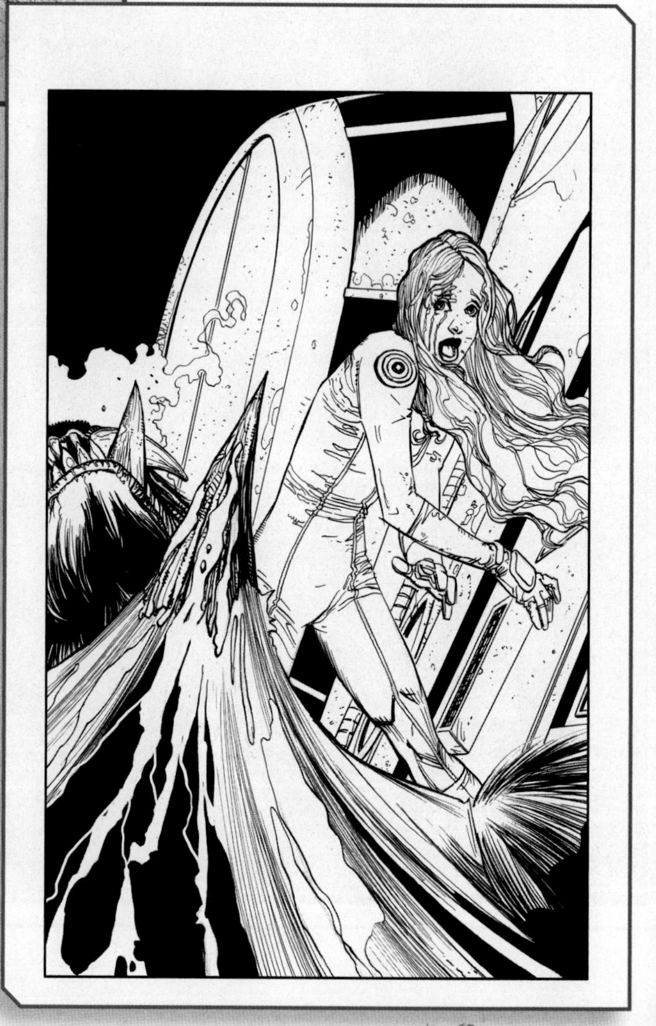

Issue 5, page 10
by ALEX SANCHEZ,
MARK PENNINGTON
& ESTHER SANZ

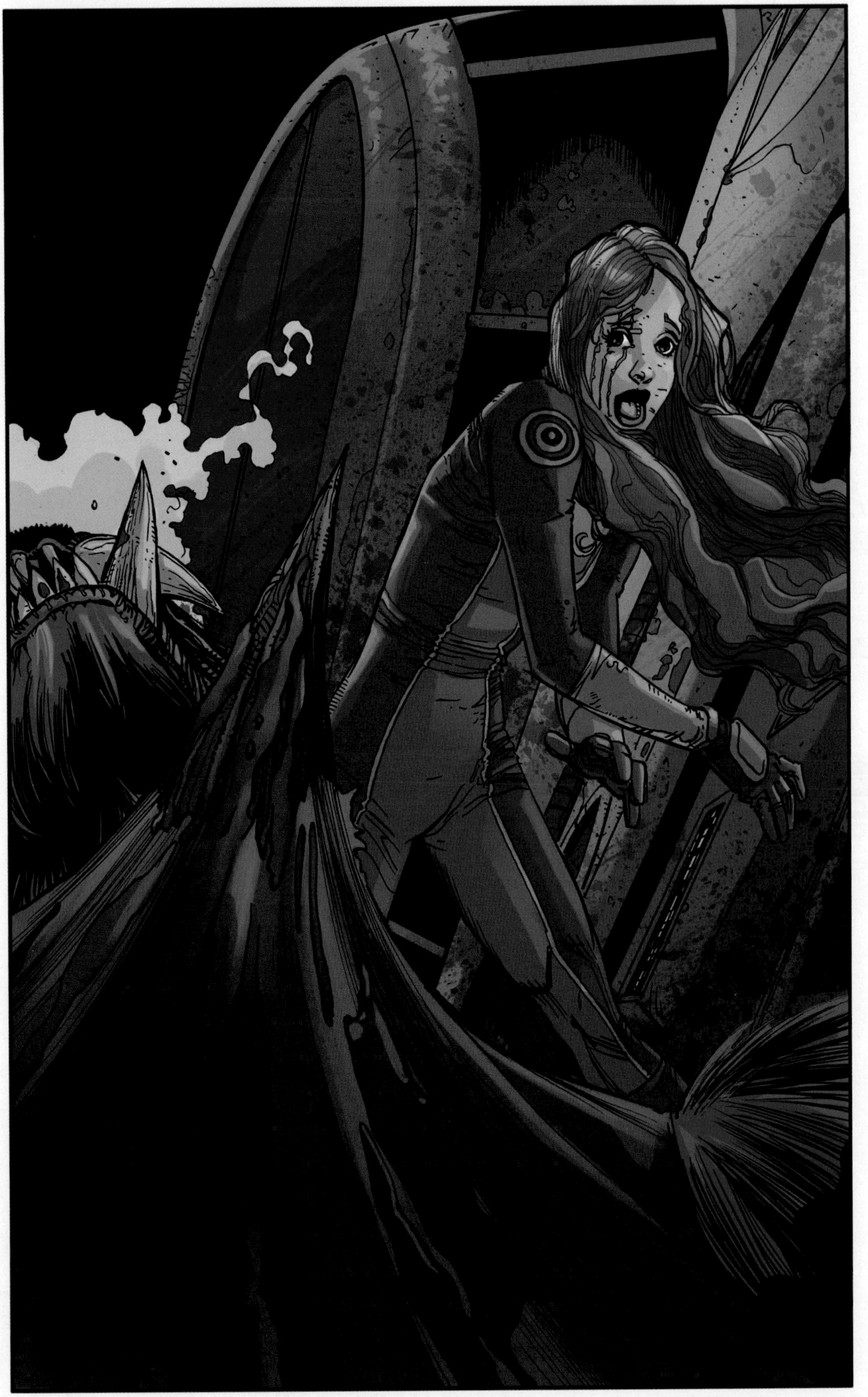

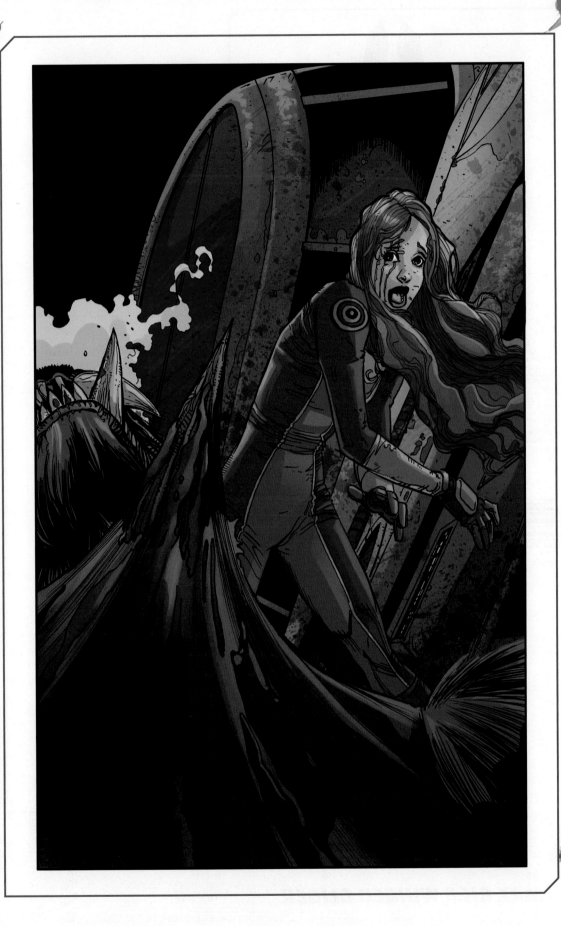

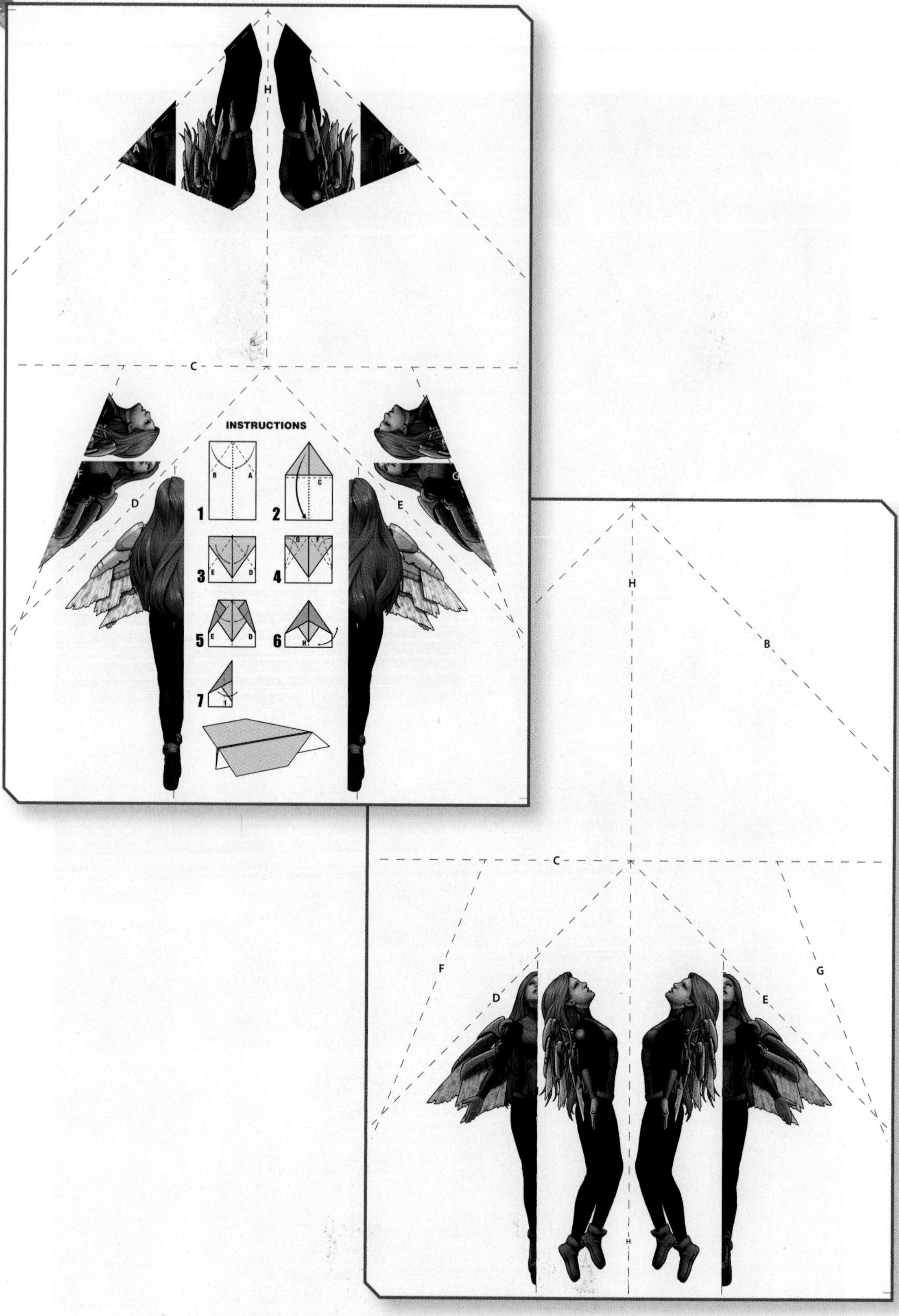
H
A
B
C
INSTRUCTIONS
1
2
3
4
5
6
7
D
E
F
G

GLIDER FOLDING INSTRUCTIONS

MAX RIDE WINGED GLIDER

promotional artwork by JOHN TYLER CHRISTOPHER

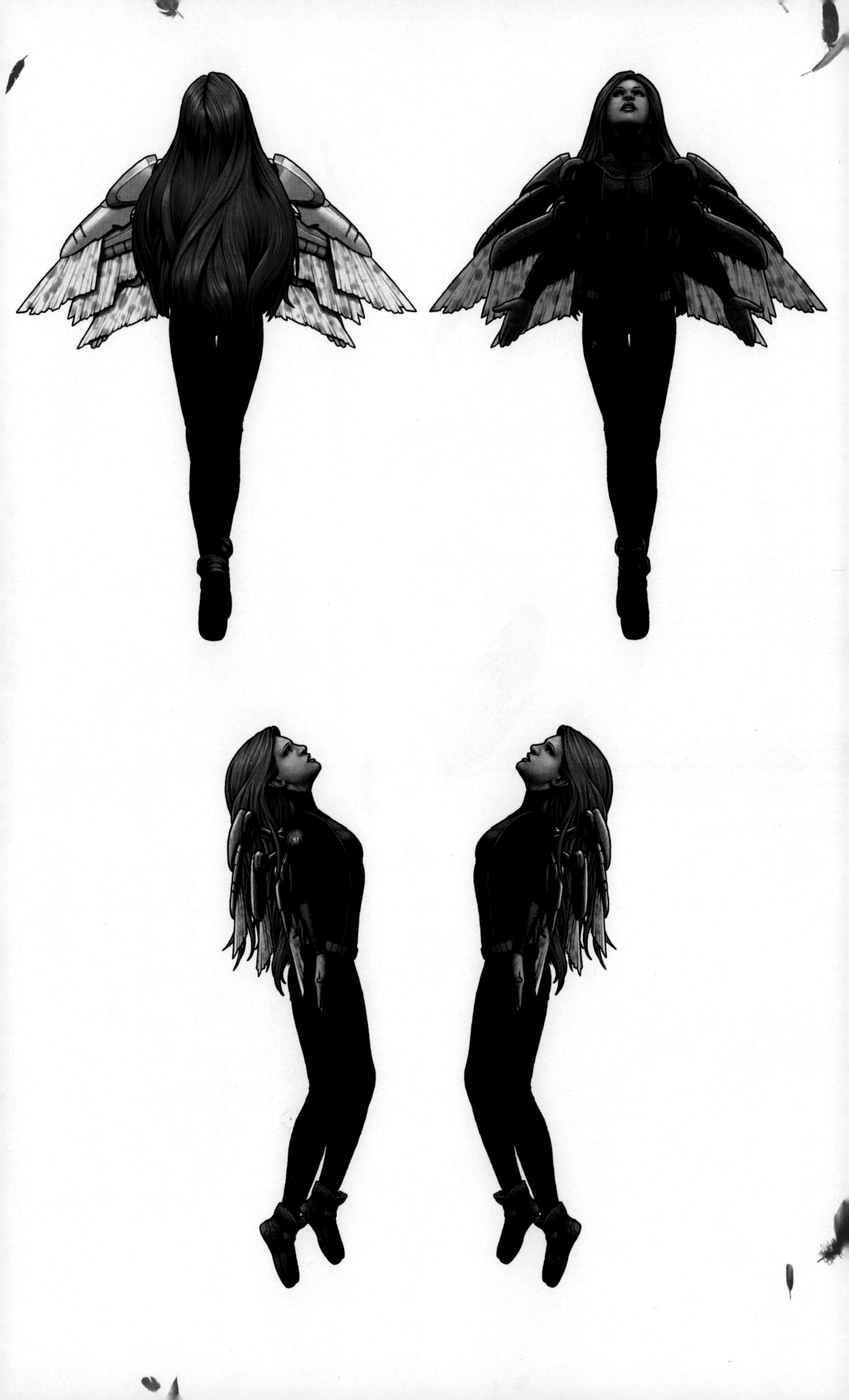

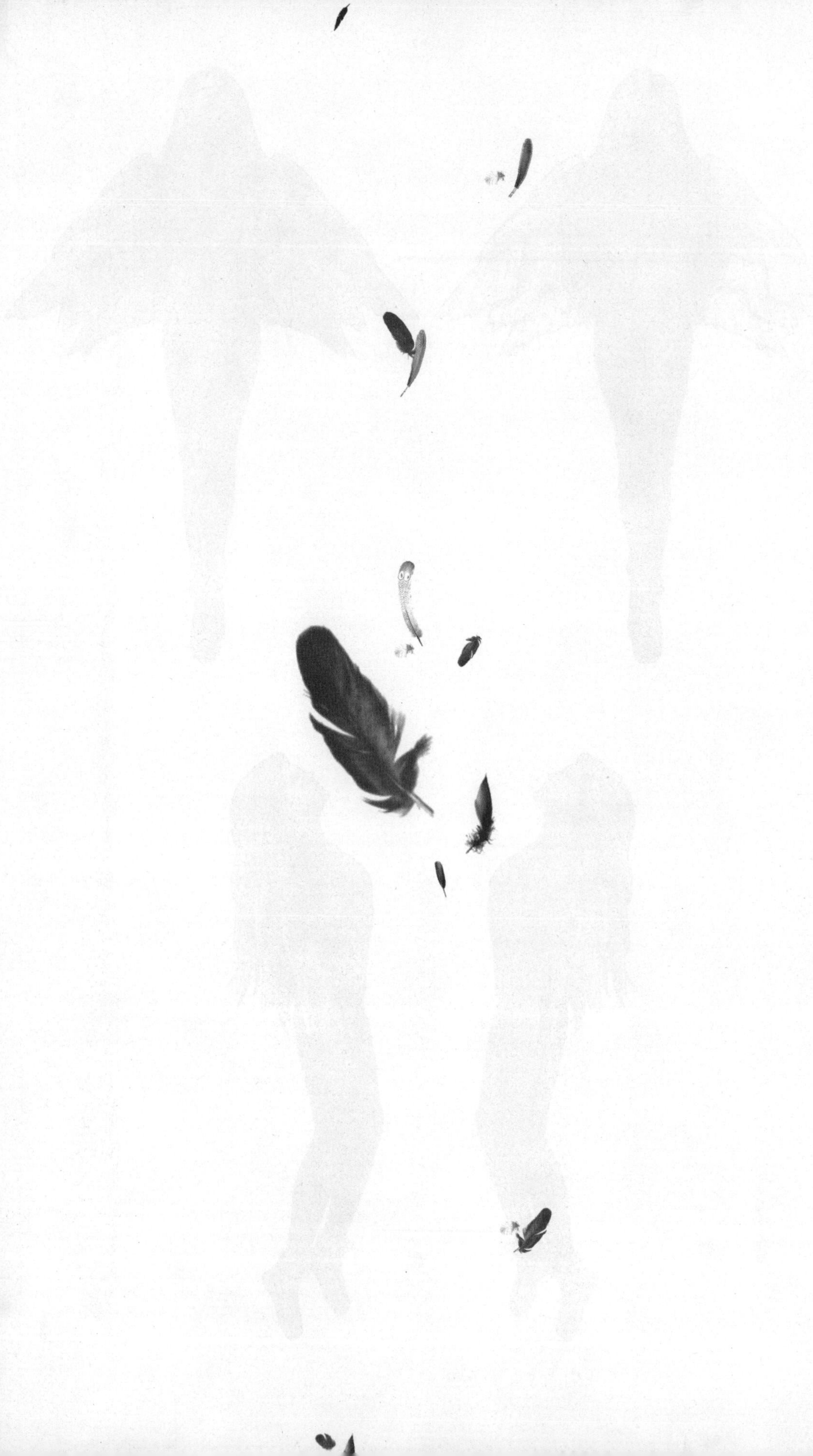